Jamie Harrison

Stripers
on the Fly

Books by Lou Tabory

Inshore Fly Fishing

Lou Tabory's Guide to Saltwater Baits and Their Imitations

Stripers on the Fly

STRIPERS
on the Fly

LOU TABORY

ILLUSTRATIONS BY
DANN JACOBUS

THE LYONS PRESS
GUILFORD, CONNECTICUT
AN IMPRINT OF THE GLOBE PEQUOT PRESS

Interior design by Compset Inc.

Library of Congress Cataloging-in-Publication Data

Tabory, Lou.
    Stripers on the fly / by Lou Tabory : illustrations by Dann Jacobus.
       p. cm.
    Originally published: Danbury, CT : Outdoor Life Books, c1988.
    Includes bibliographical references (p. 271) and index.
    ISBN 1-55821-639-1
    1. Striped bass fishing—Atlantic Coast (U.S.) 2. Fly fishing—Atlantic Coast
(U.S.)
   I. Title.
SH691.S7T335 1999
799.1'7732—dc21   98-50211
                                                        CIP

Manufactured in the United States of America
First edition/Second printing

To my wife, Barb,
for helping me create
another fly-fishing book

Contents

F*oreword*

*L*ou Tabory is one of those gifted saltwater fly fishermen who constantly experiment, reflect, adjust, and keep track of what they have done.

At the start of *Stripers on the Fly* he notes that by devoting an entire book to one species he was able to "address in detail those small but important factors that are impossible to cover" in a more general work. He has achieved his goal admirably, describing how he deals with virtually every situation a fly fisherman after striped bass might encounter. There is, to my knowledge, no other work on the subject with so much relevant detail.

Stripers on the Fly has reminded me that I am a bit short on angling intensity. "Time's wing'd chariot" drawing nigh may have something to do with this, but I doubt it. I have always tended to fish with no more than reasonable diligence, only occasionally letting the quest become fierce.

If stripers are within reach of a fly rod, Tabory suggests a way to catch them. Entire chapters, for example, are devoted to casting from ocean beaches and from cliffs. If a neophyte asks me if he should toss a fly into the open surf, I tell him to forget it, that there's little pleasure in getting hammered by combers that surge over your waders, rip your fly line from your stripping basket, or even knock you off your feet. Tabory does, one should note, caution beginners against tackling conditions beyond their skills, including the ocean when a sizeable surf is present. Almost all of my shore-based ocean fly fishing is in or near man-made salt-pond openings through a barrier beach, places where ocean waves are subdued. On the other hand, I have occasionally gone fly fishing in the open surf, and the techniques Tabory suggests for this have prompted me to try again. I'll probably never travel to where I have a chance to fly fish from cliffs, but if I do, *Stripers on the Fly* will go with me.

Tabory even devotes a chapter to fly fishing from jetties. I frequented jetties some twenty or thirty years ago, but today the jetties within my range are usually so crowded with other anglers that fly casting is almost impossible. A saltwater fly fisherman needs considerable space in which to ply his craft, and some of us also need space for psychic reasons. If jetties appeal to you, try visiting them between midnight and dawn when you will usually have all the elbow room you need.

Stripers on the Fly also prompted me to muse on what I have learned in a half century of fly fishing for striped bass. Not as much, I decided, as Tabory has absorbed in less time. Flogging the same water year after year and doing most of your fishing under ideal conditions doesn't guarantee growing competence and versatility.

I am one of those anglers who, when they find something that works at least part of the time, tend to stick with it. I am not averse to experimenting with new flies or techniques, but when some novel approach does work I don't jot it down. Eventually many such sorties into change are reduced to vague memories that might or might not come into focus when fish are eluding me. More than a score of times, I have tried to keep an angling log only to have the project expire within weeks. For me, sport fishing is a chance to relax, to absorb my surroundings. Catching fish is important, of course, as is occasionally bringing one home to eat. Where I do most of my fly fishing for stripers, such meals are quite rare. During the past several years, I've had to catch and release an average of 150 fly-rod bass before getting one that reached or exceeded the legal length limit, which is currently 28 inches in Massachusetts.

A few years ago I was given an insight into Tabory's skills and diligence. He was visiting the island of Martha's Vineyard where I live, and fishing the Dogfish Bar area of Lobsterville Beach. When conditions are right, Dogfish Bar offers some of the best shore fly fishing for striped bass along the Atlantic coast.

Over the years, I have concentrated on Dogfish Bar at dusk and thereafter. The water is shallow. Most areas that a shore-based fly fisherman can reach are not much over seven feet deep, even at high tide. The bass herd baitfish—sand eels, siversides, and various species of herring—against the beach under the cover of darkness. I have a theory that the stripers have a residual fear of attack from above, implanted when they were small enough to be attacked by sea birds, and shun their inshore movements until the light fails.

Dogfish Bar has a long, curving stretch of sand reaching out nearly 100 yards from shore that is partially exposed for a few hours when the tide is down. From time to time, I have walked out on that bar at night and caught a few bass, but have never fished it in the daytime.

Tabory, I learned from some other fly fishermen when I visited Dogfish Bar the night after his feat, had waded out on the bar, had sight-casted to some big stripers he spotted and had taken three big fish, one of 35 to 40 pounds, in the middle of a bright June day, something no one else had done in that location.

As already noted, I tend to avoid locations that are difficult to fly fish and I even go so far as to favor small flies—no more than two inches long—mainly because they are easier to cast. I prefer a floating line for the same reason, and, fortunately, I'm fishing shallow water where such a line usually suffices. Tabory, on the other hand, regards the Orvis floating line with a 10-foot sinking tip of clear monofilament as the best all-around choice for those who want to use floating lines for stripers, and in my heart of hearts I know that he is right. Habits are hard to break. Ideally, the line one uses should be tailored to the waters one fishes, and Tabory tells how to make such choices.

Perhaps I have been spoiled. The Vineyard—where I now do nearly all of my striper fishing—has many spots that offer first-rate fly fishing from shore in sheltered sounds, bays, and estuaries; and if half a gale is blowing from the wrong direction all that I have to do is wait a day or two or three. It's the fly fisher down for a week's vacation, loath to waste precious time waiting out bad weather or slumps in striper feeding activity, who sometimes makes surprising discoveries. Many such anglers will flail away in strong winds or work sheltered spots that offer little hope of success. Occasionally they catch fish and in so doing they may discover new ways to take stripers under adverse circumstances with some consistency.

Although its publication is testimony to the phenomenon, Tabory's book doesn't dwell on the growing fascination with saltwater fly fishing. When I first started fly fishing for stripers on the Vineyard in the 1940s, I devoted nearly a month of late August and September nights to it. I chose nights because I worked as a carpenter during the day. I rarely encountered another angler and never saw another fly fisherman during that period. Today, fly fishermen outnumber spin fishermen on the beaches I visit. For a decade or more, nearly all of my striper angling has been with a fly rod, but that's not because I consider it more sporting. Sometimes it's easier to take stripers on a fly than it is on a plug or jig. I have often caught bass after bass on my flies when the spinning-rod enthusiasts beside me were lucky to get an occasional fish on their lures. This usually happens when the stripers are gorging on tiny silversides or sand eels. I won't hesitate, however, to haul out a surf rod when big bass show up in the broken white water and breakers off rocky shores on the island's ocean side, water I cannot adequately cover with a fly rod.

It isn't altogether clear to me why I now use a fly rod most of the time, but one of the reasons is the small amount of gear required: rod and reel, a book of flies, some leader material, and a flashlight. Gone is the big surf stick and the tackle box or plastic bucket filled with heavy jigs and plugs. And then there's the fun of tying your own flies, dozens and dozens of them, spending only—which delights a frugal Yankee—a few dollars for hooks and materials, instead of shelling out five or six bucks a pop for a single wood or plastic plug. There's also the pleasure of fly casting. If you keep at it long enough, the line becomes an extension of your arm and body and you are in complete control even when it's so dark you can barely see your rod tip. It's an intoxicating ritual that lends itself to constant refinement. If you keep at it long enough, there will be times when you are certain that your casting is flawless grace. But if you keep at it too long on any outing—particularly after dark when you can't see what your line is doing—your rhythm will falter and your casts become sloppy. When that happens, sit on a boulder or dunnage plank and stargaze for 15 minutes. Your grace will have returned when you resume casting. A vagrant afterthought: If you are fly fishing from the water's edge after sundown, occasionally glance up and down the beach. There are quite a few non-fishing night strollers who don't realize that your backcast is reaching out 50 or 60 feet behind you. I have yet to hook one of those nocturnal wanderers, but have come close.

Again and again, Tabory tells his readers to "learn the water." Noting that the sheer size of ocean, bay, or sound intimidates those accustomed to an intimate stream or remote trout pond, he describes how to reduce a huge expanse of water to fishable segments, how to fish the bars, points, holes, rips, and channels where stripers are wont to forage. He also observes that an important part of learning the water is to visit a beach in broad daylight. Even those beaches with which one is familiar can become strange and confusing and, occasionally, ominous at night. Tabory also advises fly fishermen to try to fish at a time when the water is moving: when the tide is strong, either rising or falling.

Whether you fish casually or intensely, during the night or day, in fair weather or foul, while visiting sheltered bays, rocky promontories, or the surging surf of a secluded cove in a salt pond, Tabory has something of value for you. Indeed, he has been so thorough that I have to mention a striper-fishing tactic that I couldn't find in his book. For many years I was frustrated when bass were feeding right at my feet on shoals of sand eels they had herded against the shore. Time and again I would toss a variety of flies at them without a hit. Knowing that my fly was simply being lost among the multitudes of frantic baitfish, I wondered if other bass might be moving in from deeper water and if it might be possible to intercept them before they joined the feast. I waded out beyond the shoreside commotion, made a long cast and was immediately fast to a nice fish. This approach has worked often enough for me to want it included, albeit through the back door, in *Stripers on the Fly.*

NELSON BRYANT
Martha's Vineyard
Summer 1999

A Note on the Structure of This Book

When writing *Inshore Fly Fishing,* I began the book with fishing information first. Although different from most fishing books, this was how I wanted the book to flow. Of all the anglers who have commented on what they learned from *Inshore Fly Fishing,* no one ever mentions how much they learned about tackle. Everyone mentions the knowledge they gained about reading the water. In my fly-fishing schools and slide shows I emphasize **learning the water.** This will be the emphasis of *Stripers on the Fly* as well.

The book will contain information on tackle, knots, gear, etc., but the book's main focus will be fishing. There will be some crossover from *Inshore Fly Fishing*—this cannot be helped, as there is basic information that must be covered. I will briefly mention other species to prevent leading someone astray, particularly about tackle.

Where *Stripers on the Fly* will differ is in covering those very subtle ways to fish for stripers. When discussing one species, I can address in detail those small but important facts that are impossible to cover in a general book. There will be more talk of small flies, drifting, controlling, and mending the fly line; how new materials have influenced fly fishing; and the many new techniques I have learned since the last book. The focus of this book is reading and fishing the water types that hold stripers and how to make big waters smaller.

Acknowledgments

To Dad and Uncle Harry, for taking me striper fishing as a kid.

To old friends:
Dick Alley, Ed Boland, Jim Christiano, Jack Frech, Nick Heineman, Al Kriewald, Pete Kriewald, Pete Laszlo, Eric Leiser, Larry Merly, John Merwin, Lenny Orifice, Joe Piza, Bob Pond, John Posh, Joe Saviano, Frank Schober, Ray Smith, Ed Stallings, Irv Swope, and Paul Tabory, who helped me find stripers in my youth and still help me find them today. It was fun fishing with all of you.

To supportive editors:
Peter Van Gytenbeek at *Fly Fishing in Salt Waters;* John Randolph at *Fly Fisherman;* Duncan Barnes and John Merwin at *Field & Stream;* Nick Seifert and Ed Scheff at *Outdoor Life.* Many thanks for your continued support.

To companies:
The Orvis Company, Manchester, Vermont, and the anglers like Perk and Dave Perkins, Randy Carlson, Paul Fersen, Tom Rosenbauer, and Jim LePage, who make it so successful. Few fly-fishing companies have owners and executives who have your fishing skills.

PIC (Putnam Imaging Center), Danbury, Connecticut. This is the third book that you have helped make a success. Thanks.

Paul Guard at Action Craft, Coral Gables, Florida, for making a boat that fishes stripers so well; Mercury Outboards, Fond du Lac, Wisconsin, for a motor that keeps running; and Boat Master Trailers, Ft. Myers, Florida.

To good friends:

Chris Aubut, Steve Bellefleur, Jim Bernstein, Dave Beshara, Barry Clemson, Cooper Gilkes, Joe Keegan, Pat Keliher, Dan Marini, Mike Monte, Paul Newmier, Tom Piccolo, Dave Rimmer, Dan Shea, and Pip Winslow, who have, over the years, helped me to gather photos and given me valuable information about stripers. But mostly it is the fun times that we have spent together fishing—thanks.

To fly tyers:

Don Avondolio, Ken Bay, Joe Blados, Dan Blanton, Al Brewster, Joe Brooks, Bill Catherwood, Herb Chase, Bud Church, Bob Clouser, John D'Allesandro, Paul Dixon, Bill Gallasch, Jack Gartside, Harold Gibbs, Dennis Goddard, Hal Jannsen, Mark Lewchick, Dick Lohr, Glen Mikkleson, Ed Mitchell, Ron Montecalov, Bill Peabody, Eric Peterson, Bob Popovics, Enrico Puglisi, Gary Rowley, Ray Smith, Benjamin Van Eeden, Paul M. Van Reenen, and Frank Wentink. Thank you all for your input helping me with fly patterns for the book.

To old pros:

You all pioneered striper fishing with a fly: Joe Brooks, Nelson Bryant, Cap Colvin, Harold Gibbs, Lefty Kreh, Tom Loving, Hal Lyman, Frank Woolner. You guys made it happen.

A very special thanks:

To Nick Lyons, who patiently put up with me and produced three books. Many thanks for your help and counsel. No other publisher-editor has helped to make fly fishing so successful.

To Dann Jacobus, whose art has helped to make my writing more lucid and whose wonderful painting graces the cover. Dann, many thanks for being not only a talented artist but a fun person to spend time with.

Angus Cameron, whose insight and knowledge, as always, have made this a better book. Angus, you have helped me produce three successful books and have made me a better writer.

To Bill Bowers, whose special, delicate touch has made the writing throughout this book flow cleanly.

There are some anglers whom I have not included in the list. Please forgive me for this lapse. You know who you are—thanks. Some of you listed could fit into several categories—all of you are good friends.

*I*ntroduction

I spotted the two huge shadows cruising along a sandbar in 2 feet of water. As they crossed, moving left, I dropped a 50-foot cast in their path, letting the fly settle to the bottom. The lead fish drifted over, turned on its side, and grabbed the fly. I paused, rod under my arm, and hooked the fish with a pull from each hand. The shallow water exploded as the fish turned, rushed across the bar, and left several washtub-size eruptions before reaching the drop-off. Twenty minutes later I held the striper, nearly 40 pounds, by the tail, revived it, and watched as it disappeared over the bar. It was my third big fish in the last hour, and it was just past noon on a bright sunny day in June at a popular fishing location on Martha's Vineyard. I had just had the day of a lifetime flats fishing for stripers, but my wife and I, most of the time, were alone on the water.

This is what makes fly fishing for stripers so special: You can find them anywhere at any time. Stripers feed both day and night, in every type of water that exists in the sea. Although deemed by some anglers a mainly nocturnal species, even big fish feed in the most unlikely places at midday.

This is why stripers are both unique and the most popular fly-rod gamefish in salt water. No other saltwater species offers the average fly angler such fishing opportunities so close to highly populated areas. Stripers live and feed from the shadows of major coastal cities to remote beaches. Armed with basic fly tackle, even a novice can wander down to any striper location and experience good fishing. And at the right time and place, there is always that chance for a big fish. All of my best fly-caught stripers have been taken in waters with public access.

For me the striper has always been a remarkable fish. When I was a kid, it was the first fish I caught with artificials, and later it was the first saltwater fish I caught with fly tackle. After that experience, I was never the same.

There is something special about using fly tackle to take fish, particularly in the sea. Even a heavy fly rod seems like a delicate tool when fishing some of the striper's domain. It is this challenge that makes fly fishing for stripers so appealing. Only with fly tackle can you begin to match wits with stripers when they start to feed on small baits or when they move into shallow clear water. Fly fishing also permits control and movement of the artificial that is impossible with other tackle.

There are many ways to enjoy fly fishing for the striper: watching a bass inhale your fly in the rolling white water along a rocky cliff; hearing the crash on a dark, calm night of a striper taking a fly, seemingly off your rod tip; or casting to a fish swimming over light sand in 2 feet of crystal-clear water. The way a striper takes a fly in rolling surf must surprise the newcomer. How could a fish survive, much less feed, in water that would destroy some species? Yet the striper is at home in the roughest water—water that most anglers would pass up because they believe it could not possibly hold fish.

The key to successful striper fishing is reading the water. Once you learn where and how fish feed, you can catch them. Yes, there is more water to learn when fishing for stripers than other species, but that is an advantage. You have more types of water to choose from when fishing and more opportunity to find water that fits your skill level.

The good trout angler learns how to break water into fishable sections, to expect fish to be anywhere at any time. Although the sea looks huge and ominous, it is only a big piece of water made up of smaller sections. At times you are simply fishing small sections of water, blind casting to cover each parcel. Separating the water into fishable parts is the key to success. The secret is not just fishing a rip, but separating that rip into sections and manipulating the line and fly to fish each section thoroughly.

In this book, I will make big waters smaller—dissecting large sections into small ones. Because stripers will feed in even the smallest parcel of water, the angler must fish each piece carefully. Some of my most memorable fly-fishing events involved taking that one tough-to-catch fish, or finding fish in waters that most anglers ignore because it is the wrong tide or wrong time of day. Remember, there is no wrong time of day or tide. Yes, there are more favorable times and tides, but after many years of chasing stripers I have learned never to disregard a time or place because it is "wrong."

As I cover the different types of water and how to fish them, you will see a situation and say, "Why didn't I think of that?" This is a reaction that we all have; it is certainly how I learn from other anglers. You can learn something, not only when another angler tells you where and how he took fish, but even when someone tells you about an event, positive or negative, that might shed light on how to solve that puzzle, explain that mystery. Even if it's just for one night, one tide, or one location, it is unlocking the puzzle that makes fly fishing fun. Yes, it is exciting when fish are feeding and taking everything that lands in the water. But even if you land only one fish, or make just one fish take your fly, if you have discovered something new, it makes fishing truly rewarding. To me, it's more than catching numbers of fish that makes fly fishing special—it's catching that one fish.

The Striper's Habits 1

*T*he resurgence of striped bass is the reason the Atlantic coast has become a fly-fishing Mecca. *Morone saxatilis* is also called linesider, greenhead, or squidhound, and south of New Jersey, rockfish or rock. By whatever name, they are the mainstay of the New England and mid-Atlantic sport fishery. Along with codfish, stripers helped feed the colonists in the early history of America. Stripers have seven to eight dark stripes running laterally from just past the gill plates to the base of the tail. The back color varies from very light olive to dark olive to a blue-gray, blending to a silvery-white underside. Fish living in rocky areas are darker; fish over light sand will be almost beige with a hint of olive. Like many species, the striper blends well with its surroundings.

Today the striper is the most important fly-tackle gamefish from Maine to the Carolinas. On the West Coast, the once-popular fishery in San Francisco Bay has been reduced to a trickle. The future looks bleak for the runs of fish in Coos Bay and the Umpqua River in Oregon as well, and for other scattered pockets of West Coast stripers. The rivers in South Carolina and Georgia still have good fishing, but not the healthy stocks that once existed. Without strict conservation measures, we would not have the excellent fishing that we enjoy today in New England and the mid-Atlantic.

Because it is fine table fare, the striper is a popular food fish. As this book goes to print, sportsmen are fighting to preserve the fishery. Only in fresh water do stripers enjoy the security from commercial fishing that can, as we have witnessed, quickly decimate their numbers.

Luckily, the striper is robust and adaptable. A fish that survives and spawns in the Hudson River can learn to live anywhere. The Hudson's spawning populations supply the surrounding New York areas and parts of New Jersey and mix with Chesapeake Bay fish in Long Island Sound. Chesapeake Bay and the river systems that run into it are the major Atlantic spawning areas. The bay produces tremendous numbers of stripers and populates the rest of their range.

Water Temperatures

Temperatures have a strong influence on the striper's life. Although stripers become active at 40 degrees Fahrenheit, intense feeding occurs at temperatures from the high 40s to the mid-50s, associated with spawning or migration. Water in the mid-70s slows the striper's metabolism, bringing about less activity and mostly nighttime feeding. Water temperatures in the low 40s and mid- to high 70s have a similar effect on stripers: They feed less and are less active. Ideal feeding temperatures range from the low 50s to about 70 degrees.

Migration

The spring and fall migrations of stripers along the Atlantic coast bring an annual run of fish through the area. Some fish migrate hundreds of miles, traveling the outer beaches from Virginia to Maine. Most Pacific migrations occur within the river and bay systems; there is no significant movement of stripers along the outer coast. This limits most Pacific striper fishing to bays and estuaries.

Some fish begin migration in their second year, although until recently, most schooling stripers were third-year fish, averaging 14 to 16 inches. Several years ago, large numbers of 8- to 12-inch fish flooded the Atlantic coast. Perhaps because of scarce food supplies in their nursery areas, many 2-year-old fish moved to better feeding grounds.

The spring run begins in the southern locations, moving north as the water warms. As the temperature rises into the 40s, fish begin moving north, reaching Cape May by mid-April, Cape Cod by mid-May, and the Maine coast by the first of June. These times vary, and the earliest signs of fish are generally holdovers that become active on warm days. Smaller fish show first in the spring; in the fall, the appearance of large numbers of small fish signals the season's end.

The fish begin moving from Maine in mid-September and from Cape Cod by the first week in October, forming good numbers of fish at Cape May by December. Chesapeake Bay has fish activity throughout the year if the winter is mild. The major departure of stripers from the Chesapeake Bay begins in late March to mid-April; the fish begin returning from the end of October to Christmas.

Stripers spawn up rivers in mixed fresh and salt water. In some locations, the eggs differ slightly to adapt to the river's environment. Pollution and the damming of whole river systems have altered the striper's spawning grounds, but luckily the fish have adjusted to their changing environment. Stripers are tolerant of all salinity levels and are at home from pure fresh water right out into the sea. Because they can adapt to any water conditions, they can live and feed anywhere.

The striper's growth rate varies only slightly in different locations; water temperature is not a factor, as it is with some species that grow more slowly in colder waters. At 1 year they average 5 inches, by the third year they are 15 inches, and a 6-year striper averages 24 inches.

Stripers are built like armored tanks. They have heavy skin; large, heavy scales; large fins; and a big tail. They will feed in the heaviest surf, and only too much sand suspended in the water will drive them offshore. Beware: The dorsal and pectoral fins have long, sharp spines. The gill plates are also sharp, but handling the striper is easy because there are no teeth—only a rough, sandpaperlike coating on both lips. Gripping a striper by the lower jaw will temporarily incapacitate the fish.

The striper's husky build, armored scales, and powerful tail allow it to roam in many different waters.

How and Where Stripers Feed

Stripers prefer feeding at night or in low light; with a plentiful bait supply, there would be less daytime feeding. The large numbers of fish that are now feeding in bright daylight indicate that stripers have changed their habits. Certainly this is true in summer, when many locations just 10 years ago would have seen only late-night feeding. The only exceptions are deeper, secluded offshore rips, which have always held daytime-feeding fish all summer. The numbers of fish feeding in clear water on light-colored, shallow sand flats are significantly greater than they were when I started fly fishing years ago. With fewer large foods, the stripers needed to adapt to feed in the daytime on smaller baits in shallow water. This change is certainly desirable for fly fishing, adding new fishing opportunities. Sight fishing in the shallows, as well as larger numbers of feeding fish along the cliffs, in the estuaries, and on the big reefs at midday, are among the benefits we are seeing. Today anglers in some locations can take large numbers of fish—and some good-size fish—all summer and never fish at night. That would have been difficult 30 years ago.

Estuaries perhaps offer the most variety for the fly rodder. Many of these sheltered sanctuaries have stripers feeding and holding in waters that are completely

Stripers feed in the white water rolling along this rocky shore. Very few other gamefish will feed in such diverse waters.

landlocked at low tide. As the tide brings a fresh flow of seawater and food to these locations, the feeding begins. On falling tides, the mouths and edges of the estuaries become traps for many types of food, with hungry stripers waiting to ambush the helpless sea creatures. Waves rolling along an open beach or swelling against rocky structure create similar traps for the bait and similar feeding opportunities for stripers. I believe stripers are the most opportunistic feeders in the sea. No section of water is out-of-bounds to the striper, and it will consume any likely food sources. Yes, there are the staples and favorite baits, but even big fish will eat dime-size food if it's available and easy.

The Basic Foods

The important striper foods for fly fishing are sand eels, spearing, and anchovies, as well as juvenile herring and menhaden. In the spring, adult herring bring big fish into estuaries to feed, but the big flies used to match the baits are tough to cast. However, in some shallow waters, crabs, shrimp, and worms, as well as a host of other small foods, make up the striper's diet. The recent switch to small foods, like daytime feeding, has been a great benefit for fly anglers. Stripers feed on a greater variety of foods than any gamefish I know.

Stripers do not make sizzling runs or spectacular jumps as some gamefish do. They fight hard, but not like a bluefish, tuna, or jack. Bigger stripers give powerful runs and use water flow to their advantage. It's not the fish's power itself that makes a striper tough to land, but the environment in which it lives. However, the striper's appeal comes from the many different places you can catch them and the way they take a fly. Of the many different species of gamefish I have caught, none offers the variety of fishing opportunities that stripers do. Like the trout, the striper is an exceptional fly-rod fish.

How to Begin 2

*P*erhaps what overwhelms most anglers, even veteran freshwater fly rodders, is the sea's sheer size. The first look at big water will unnerve most who have never fished the ocean. Looking at heavy surf pounding a shoreline and wondering where and how to fish can make even the experienced angler skeptical. I have had novices ask, "How can I fish a beach when the surf is so big I cannot get close to the water?" The answer: You don't. You go to a protected, easy-to-fish location because that is where the fish are feeding and where you can reach them. Most beginning saltwater fly anglers try to fish water that is beyond their skill level. Even seasoned fly anglers will stubbornly take on water that is too difficult for fly fishing.

"Don't fight the plug" is the best advice on plugging in an electrical appliance I have ever read. There is a large side and a small side to an electrical outlet, which receives a plug with the same setup. If it's reversed, the plug won't fit. Don't fight the water! If you are battling conditions that make fly fishing difficult, find water you can fish easily. Choosing fishable water conditions is the key to successful fly fishing in the sea. But first you must choose tackle.

Start with tackle that fits your skill level, size, strength, and the waters you plan to fish. (See Chapter 14, Choosing an Outfit, for tackle selection.) When attempting anything for the first time, try it under favorable conditions—a dark windy night is not the time to learn saltwater fly fishing. Daytime in calm, sheltered water is the proper time and place to begin. If you do not fight the elements, learning will be easier.

Selecting a Location to Fish

In each chapter, I will discuss where and how fish feed. However, there are some fundamental signs that reveal the presence of fish. The sight and sound of feeding fish or birds feeding in an excited state are sure indications. Baitfish are usually placid, but the presence of gamefish will keep them in an agitated state. If baitfish are skittish, stripers are around. Be alert for the smell of fish or bait. Many anglers along a beach could mean there is a good run of fish. Finding large concentrations of bait in an area is another positive sign. Remember, unlike trout that hold in a stream, stripers keep moving, hunting for food. Stripers do hold in the same locations and frequent the same feeding areas, but food is the key. Places without food will draw few fish. The good striper angler is a good hunter.

At first light, look for dead bait along the shoreline. On a calm morning, search for surface activity that might indicate the presence of baitfish. Wade out into the water and stamp your feet on the bottom. If sand eels are holding in the sand, they will jump into the air. At this time of day, the stripers will find the bait when it leaves the sand, creating a feeding spree. Hatches and swarms of food occur at different times, and after several fishing seasons you will learn when these events occur and plan for them. I will cover this in more detail later, but begin to think of—and look for—the basic signs on your first outing. It will soon become second nature to identify the signals that there are fish in a given location.

Fishing for one species helps you to focus on that fish. Anglers who fish in one environment for one type of fish become very accomplished at that style of fishing. However, there are some drawbacks. What sometimes happens to anglers, myself included, is that we become so focused on one water type that we do not see the forest for the trees. Learning and fishing many water types helps us acquire a wider range of knowledge. One method might work for several water types, but if you did not learn a certain technique by fishing one water type, you cannot apply it to another fishing situation. It is important to keep an open mind and to keep trying different techniques until you find the key to that puzzle.

I plan to cover each water type in precise detail. Learning how to fish many types and conditions of water will help to prevent tunnel vision. Even if a water type does not appeal to you, learn to fish it. The knowledge gained might, one day, help to unlock that riddle.

Choosing the Right Fly

The first consideration here needs to be casting—can you handle the fly comfortably? Some patterns are too heavy or too bulky and dangerous for the average angler to cast. A fly might be very effective, but if it causes casting faults and makes fishing miserable, choose one you can cast well instead. Unlike trout, stripers will usually take a variety of patterns resembling the bait in the water. Start fishing with an all-black, all-white, or all-chartreuse Deceiver or Snake Fly that matches the size of the baitfish. Keep your fly selection simple, with several basic patterns in three colors tied on #2 to #1/0 hooks, 3–6 inches long. Once you become familiar with the fishing, you can build a selection of flies based on food type, water conditions, and time of year. I will detail the important food types and fly patterns in Chapter 17. A white or black, 4-inch-long basic fly pattern is all you need to begin striper fishing.

A 9-foot knotless tapered leader looped to the fly line's end is the best leader system to start with. Before each outing, check the leader for wind knots or nicks from the end of the fly line to the knot at the hook's eye. If there is any sign of wear, test the worn spot by pulling with your hands. More advanced anglers should check Chapter 16 for other knotting systems.

Removing the Kinks and Coils

Begin by stretching the fly line. Either pull small sections with your hands, or hook the loop at the end of your fly line to something and pull the line to stretch it. This removes all those coiled loops that can knot inside your basket when casting or when a fish runs.

Removing the memory—the coils—from the fly line makes fishing easier. Either use your hands to stretch small sections of line, or stretch the entire line.

Learn to use a stripping basket (see Chapter 14, Choosing an Outfit) whether fishing from shore or boat. Fish only the amount of fly line that you can cast easily. If you rarely empty the basket with your best cast, reel up the excess fly line; every third or fourth cast should pull all the fly line from the basket. When the cast pulls the line tight, slapping it against the rod, it helps the fly line to land on the water in a straight line and keeps clearing the basket, preventing most tangles. When fishing in low light, it's a necessity; for now, it's a good habit to develop.

Line control is essential—in some locations, it is much more important than distance. Long casts are unnecessary, even unwanted in some situations. Keeping contact with the line and fly is always important. Each season, many stripers take a fly presented with a short cast, but anglers catch few fish when not in contact with the fly. If attempting longer casts is causing the line to land with too much slack, shorten the cast.

Line Handling

Learning to maintain fly control while manipulating and managing loose fly line will frustrate the novice. Even many trout anglers will find this a chore because saltwater fishing requires much more line than most trout-fishing situations. Many anglers use a two-handed retrieve, tucking the rod under the arm and using both hands to manipulate the line. The two-handed retrieve offers many advantages. It works well with a stripping basket; the casting hand gets a rest when you place the rod under your arm. The arm covers the "mousetrap" parts of the outfit—namely, where the reel attaches to the rod—as well as the reel handle, so there is little chance of the line snagging behind the reel or on the reel handle when a fish runs. When hooking a fish, you have both hands to manipulate the line when the fish runs. Hooking a fish with a hand-over-hand retrieve gives a more positive hook-set than using the rod to strike the fish. Also, if you miss the strike when hooking with your hands, the fly remains close to the fish; using the rod to strike takes the fly away from the fish.

Using both hands also allows a larger variety of retrieves. Some anglers prefer to use a one-handed retrieve. This is purely personal preference, but if you are a beginner, I recommend you learn the two-handed retrieve.

Line Management

Line management is the key to fishing for stripers. Learning to handle the fly line, using your hands to retrieve, to hold, or to feed line is an integral part of the sport. There are times when you do more line handling than casting. Fishing the wash along a beach or fishing the rolling surf along a cliff might require, on one cast, both retrieving and feeding the same section of line several times before finishing the drift. As with retrieving, each angler must develop a line-handling system that works. How well you handle and control the fly line will determine how well you fish. Learning to manipulate the line is not difficult; it just takes practice. Stretch the fly line, and be sure it's clean and is not twisted. If you don't, learning will be a hassle, and later on fishing will be difficult.

Rod position is also important. Hold the rod low, with the tip just above or even touching the water when wading or fishing from a boat. Keep the rod pointed at the water in the direction of the line. Maintain a straight alignment with the rod and fly line. The rod should never be at an angle to the line, either up and down or sideways. In a current, or with wave action, move the rod so it follows the line's and the fly's position.

Retrieves

Retrieving moves the fly, gives it action, and helps to maintain contact with the fly. There are many ways to retrieve a fly. Throughout the book, I will give advice about retrieves and which ones work best in different situations. Each angler must develop a system of retrieves that will work the fly properly in different waters. One is a survival retrieve to use when the angler is tired, bored, or has lost confidence but wants to continue fishing. This should be a simple means of moving the fly without requiring thought, a retrieve that you can perform in your sleep. It will become a retrieve that you use often, a steady, slow-to-medium movement of the fly. Working the fly quickly requires more skill in line management. If adding long pulls to a fast retrieve, line management becomes even harder.

After some fishing experience, the number of retrieves you know will increase. In most cases, the seasoned angler will employ fly movement instinctively, using a retrieve that blends with the water's flow. **Learning the water** helps the angler to apply the retrieve that works in a given situation. Consider the following as well:

- Fly type, along with the bait type you are trying to match, sometimes dictates the speed and style of retrieve.
- Some retrieves do not make the fly swim like a normal baitfish, but stripers react to a bolting, pulsating retrieve because the fly looks like crippled prey.
- The water's flow and speed, and the depth you plan to fish, are factors to consider when employing retrieves.
- Different line densities require certain types of retrieves.

There are also times when you will catch fish using a retrieve that seems totally improper. Finding the correct retrieve is part of solving that fishing puzzle. The better anglers keep trying different methods until one works.

That First Cast

Most anglers should start by fishing moving water. Flowing water makes fish strike more aggressively; it disrupts the bait, helps impart action to the fly, and keeps the angler in contact with the line. One early morning, while sitting on the Vineyard Haven ferry, I saw an excellent example of the importance of water movement. Even though the flowing water was artificially created, it triggered the stripers' natural feeding instincts. When the captain used the bow thruster to maneuver the ferry, it sent a billow of water swirling away from the boat. In the area illuminated by the dock's lights, I saw boils appear in the swirling water as stripers began feeding. The swirling water disrupted the schools of spearing that congregated around the docks, flushing them out to the waiting fish. Each time the thruster operated, the fish would feed in the moving water. I wanted to start casting.

Some locations in the sea are called rips. The name comes from the choppy appearance of the water's surface—a rip line. Actually most current flows are called rips.

To get a feel for line control, find some ripping water and fish it in daylight. Cast a neutral-density fly, such as a Deceiver, at different angles to the current and see how the fly swings. Casting straight across or upcurrent makes the fly swing faster and lets it settle into the water column. You will notice a bow in the line, and at some angles to the current, fly control becomes more difficult. Casting downstream gives little swing and less depth to the fly, but positive control without slack line. In slower water, it is easier to maintain line control when casting at different angles to the current.

Remember that the more line you cast, the harder line control becomes. And different fly lines, such as floaters and slow and fast sinkers, feel and fish differently. Each line type requires time to master in different situations. Equally important is learning to fish the different types of rips that occur in our waters. I will discuss detailed fishing information for each water type, but to avoid redundancy I will discuss basic rip fishing, which will work for most water flows. Fishing a rip is the foundation of saltwater fly angling.

How Rips Form and How to Fish Them

In salt water, the rising and falling of the tide creates rips and produces the most consistent and predictable flow. Flow produced by wave action is more of a surge than a steady flow. With a tide chart, you can predict rips at the mouths of outlets, over reefs and bars, and along shorelines.

Rips vary, both in the length and duration of the flow and in the speed and power of the flow. Faster, deeper rips can flow for great distances, even when they reach deeper water. Over a flat, a rip will flow well for the length of the flat, but once it

A rip provides easy feeding for stripers. The choppy surface is a telltale sign of moving water.

reaches deeper water it dissipates quickly. A rip does not have to be big, deep, or fast to produce fish; any moving water provides a good feeding environment for stripers.

Rips form when flowing water is constricted. A bar, a point, or a sudden change of depth causes a funneling effect that accelerates the steady flow of the tide. On a calm day, even a small rip shows up well; at times wind enhances a rip's appearance, making the choppy line stand out.

The secret to fishing a rip is to make the fly swim through the flow so it looks alive and helpless. In a slow rip, you can cast at any angle and—just by varying the retrieve—make the fly look natural. Use a faster retrieve when moving the fly downtide; a slower retrieve going into the flow looks real and keeps positive contact with the fly. The trick to fishing flows is moving the fly around, casting at different angles until you find the right one. Slower flows are best for the freshman because they are easier to fish, particularly in areas with constant water depth.

In faster rips with changing water depth, fly placement and fly control—as well as your position along the rip—are all important factors. I'll discuss shallow rips first, fishing with a floating or intermediate line.

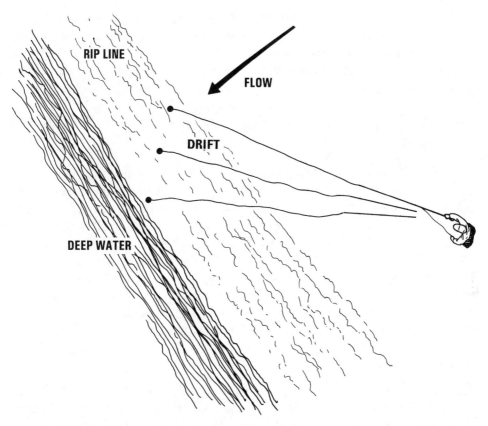

When fishing a rip, cast above the rip line and at different angles, and let the fly drift or swing into the drop-off.

We are standing or anchored several yards above the rip line on a long gravel bar that runs out 70 feet. The flow is slow, and the water depth is 5 feet. Begin casting just up-current of the rip, letting the fly swing into the deeper water. Let the line settle into the slower water before retrieving. Keep the rod pointed at the line, following it as it flows downcurrent. Make several casts of different lengths in that same zone, retrieving slowly after letting the fly swing. Then cast at different angles both above and below the position of the first cast, again varying the casting length. On some casts, allow the fly to drift longer, but begin retrieving immediately on a few casts as well. This moves the fly around and changes the fly's swimming angle while working it through all the water. You are fan casting, casting at various angles to find the best way to present the fly.

Keep working this routine while moving down the flow a few yards at a time. If wading, I might move only several steps if the rip is not very wide. If the bar is 50 feet wide, I might make the moves longer. After learning a location, you will know exactly the distance and angle to cast and what retrieve to use in certain water conditions: **Learning the water** is so important.

A fast-sinking line takes more skill but offers more possibilities, because you can work different levels even in fast water. Use the fan-casting technique, moving the fly around. A sinking line has less bow because the line diameter is smaller. On longer casts, let the line and fly sink by casting well upcurrent, dead drifting most of the cast. Try retrieving downcurrent on some casts, moving the fly with quick, long pulls. This can be very effective with big light-colored flies.

In a boat drifting down a rip, fish the same way by casting in different directions around the boat. The only difference is that the boat is drifting downcurrent at the same speed as the rip. Unless there is wind that alters the boat's drift, you are actually fishing flat water because you are moving with the flow. Drifting allows deeper fly penetration even in a fast rip, but keep a sharp watch to maintain contact with the fly. Wind alters the boat's flow, so you need to find the best casting angle to get the line down without losing contact with the fly. Wind against the tide can be tough; cast angling upcurrent, and fish the fly across current to the boat as it flows upcurrent. Drifting in a wind is trial and error because there are so many variables.

Mending Line

Once you get a feel for working rips, try mending the line to alter the fly's flow and speed. Mending line can get the fly down somewhat without using a fast-sinking line, but the main reason for mending is to change the fly's speed and direction.

Mending upcurrent slows the swing, keeps the fly facing upcurrent longer, and lets it settle. A downcurrent mend makes the swing faster, makes the fly face across or downcurrent, and keeps the fly up in the water column. A floating line allows mending at any time in the swing; with sinking lines, you must plan the mend and the drift in advance. However, a sinking line allows many different options and much better penetration than a floating line. In deeper water with a fast-sinking line, mending will make the fly "talk." Throughout the book I will mention different mends; be sure to keep experimenting to improve the fly control you get from mending.

The Sense of Touch

Once you begin to feel the fly's resistance, try closing your eyes to instill a sense of touch to your hands. Even in bright daylight, most striper fishing requires more feel than visual skills. Developing a good sense of touch is vital to becoming a good striper angler. Closing your eyes is a good way to learn how to fish at night.

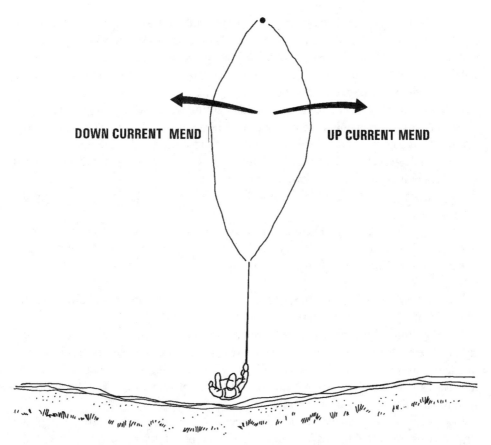

DOWN CURRENT MEND   **UP CURRENT MEND**

Mending line is good way to set up a drift, let the fly sink deeper, or change the fly's angle in the current. You can mend in either direction to the current, with the line at any angle to the flow.

Terms to Learn

Below is a list of terms and their definitions. The definitions are brief, explaining just enough for the angler to understand what I am discussing. Most of the terminology is basic; the experienced angler will know it. A beginner should learn the terms—they will make the text clearer. In different sections of the book, I will cover the terms in detail, but learning basically what they mean will give the reader a head start. Use this list as a reference.

    Bait—Any foods stripers will eat that the fly rodder can imitate with a fly—crabs, all baitfish, shrimp, eels, worms.

Bars—Although stripers have driven us all to drink at times, a bar in the sea is not for the intake of spirits. These bars are mounds of sand, gravel, mussels, oysters, or embedded rock. They form barriers, create rips, give shore anglers wading access to holes, and help form ocean holes. Some are small mounds, 6 inches high, but bars can be many feet tall with severe drop-offs.

Boiling water—A very strong current that churns like a pot of boiling water.

Breachway—An opening from a salt pond into the sea, with rock jetties on both sides. This is a common term used in Rhode Island for the pond openings.

Cut—A deep section of water between two bars or between a bar and shore. Cuts funnel water and bait, and can form strong currents.

Dead drift—A method of working a fly with no retrieve, letting it flow with the water's movement.

Drifting or **drift fishing**—Fishing from a boat that is moving with the current or wind, or drifting along a shoreline or down a rip; fishing without using any source of power.

Drop-off—A location where the water plummets from shallow to deep very quickly.

Fan casting—Casting to different locations in a fanlike pattern, covering all sections of water in front of the angler.

Feeding lane—The section of water that forms a line between the faster flow of a rip and the back eddy. The mouths of outflows or the cuts between bars will have a distinct line—or wall of water—which is very visible in faster currents. Also, a line that forms between two currents moving in different directions. The same sort of feeding lane develops in a trout pool.

Feel—The sense of touch needed to detect a strike or to feel the fly through the line. Having good feel means knowing when there is a tight connection between the line and fly.

Line control—Using your hands to hold, retrieve, slip, or move the fly line, either to work the fly or to maintain contact with it. Fishing the wash along a beach might require walking with the flow, but your hands are the major means of controlling the line.

Mending line—Using the rod tip to manipulate line, to feed line to alter the fly's movement, or to make the fly settle deeper. Mending means throwing a section of fly line in a U-shaped bend up, across, or downcurrent after making the cast.

Mung—A reddish, fine weed that collects along some beaches after a prolonged onshore wind.

Ocean hole—A section of deep water along an ocean beach. Ocean holes develop mostly along large sand beaches, but they also occur on hard-bottomed beaches. Many holes are framed by submerged sandbars and look like a blue-green pool in the middle of a tan field.

Outflow—Any location where a large volume of water funnels through a small opening, creating a flowing stream of water. Creek mouths, river mouths, and openings to saltwater ponds all have outflows.

Pocket—A section of water that holds fish and bait. A location of deeper water, or a corner that offers protection from wind or heavy surf.

Point—Any strip of land that protrudes into the water. A point of land is large, but some points, particularly along ocean beaches, might be only the size of a tennis court, and they seem to vanish once you reach them.

Release anchor—A float that snaps to the anchor line, allowing you to drop the line overboard and chase a fish without pulling the anchor.

Rip—A current that forms with tidal flow. Some locations have a choppy appearance—a rip line. Actually, most moving water is called a rip—this is a common term referring to current.

Rip line—The dark choppy line that forms from the movement of tide over any structure, bar, or reef.

Slipping line—Feeding line with the retrieving hand. Slipping is used when fishing in the surf to allow the fly to flow with the wave's pull.

Slope—The grade along a beach. This term is generally used to describe a steep beach.

Smelling fish—Feeding stripers and baitfish give off an odor. At night, or when there is no visible presence of fish, the scent can help locate them.

Strike zone or **sweet spot**—The section of water that gives the best chance to hook a fish. Also a good holding location for fish, or a spot that keeps producing strikes.

Tidal flow—The current that forms from the tide when it moves.

Two-handed retrieve—Using both hands to retrieve, holding the rod under the arm.

Wash or **trough**—The section along a beach where the waves roll down the slope and spill into deeper water. The white rolling section of the surf. Generally seen along steep ocean beaches, but there can be a wash along any shoreline with wave action.

White water—The rolling white section of a broken wave, or the white frothy part of a wave that flows until it stops moving. After breaking, white water can flow up a beach or cliff, then flow back into the sea.

Smooth, Sheltered Beaches ③

When there is little wind or wave action, many beaches have docile periods. Even open ocean beaches on calm days can offer easy fishing. Beaches inside small estuaries and locations protected by surrounding land masses seldom get heavy water rolling in, but most locations are affected by wind. A smooth, sheltered beach is one that is easy to walk, with no large rocks and free of rolling ocean surf.

Lobsterville Beach on Martha's Vineyard is a fine example of an easy-to-fish location with these characteristics. Several miles long, it is perhaps the most heavily fly-fished beach in the world. I first fished Lobsterville with one of the "mayors" of Vineyard fly fishing, Cooper Gilkes. It was the wrong tide, dead low, but Cooper wanted to try it anyway; he has that knack for finding fish. His years of fishing gave him enough confidence to trust his instincts and try a location at the wrong time or tide. This is the mark of a good angler and something to always remember: Believe that gut feeling and don't be afraid to take a chance.

We started working the water from the parking lot, moving east to the bowl down the beach. The bottom was gravelly, with round stones from marble to baseball size. The current was slow, but Cooper said it would get better with the coming tide. We ran into several other anglers, but they left, grumbling, "It's too low to hold fish." Coop just smiled and said, "There will be fish here, captain, just hold tight." And as usual, he was right. We did not set the world on fire, but we took fish. Lobsterville is one of those places that holds fish anytime, at any tide, but as at most beaches, you

A smooth, open beach is a good location for beginners and can provide excellent fishing.

must sniff them out. There are nights when fish are everywhere, but many times fish hold only in certain pockets along the beach. On slow nights, you must keep searching; there are fish feeding somewhere.

The first task is looking for concentrations of foods like baitfish, shrimp, squid, or crabs. With concentrations of bait along a large section of beach, stripers might be scattered. If one small section along a beach holds baitfish, keep fishing that location. This is the main difficulty when fishing a sheltered beach when there is no structure or area of moving water to concentrate the fish. The actual fishing—walking, casting, and covering the water—is easy, but finding fish can be difficult, because there are no obvious, good holding areas. Once you learn a beach, the better spots will become apparent.

Finding Fish

With no evidence of feeding fish, I like to walk and cast, working downcurrent. If there is good overhead sun and clear water, get up high and look for fish. In low light, let the fly do the searching, casting at various distances and at different angles to the shore, and retrieving at different speeds. When searching a beach, several anglers can cover the water better than one. If fishing alone, I will work a likely section, then fish it again with a different fly and technique.

Wade carefully, and keep watching the water near the shoreline. In low light, stripers feed right along the shore, even without wave action. Some anglers wade too far, walking where they should be fishing. Particularly along beaches with gravel bottoms, the fish feed in close. I remember fishing a unique section of beach on Nantucket. Several spin anglers told me a secret: They would never wade at all, but would drag their swimming plugs so the hooks hit the gravel bottom along the shore. If they waded beyond the gravel, fishing the deeper water, they caught few fish. Lobsterville Beach is another prime example of this. Each season, many stripers take flies just a few yards from the shoreline. Wade only when necessary; on calm nights, wade and walk quietly.

Look for small points, coves, and pockets along the beach. Low tide with overhead sun will reveal many features of a beach's character. Note these features with landmarks along the shore if you plan to fish at night. Daytime observation will give the angler clues about water, tide movement, and bait type. You may also be shocked by the fish activity along some beaches at midday.

Working the Fly Close

When fish strike close to shore, work the fly right to your feet. In locations that require a long cast, roll casting before you pick up helps to avoid making many false casts. Stripers will track a fly for some distance, striking when the fly appears to be escaping into shallow water. Rod-tip strikes are common, and fishing the fly to your feet is a necessity. With approximately 15 feet of fly line outside the tip, lift the rod by slowly raising your arm above your ear. Keep working the fly by twitching the rod tip. When the fly is close, make a roll cast, pick up the line, and cast out. If a fish takes when the rod is in the air, make a hard roll cast. With sharp hooks, you will hook most of the close takers. With this technique, you can work a fly very close without having to make numerous false casts. (See Chapter 20, Hooking, Fighting, and Landing Techniques.)

To prevent retrieving too much line inside the tip, mark the line by putting several nail knots in the fly line close to one another, using sections of 10- to 15-pound-test monofilament. When you feel the nail knots while retrieving, you will know how much line is beyond the tip. Putting a mark 40 feet from the end of fly line gives you a good reference point. A mark at 40 feet leaves 30 feet of fly line beyond the tip—a good standard casting point. When you feel the mark, keep retrieving—perhaps fifteen pulls, which should be another 10–12 feet. Each angler must develop a system to establish the proper amount of line for casting. When I feel the fly line's diameter increase, I count the retrieves. After a time, it will become automatic; you will not need to think about numbers of retrieves, and your instincts will adjust to each situation. However, for the novice, a set mark on the fly line makes low-light fishing easier.

If you determine that the stripers are feeding near the shoreline, reel up some of the fly line and concentrate on the water next to shore. There are times when a 30-foot cast works well. When using less fly line, fishing is easier because there is less line to control, less line to clear after hooking the fish, and a more positive hook-set. A major fault of some anglers is trying to fish too much fly line. Use only enough line to reach the fish—put the rest back onto the reel.

Coping with the Wind

Wind affects any beach. A wind of 10–15 miles per hour creates waves. If the wind travels over several miles of open water, it can form rollers along a beach. Wind creates line-control problems. First, casting into the wind stacks up the line; the leader will certainly pile up. Excess fly line on the water prevents fly control, because you are not in contact with the fly. On flat calm water with little flow, this is usually not a problem, because the retrieve tightens the line quickly. In moving, wavy water, excess line makes fly control impossible. In broken, choppy water, a short, straight cast gives the best line and fly control.

Casting straight into the wind, using short casts, should keep the line straight. Yes, fighting the wind, shooting right into its teeth, makes casting difficult. But with a low, short cast, you can at least keep the line straight. A quartering wind blows the line, and the waves then wash the line sideways. Sometimes a quartering wind makes fishing very difficult. With a quartering wind, cast straight into the wind, keeping the line at an angle to the beach. After casting, walk downwind to maintain a straight line between you and the fly. By walking with flowing water, you keep the line perpendicular to the beach. Along ocean beaches with big surf, this is essential. (See Chapter 4, Ocean Beaches.)

When fishing with an onshore wind that is not overwhelming, try casting at different angles to find one that allows line control. Current flowing against the wind (for example, a quartering wind from the left into a flow from the right) can give a neutral effect, preventing the line from swinging too quickly to one side. In this situation, picking the proper angle makes fishing easy. Remember to try casts of different lengths to determine the amount of line you can control.

Coping with Fast Water Flow

Wind and water flowing in the same direction will swing the fly very quickly. This requires the angler's full attention because the fly remains in the strike zone for only a brief moment. When the line and fly are perpendicular to the shore, the fly remains in

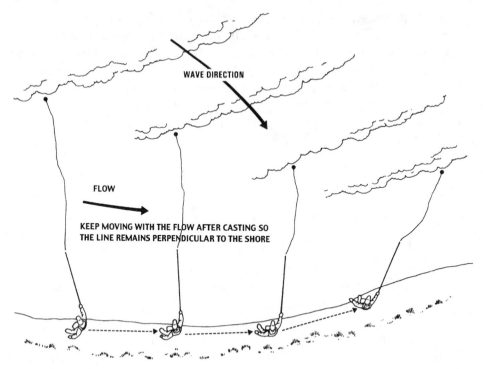

WAVE DIRECTION

FLOW

KEEP MOVING WITH THE FLOW AFTER CASTING SO
THE LINE REMAINS PERPENDICULAR TO THE SHORE

To maintain line control, you must move with the flow along the beach.

the strike zone. If the water pushes the line and fly quickly to one side, a fish has only a brief time to take the fly. This is the reason you sometimes need to walk with the flow to keep the fly in the strike zone.

When fishing fast-flowing water along a beach, use little or no retrieve. Keep casting, let the fly swing, then pick up and cast again. This takes smooth, quick line control. Most beginners have problems handling the line efficiently enough to work such water. When the fly and line land, you must be ready with the rod in position, line in hand. Keep the rod low and take in line until you can feel the fly. If you feel any resistance, make a strip strike. Depending on conditions, there might be a large bow in the line, and the strike will be a subtle tap. I fish with the rod under my arm, using both hands to retrieve. With even the slightest bump, I begin taking line with a quick hand-over-hand retrieve. If there is any resistance, I keep taking line until it tightens. Then I set up with a firm pull. Striking before you have a tight line will result in many misses.

When not fishing water with a very fast flow, try different retrieves depending on water conditions. On calm nights with slow water flow, mix up the fly's movement. Sometimes a fly with a spun deer-hair head that pushes water draws stripers; in still water, a surface wake can drive fish crazy. Try a fast retrieve with a small fly as well. Generally a slower retrieve works better at night, and a faster retrieve works better during the day, but keep experimenting until something works. In moving, broken water, remaining in contact with the fly and keeping it in the strike zone are your main concerns. In broken water, the fly gets its action from the water movement. Maintaining line control keeps the fly swimming, looking natural. Baitfish dart, glide, and suspend in their surroundings, flowing with the water. A fly that moves with the flow looks natural; a fly that shoots against a surge of water does not. When you retrieve, use the fly's movement to keep it swimming as a natural bait would. Remember, retrieving is more than moving the fly; it should be used to keep a tight line and to keep the fly in the strike zone.

What Wind Does to Fish

Wind not only affects casting and line control, it also makes the fish feed differently and moves the bait to different locations. Wind blowing straight onto a beach puts bait right on the shore. Wind blowing along a shoreline pushes bait into a cove or against a point on a beach. If you catch fish along a section of beach and the next day the wind is from your left, begin fishing in the same location and work right. Blows and coves collect baitfish when a wind blows along a shoreline, pushing the bait into the pockets.

Offshore wind makes casting easier and flattens the waves along a sheltered beach. A strong wind from the land can push the baitfish into deeper water. Along some beaches, expect to find the stripers farther from shore with a stiff offshore breeze. A light wind keeps the bugs down and leaves a calm section along the shore. Look for feeding fish in this slick water.

Use Your Senses

Wind takes away your eyesight and hearing, but it helps your sense of smell. If you notice a smell like melons, or any fishy odor, it is probably from bait or fish, or both. At times the scent is light, but with heavy concentrations of fish and bait it can hit you like a wall. Investigate even the faintest aroma of fish and keep working upwind until you find them. With a quartering wind, the fish will be beyond the smell, upwind. An onshore wind will have fish right where you smell them, if you can reach the fish. If the fish are offshore, beyond casting range, stay with the smell and hope they move in.

On calm nights, the sounds of feeding fish travel some distance. Listen for pops, splashes, and at times explosions if big fish are crashing fast-moving baits on the surface. Fish sipping small baits make little noise, but they still show up on a calm surface. In the right light, even at night, you can detect surface-feeding fish. Depending on the amount of light and the sight angle, you can see fish for some distance. At night, keep your senses working, and not just for signs of fish. Light shining along a beach means fish activity, as does the sound of a reel drag. Good anglers use every possible signal when looking for stripers.

Line Choice

The intermediate fly line covers most conditions along smooth, sheltered beaches. I recommend this line for a good portion of our fishing, because it evades the wind's effect and tracks better in broken water than a floater. A floating line or clear sink-tip line works well on warm, calm nights when fish are feeding right on top. From summertime to early fall, locations south of Cape Cod have many balmy nights when a surface line works well. In flat, calm conditions, either line will work; the intermediate works better in broken water. If you plan to own only one fly line, the clear-tip line—a floating line with a clear, intermediate 10-foot tip—is perhaps the best choice for sheltered beaches.

Using a Boat

Fishing from shore or wading is the smart way to work most sheltered beaches. For secluded locations without shore access, a boat can be effective. Onshore wind makes boating difficult if you must get close to shore. Drifting in with the wind and anchoring is the only way to work the water, because along any beach, running an outboard motor is poison. You must use a paddle, pole, or electric motor. Most electric motors do not have the power to fight a strong wind with a boat longer than 16 feet—forget poling and paddling. An onshore wind will make boat fishing impossible if you want to cover the shoreline as completely as a wading angler can. The electric motor works well in light winds, allowing you to move along, searching for fish. On very quiet nights in shallow water, boat anglers must make each move with care, because one mistake—one loud thump on the boat's bottom—will drive fish from an area. Use the same caution and care along shallow beaches as you do when flats fishing. On a calm, still night, you need to be even more cautious.

The water depth and the boat's size govern how close you can work to a shoreline. There are locations unsuited for boat fishing. Any shoreline with easy access will have wading anglers; the intrusion of a boat is unpopular. Shorelines lacking deeper water near shore are best suited for wading. To fish a beach from a boat, keep about a fly cast away from shore, land your fly in shallow water, and work it back to the boat. When fish are feeding tight to the shoreline, strikes might occur just as the fly hits the water. Use the same techniques from a boat that you would use from shore. Keep moving the fly around, try different retrieves, and keep watching. The added height advantage in a boat helps you spot fish.

If there is a good current, anchor the boat and fish by casting at different angles around the boat. Concentrate your efforts along the shore, letting the fly swing from the shallow shoreline out into the drop-off. Make the fly look like a baitfish flowing from the still water along the shore into the moving water in the drop-off.

Most sheltered waters do not have major movements of migrating fish; rather, the fish move in and hold for a time, but few reside there. There are times when traveling fish invade sheltered locations, and some beaches have steady feeding activity all season. However, you will seldom find the concentrations of fish that occur along the outer beaches of Cape Cod or at Montauk Point, where floods of fish overwhelm some locations. The good sheltered beaches are very consistent, but most do not have the deep water, structure, and heavy concentrations of bait that make some outer-beach areas classic.

Choosing the Best Tides for Sheltered Beaches

Places with small tides (2–4 feet in depth) should have fishable water on all tides. Beaches in many areas of the bay side of Cape Cod dry up at low tide. All beaches are different. To learn where the fish might hold at different phases of the tides, look at the locations at low tide. Many times I take a walk with my tackle and wade around to learn a location well. Look at the beach's angle and the slope between the high- and low-water marks to determine the water depth at different stages of the tide. If the slope is steep, there will be enough water at high tide to hold fish. If the beach slopes quickly into deeper water, you can fish it at any tide. Some beaches give access to large flats at low tide. At the low stages of the tide, you can fish the flats, and work along the beach when the tide is up. Locations with bigger tides have the most variety, changing to greater extremes and changing more rapidly throughout the tide. Places with small tides might have only subtle change throughout the tide; a 10-foot tide will alter some locations drastically. Picking the right tide comes with experience. A good bet is the last 2 hours of coming tide and the first 2 of falling tide. You will discover the prime tide by spending time fishing a location—by **learning the water.**

Wading is the most effective way to fish most sheltered beaches. Remember, wind can change conditions tremendously, making fishing difficult, but wind might also put fish along the beach. For most fishing conditions, an intermediate or sink-tip fly line works well with a 9-foot rod for an 8- or 9-weight line. Without heavy rips, even a big striper will not make an extremely long run, so 150 yards of backing on a mid-size, single-action fly reel works well. Sheltered beaches in most conditions are ideal for a wide range of fly-fishing skills. They are the perfect choice for the newcomer to wet a line.

Ocean Beaches 4

T he water was working perfectly, breaking into a point located along the beach. The beach was an ideal ocean shoreline, with sandbars located along the beach forming deep pockets between the bars and the shoreline. Waves breaking over the bars and into the points caused good water movement in the holes along the beach. The waves rolling onto the beach and flowing into the deep trough to my left looked ideal, yet cast after cast proved fruitless. I tried every angle with several flies, but not a bump. The right side of the hole looked good but didn't have the deep holding water like the location to my left; it did, however, have fish. The shallow bar that ran from the beach to the drop-off and the hole to the right provided action for more than an hour. Apparently the quartering wind pushed the bait to the right side of the point I was fishing. Standing on the point, viewing the water on both sides, I would have bet money on the left side. I would have lost my shirt. Fish move into a beach to feed; they go where the food is. If there had been bait in both locations, the better fishing would have been in the deeper pocket to the left. It offered more protection and easier feeding for the stripers. But the right side had the food, and that is where the fish were.

Ocean beaches are a mixture of fine to coarse sand that is mixed with large gravel in some places. The outer beaches of Cape Cod, from North Truro to Chatham, are classic examples of what an ocean beach looks like. The moving sand forms deep holes along the shoreline. Waves rolling against the beach create offshore sandbars

Rolling surf along a steep beach can put fish right at the angler's feet.

and points along the beach. The holes that form between the points and inside the bars create a steep section of beach in front of deeper holes. A typical ocean hole, viewed from above, would look like a pond with a beach on one side and submerged bars on the other side separating it from deeper water. In some cases, there is a series of holes leading into deeper water. There is no one shape to ocean holes, and their configuration keeps changing. Some are small, but most spin anglers cannot cast across the better ocean holes. Locations with smaller tides have miniature holes that are more like troughs and might run dry at low water. The bigger holes always have water, even with moon tides. When locating ocean holes along a beach, look for sections of deep, blue or green water surrounded by light-colored bars. If the water is clear and there is enough light, the holes show up well.

In some locations, fish hold and wait for the bait to come to them. Along ocean beaches, fish feed where the food is located. When you find bait, the fish will be there. Fish are not always active, feeding on certain tides or at different times of day, but they remain close to the food and keep coming back once they find easy feeding. Unfortunately, the food keeps moving, so the good beach angler must continually search the beach to keep pace with the moving bait. Often the move is short, but wind or heavy feeding activity might drive the bait some distance.

At times, ocean beaches have large numbers of fish—and big fish—feeding within easy fly-casting distance. On big beaches, the three challenges for the fly angler are finding fish, selecting fishable water, and line control. If there is even a modest sea running, choosing the right place and keeping in contact with the fly will frustrate the novice.

Selecting the Right Water to Start

Choosing water that you can comfortably fish is the primary goal. The water along open ocean beaches can roll with such force that even spin fishing is difficult. A moderate sea—2 to 4 feet—allows fly fishing on most beaches if the slope is steep. Fly fishing on long, flat ocean beaches is tough unless the sea is flat. You will seldom be able to reach the fish, and wave action will make wading impossible.

Steep beaches like Cape Cod's Nauset Beach or Nantucket's Madaket are ideal locations that remain fishable in all but the largest seas. The outer beaches along Long Island, New Jersey, and down into Virginia have smaller tides with generally less slope to the beach. The holes are usually smaller, ideal for fly fishing if the sea is not too big. A classic steep beach slopes quickly into deeper water. In locations with big tides, some areas might drain out at low water, leaving them too shallow, but some sections usually remain fishable even at low water. When the sea is heavy, the outer bars help break the waves' force, making some sections fishable only at low tide. With normal sea conditions, the higher tides are generally ideal times to fish. Because of changing conditions, the waves' size, different tides, and different wind directions, learning ocean beaches requires more time and skill than learning sheltered beaches.

Your first consideration should be the sea's size. If it looks big from a distance, it will be even bigger when you get closer. Most fly anglers would have trouble fishing with 6-foot surf rolling into the beach. A wave of this size rolls up a beach with tremendous force. It can rip a fly line from your hand and knock a careless wader into a tumbling sea. In big seas, **do not wade.** (Beginning on page 42, there is a short section on safety and survival in the surf. If you have little surf experience, pay close attention to this section.)

The first time you try surf fishing, choose small, 1- to 3-foot seas. This gives good water movement without harsh conditions to fight, and the sea is not large enough to hurt you.

Reading a Beach

Water along ocean beaches is perhaps the most difficult of any water in the sea to read. Its appearance varies constantly, and the beach itself might change, sometimes daily. Most ocean beaches change each season. Frequently sections of shoreline alter so drastically that you will not recognize them the following year. Each spring, I check locations in the daytime before fishing in low light.

A wave that breaks, then dissipates, is a sure sign of deeper holding water right near the beach.

When searching for fishing locations, there are several basic features to look for. The beginner should research the beach in the daytime, looking for a deeper blue or green section of water surrounded by light-colored sandbars. Some areas next to shore are not framed by bars—there will be just a deeper section along the beach. These pockets hold bait and fish. Ocean holes range in dimensions from small pockets to massive areas the size of many football fields. The smallest holes, some the size of a backyard swimming pool, are easier to fish, but hold stripers mostly at higher tides. These are not the most desirable locations, but they are good places to learn and do offer good fishing at times. Choose smaller water at first, locations where you can move along and cast, covering most of the hole. Or, choose a section of beach with deep water right against the shore that you can fish with a short cast.

Reading the White Water

After locating a hole, watch how the water works as it breaks over the bar and how the waves flow against the shore. Look for patterns. Watch how the water flows in and around the hole. As waves break, white water should form and roll over the bar, spilling into the hole. Waves break onto the shallower bar, then roll over the bar, and the white water spills into the deeper water. When white water forms, then just disappears, it is spilling into a hole. If white water forms 100 feet from shore and rolls into the beach without interruption, there is no deep water inside the bar. Only on a calm day could you fish this area, because line control would be difficult in big surf. Fish do feed in these areas, but they are not ideal fly-rod locations in heavy seas.

Where white water spills into a hole is prime feeding location. It is possible to reach this water when fishing a small hole—larger locations are well beyond the reach of the fly rodder. Only the edges might be reachable if the bars cut right near shore. Here you can work the water breaking over the bar that drops into the hole, as well as the flowing water between the bar and shore.

Fishing the Drop-offs Behind the Bars

What mystifies most anglers is that stripers really do feed in that rolling water. The fish hold in the deeper water just where the white water spills into the hole. Wade out at low tide and see what the drop-off behind a bar looks like. Some locations drop so severely that one step off a dry bar would put most anglers over their heads. Even though white water is thundering over the bar, there is good holding water below the drop-off.

Fish must feed aggressively in this rolling water. Drop a fly into the water on the bar and work it through the moving water into the drop-off. Casting across the flow and letting the fly swing into the deeper water works best. The fly flows into the hole looking like a baitfish caught by the white water. When the white water is big, use a short line, letting it dead drift. If you are having trouble controlling an intermediate line, use a fast-sinking line. Depending on the speed and amount of water flow, you might need to retrieve to keep in touch with the fly. Feel is important. Keep in contact with the fly, or you will miss most strikes. If you must use a long cast to reach the location, begin retrieving immediately after the fly lands.

Watch to learn how the line and fly work in this water. This will help when fishing in low light, when you must rely totally on your sense of touch. Developing the feel and being able to visualize what the line and fly are doing even when you can't see will improve your success rate. Remember: Even with overhead sun, you constantly use your sense of touch when fishing in rolling, discolored water with a sinking line.

Casting directly into breaking water demands quick and positive line handling. Retrieve the line as soon as it lands, and keep it moving quickly; otherwise, you quickly lose touch with the fly. This is like casting upcurrent in a trout stream or straight into a rip, where you must be ready to retrieve when the line hits the water. Depending on the water's speed, alter the retrieve to maintain feel of the line and fly. When fishing straight down any flow, the fly must move at the same speed or faster than the mov-

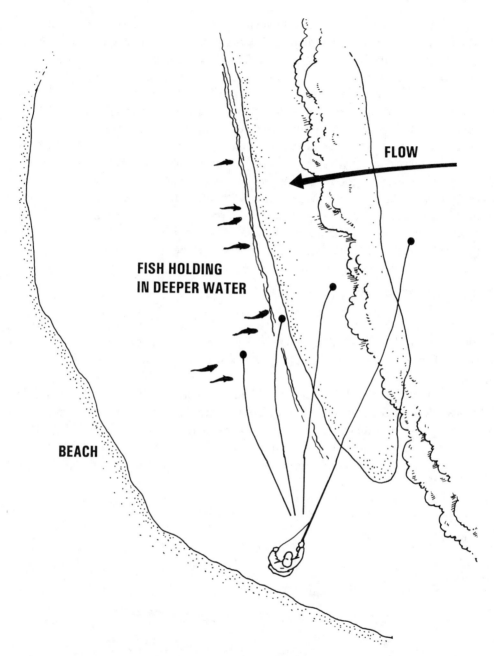

FLOW

FISH HOLDING IN DEEPER WATER

BEACH

Work the deeper water behind the bars by casting into the white water, letting the fly flow over the bar with the white water into the hole.

ing water. If the water pushes the fly, there is slack line and no contact with the fly. Maintaining fly control when fishing the line in the same direction as the flow requires constant alteration of the retrieve. The pulsating push from the surf adds another challenge. Don't be discouraged—this takes time and practice to learn.

In daylight, poppers work well, fished on the bubble-covered surface just below the white water. Poppers show up well, and as long as the popper is splashing, there is good contact between line and lure. Surface commotion attracts fish, particularly in bubble-filled water. Here the fish comes to the noise, sees movement, and takes. Poppers are effective in light to moderate water; they are hard to control in heavier water. Poppers are always a good bet in the daytime when line and fly control is difficult. Many times, even if fish do not take, they will look at the popper, leaving a swirl behind it. They are good searching tools because you can see any action the popper generates. An intermediate line works with a large popper if you begin retrieving just as the line hits the water, but a floating line works much better.

Working the Wash

The wash, the rolling water along the beach's edge, is a superb location for fly fishing. Waves rolling or breaking along a beach create the wash. A wave will hit the slope of the beach, break and roll up the beach, stop, then flow back down. The wave's force drives it up the beach above the actual water level, then it spills down the beach, crashing back into the sea. When this section of water is calm, fish it as you would a smooth, sheltered beach. Usually there is some wave action, and when there is active surf, this moving water confuses many anglers—as it should, because it is changing constantly. This section of water that rolls up and down the slope of a steep beach is also called the *trough* or *slough*—both words meaning "hollow" or

The trough along a beach is a favorite feeding location for stripers.

BEACH

WASH

FISH SOMETIMES FEED RIGHT IN THE WASH

"depression". The wash section of a beach is actually the portion of the slope where the wave rolling off the beach spills into water deep enough to stop the flow. It looks bowl-like, but it is just the refraction of light that makes it look hollowed. The slope of a beach is actually straight when viewed at low tide. Only where the slope meets the flatter bottom of the ocean's floor will a hollow form.

With moderate surf of 1–3 feet, an intermediate line works well. With larger waves in the 4- to 6-foot range, a Teeny-style line is a better choice. Teeny, Depth Charge-style line, consisting of 30 feet of fast-sinking line with an intermediate or floating running line, tracks better in the heavy roll and gets the fly down into the trough. However, these lines are more difficult for the beginner because the line sinks quickly, requiring fast line handling.

How the Wash Moves

What puzzles most anglers is the many directions this water moves in, seemingly at the same time. The possibilities are endless. Luckily, several patterns develop that are important to the angler. One water movement is up and down the beach; the other is sideways. You control the effects of the water that flows up and down the beach's slope with retrieve. The effects from the flow to the side you control with rod angle and footwork. In big surf, footwork is also necessary to control the up and down. Because the wash moves a greater distance in bigger surf, at times you must move up and down the slope to keep the fly in the strike zone. This requires experience; it's not for the beginner.

The flow of water up and down the beach is the most difficult water movement to deal with, particularly in midsize to large surf. Usually there is no pattern to the speed and force of the surf. Depending on speed, size, power, and direction of the waves, this can be one jumbled mess. If there are both ocean swells (waves from an offshore storm) and wind-blown waves, there might be two waves breaking at the same time from different directions. This causes a mixture of water movement that might be unreadable and difficult to fish. When the water is very confused, use only the amount of line that you can easily handle to keep the fly in the strike zone. Land the fly just beyond the break line of the surf, 10–15 feet out. This will put the fly right in the wash. After casting, try to keep a tight line, letting the fly hold in the wash or just outside the flow. If you cast when a wave is flowing away, straight down the beach, you might need to feed line or walk down the slope to keep the fly in the wash. As the next wave breaks, a fast retrieve or walking back up the slope might be necessary to keep in touch with the fly. This is a constant game of give-and-take to keep in contact with the fly. In lighter surf contact will be fairly constant, but in heavy surf there will be periods of total loss of control. Some days you will be lucky to maintain fly contact 50 percent of the time.

You sometimes need to move both up and down a beach, as well as sideways, to maintain fly and line control.

With normal conditions, work the fly as you would in rolling water along a smooth beach. The only difference is that a steeper beach has a heavier flow, and the flow changes are faster and more abrupt. Only occasionally will you need to feed line along a shallow beach. Feeding line is a necessity, even in small surf, along some sections of a steep beach. Here is where a two-handed retrieve works well. With both hands retrieving into a basket, there is better line control and a quicker take-up. Obviously, fishing without a stripping basket would be impractical; line management would be impossible.

How to Feed Line

Feeding line to a surging wave takes time to master; it's all in the hand, but you must use your eyes, too. Feeding too much line creates slack; feeding too little makes the fly bolt upcurrent like "superfish" swimming into a flow it could not possibly fight. The trick is to be ahead of the flow by watching the water's movement. An oncoming wave that walls up pushes the line and fly into the angler. The reverse happens if the wave is pulling away. Reacting by retrieving or slipping line before you feel the pull or slack helps keep you ahead of the flow. The real sense of touch comes in when you see a wave walling up but don't see the whole wash dropping down the beach. Here the hands take over, feeding line even though your eyes tell you to retrieve. The hands also will learn to distinguish between a strike and a wave's pull. A good trick is to keep pinching the line as you feed it. Tapping the thumb and forefinger together on the line will detect a strike. A wave pulls line smoothly; the weight of a fish will be a sharp tug. After following and taking the fly, most fish will flow out with the wave. By tapping the line, you will feel the fish's weight. When the fish is surging away with the wave, just hold the line, letting the fish hook itself. Setting too hard might break the leader, because the fish and wave are surging away together, creating a sharp pull. If you add another sharp pull, you literally create two jerks on the end of one line—you are the jerk who should not jerk!

Mending Line

If the surf is not too big, you can mend line to keep it in the strike zone and maintain a flow with the wash. In cases where the waves flow at an angle, keep mending line into the flow. Also try mending to make the fly run along the beach. Land the fly just beyond the white water and throw a mend down the flow. This will make the fly work along the beach down the flow and get the fly a little deeper into the water column. You might need to move along the beach in the direction of the flow to keep ahead of the fly.

Places along a beach where billowing areas of water form attract stripers because the turbulence disrupts the bait.

Mending works well when fishing the small billows of white water that form in some sections along the beach. Beaches with small gullies that are perpendicular to the surf create mushroom-shaped flows of white water. They look similar to the flow of white water that rolls off a cliff. In the proper wave conditions—usually small— these locations hold fish. Cast near these flows of white water, getting the fly to move with the white water into the trough. Cast the fly into the flow and mend line to one side of the white water so the fly swings along the edge of the flow. Mending line is a good way to make the fly flow at different angles to the beach or at angles to the flowing water.

The flow of the water along the beach should be more constant. In some locations, there will be a steady current. Waves breaking at an angle to the beach create a surging flow to the side—waves from your left will flow to the right. In big surf, this will have a strong force, sweeping the line quickly to one side. As when fishing angling waves along a smooth beach, you must move with the flow to keep the line perpendicular to the beach. (See Chapter 3, Smooth, Sheltered Beaches, for information.) At times you will need to walk at a steady pace to keep the fly in the strike zone. With a

Billows of white water form along some sections of beach. Fish the edges of these sections; they are locations that offer easy feeding for stripers.

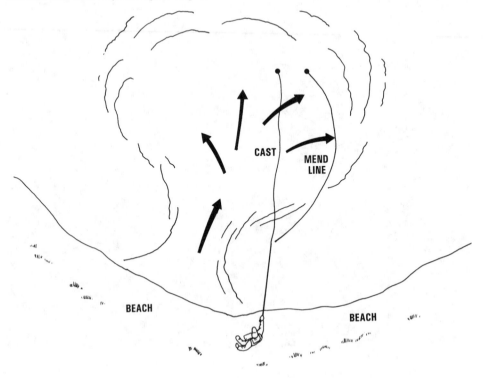

heavy flow, you must be content to keep the fly in the strike zone for a short time. Casting up into the flow helps to keep ahead of the moving water. There will be areas along the beach with water that is moving too fast for fly fishing. Choose areas with less water movement. In smaller surf, some locations will fish just like a smooth beach. Areas with current flow against the wave flow are easier to fish. In big surf, you need the flow against the waves because fishing is very difficult if the flow and waves are from the same direction.

You must keep watching the water's movement even in low light. If there is not enough light to see the waves forming, beware. You can fish an ocean beach on a very dark night in small surf. But do not attempt it in big surf unless you know it well. In big surf, you need to keep moving up and down the beach to keep close to the wash. If you cannot see the waves coming, trouble is inevitable.

Times of Flat Water

When fishing an ocean beach at calm times, work the water as you would a smooth beach. The holes and steeper shorelines will have feeding fish right along the slope; cast at different angles to the beach, or work the fly right along the shore. Wading out in the shallow water off the points allows access to water that is unreachable when there is surf. At lower tides, many areas offer large shallow locations where you can stalk fish, working the holes from dry sandbars. In big-tide locations like Cape Cod, numerous possibilities open at low water. But watch out! It is easy to lose track of time and the coming tide. This water is big, and you can get trapped on these bars. The tide rises fast and the coming tide might bring up a swell. Remember the route back to shore, and don't press your luck. Leave as the tide begins covering the bars. You can fish many of these places as you would fish a flat. (See Chapter 6, Flats and Shallow Water, Mud, and Sand, for more information.)

Fishing the Small Holes

Wave action along a beach creates continuous water movement inside the holes. The waves flowing over the bars fill the holes to a higher level than the surrounding sea. Water seeks its own level. When the water level in a hole overfills, it runs out through the paths of least resistance—usually through the cut between the bars.

Sandbars that run along ocean beaches usually have a trough, a deeper section of water between the bar and the beach, with openings at each end. I call these "miniholes." They look like drainage ditches at low tide. Some are quite small, the size of a school bus. Waves breaking over bars fill the trough to a higher level than the surrounding water. This creates current, a rush of water flowing from each end of the trough. The moving water is a good feeding area, along with the drop-off on the backside of the bar. If

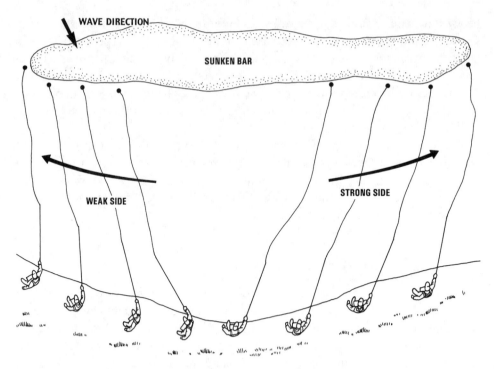

Miniholes offer the fly rodder good fishing in smaller surf. Concentrate on the drop-off behind the bar and the flow at the ends of the hole.

you can cast onto the bar, work the entire area from the bar's drop-off to the flowing water at the mouth of each opening. The water flowing over the bar offers a combination of wave action and flowing current. If you start from the middle of the trough, work to one side, fishing carefully right to the opening. Then move back to the middle and work the other side, again to the opening. Cast straight into the waves, starting your retrieve as the fly lands. Try to get the fly to swim with the waves that are flowing over the bar toward you, then let the fly swing into the hole, and keep retrieving to work the fly across the current. When possible, let the fly flow with the current by slowing the retrieve once it reaches the current, but keep retrieving enough to feel the fly. In low light, keep a more positive retrieve—not fast, but keep it moving so you maintain contact with the fly. In daylight, try a popper or a surface fly. A black Snake Fly works well even with an intermediate line, because the line pulls the fly under after several surges on the surface.

If the waves are breaking straight into the beach, both sides of the hole will have nearly equal flows. When the wave direction is on an angle and the waves are flowing into the beach from a quartering direction, one side of the hole will have a stronger current. Waves flowing into the beach from your left side will produce a stronger water flow from the right side of the hole. The reverse is true with waves from the other side. The side having the stronger water flow generally is the better side to fish.

Fishing the Points

Points along ocean beaches help create the holes that form along the beach. Unlike points of land, the points along a beach are usually smaller. They appear larger from a distance, shrinking in size and stature until almost disappearing once you arrive at the point. This makes finding a point at night challenging, and this is why it's necessary to pick a landmark other than the point itself when trying to locate one in the dark.

A typical ocean hole has a point on each side of the hole. Points do occur along beaches even where there is not a defined hole. The point will have deeper water to one or both sides, but there may not be a defined hole associated with the point. The deeper water along a point holds fish. The best location is where the waves roll across the point and into the deeper water. This will look similar to water flowing over a bar into an ocean hole, and it's really the same condition, identical to the corner of an ocean hole. When fishing either location, cast the fly onto the bar and let it flow into the deeper water. Most points have water shallow enough to break the force of all but the heaviest surf. With bigger waves, these pockets are the fly rodder's haven. If there is too much surf to fish here, leave the beach and find more sheltered, inside waters. Keep working the water, casting at different angles to get the right flow, casting and letting the fly dead drift if the flow is strong. You will be fishing at the corner of a rounded triangle. Concentrate mostly on the drop-off of the outer bar, but keep fishing the inner shoreline—the inside corner of the triangle—as well. Make some casts along the shore, or move and fish down the inside shoreline. In moderate surf, this entire beach should be fishable; in big surf, only the pocket will offer shelter.

If you can, fish both sides of a point and the shallow water over the point. A point with deep water on both sides offers some protection with any wave direction. You can always work the lee side. When waves are breaking straight into the beach, both sides of the point should produce good working water. At times, the shallow water right at the point will have fish. On a calm day, this is the only location that will have current. Rips will form along some bars at certain tides. Local knowledge—**learning the water**—is important, because these rips may appear for only a short time each tide. Calm water along an ocean beach generally scatters the fish; points collect fish in calm conditions.

How an Ocean Hole Works

Waves breaking into an ocean hole, over bars, and over a point create constant water movement. Rips formed by an ocean hole, or flowing between two bars, can have tremendous force; a good swimmer could never fight this flow. The water rushing

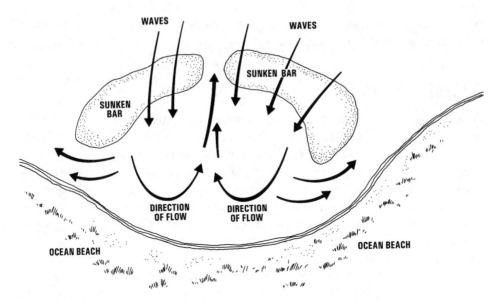

An ocean hole works in many ways. Sometimes there are several different flows within a hole. Reading this water can be tricky.

from the hole's center back out into the ocean is usually the strongest flow, but the water flowing through a side cut in the bars can also be strong. At times this force begins on one side of the hole, flows in a semicircle, then rushes out into the sea. As a young surfer, I learned to respect this flow and learned how it worked. Inside an ocean hole, the water usually flows along the inside edges of the bars, meeting in the middle, then rushing out through a cut in the outer bar. Viewed from above, if you were facing the ocean, the water to the hole's left side would flow counterclockwise, meeting the water from the right flowing clockwise, like two gears spinning in opposite directions inside a football-shaped sphere. The water along the shore on the left side of the hole would be flowing to the right—on the right side it would be flowing to the left. In the center, along the shore, the water might have little flow, but this slack water will shift from side to side as the force of both flows changes.

A large set of waves breaking into one side of the hole will give that side more flow. The flow of water in the corners will maintain the same direction, but the amount of water entering the hole will vary the flow's speed. This is only a general description, because wave size and speed, numbers of waves, and tide size can all influence how the water in the hole will work.

Cuts between the bars provide ideal feeding locations. The water funnels the bait out through the small openings, giving the fish moving water while gathering the bait for easy feeding. Along beaches with big tides, low water might be the only time to fish these cuts, because they are usually beyond casting range. However, the cuts between the outer bars and the shoreline might be close enough to reach.

If you can wade to one of the bars, cast across the cut's opening, working the water by placing the fly in different locations in the flow, as in fishing a rip. Also work the water in front of you using short casts, and fish where the wave washes from the bar into deeper water, on both the back and front sides of the bar. This is similar to fishing a minihole.

When fishing from shore, cast straight out into the cut, working the water on both edges where it flows from the cut into deeper water. To work the flow, make a quartering cast across the opening so the fly can swing downcurrent, working the mouth of the opening. Try, on some casts, just pulsating the fly as it swings. With this flow, you should have good line control to work the fly at many angles. If you can reach both edges of the flow, make the fly swim through the feeding lanes. (For more detail on feeding-lane fishing, see Chapter 10, Estuaries.) Stripers, like trout, will hold on the edges of feeding lanes waiting for food.

Weed Problems

Onshore winds along a beach cause weed to collect in some locations. There are times when this weed hinders fishing or even makes it impossible. Called mung, this

Mung weed will collect along a beach, making fishing difficult.

fine red weed coats a fly line like wet snow on a power line and sticks like molasses. When it's bad, the weed buildup at the rod tip will stop the retrieve. Mung collects in pockets along the shore, clogging some holes or sections of beach, but leaving others free of weed. If you encounter weed in one hole, keep moving until you find clear water. At times, it affects only one side of a hole, leaving the other side fishable.

If you encounter weed when fighting a fish, keep as much line above the water as possible, and keep shaking the rod tip. Quick snaps with the rod shake the weed off. But when it builds up, weed can clog the line at the tip. I have watched anglers handline a fish in because the tip and guides were clogged. Expect to find mung after storms with several days of steady onshore wind. It will clear with one tide and offshore winds.

Boating

Using a boat to fish most ocean beaches is out of the question. Usually, the best fishing is right next to shore. Light seas will allow sensible fishing for the experienced boat angler. As long as there is no white water breaking over the deeper bars, you can work the water around them. This is similar to working open water. (See Chapter 11, Big Rips and Open Water.)

Hazards Along a Beach

Safety must be your first consideration if the seas are big. As a surfer, I found out what a wave can do to a person. A slow 3-foot wave on a long, sloping beach will push you; a fast 3-foot wave snapping over a steep bar feels like getting blindsided by a pro linebacker. A 6-foot breaking wave could tumble a pickup truck. Getting caught and pulled into the wash along a beach is not a joke.

The first rule: Never turn your back to the sea. When you need to tie on a new fly, walk up the beach well away from rolling surf. If you turn your back to the sea, either on shore or in a boat, it will bite you. When fishing, keep to the crest of the beach, venturing down only if you can stay in water less than knee-deep. When fishing the wash, if you are moving up and down the beach's slope, keep watching for large waves or waves that double up.

All beach anglers get caught wading too deep. You get careless and bang, you are waist-deep, with a wall of water trying to suck you into the sea. If you get caught, move immediately with the flow up the beach. Remember, the wave flows up the beach first, holds, then flows down the slope. When caught, the more ground you can gain up the slope before the flow starts down, the better chance you have of staying on the beach. As the wave begins flowing back into the sea, stand sideways to the flow, planting your lower foot. Lean into the rushing water, keeping your feet planted. If, by chance, you get sucked into the wash, try to move away from shore unless there is a chance of getting back up the beach on the next wave. The best choice is swimming to deeper water. This

A sand wall is a sure sign of an ocean hole right along the beach.

gets you away from the pounding waves in the wash and gives you time to plan your escape. Prevention, however, is the best cure.

Avoid walking against a large dune or embankment. Some locations, such as the northern end of Cape Cod, have long stretches where the high dunes run right into the ocean. If trapped by a big sea in this location, you have nowhere to go. When walking along a shoreline, watch for the sharp drop-offs near the holes. Steep walls will form at the center of the deepest holes. They run sometimes head-high from the center, tapering to each end. Stepping off one of these drops will cause a bad fall. Driving your four-wheel-drive vehicle over a bank will be very unpleasant. Finding walls along a beach, by the way, means you have discovered a good fishing location.

Finding and Marking Beach-fishing Locations

Ocean beaches require research. Even the veteran surf angler keeps a constant watch over the beach. First you must learn to find and identify the better locations. As mentioned above, a wall along the shoreline indicates that there is deep water along the beach. With good overhead sun and clear water, the holes will show up blue or green ringed by lighter tan bars. If the water is riled up and discolored, look for waves that break, then disappear. Watch the white water from a wave as it breaks over a bar. If the white water rolls, then disappears, there is deep water between the bar and shore. The breaking water might be some distance from shore—some holes are very large. But even locations with a bar 75 feet from shore can be good holes. Actually, they are more suited for fly fishing. Most holes are shaped like footballs. In breaking surf, the outer bars will show up white, ringing the deeper water. Viewed from a high perch, the holes are easy to spot. When you run along a beach in a vehicle, the white water and the sand walls help locate the holes.

If you plan to fish in low light, mark the holes, choosing a landmark you can find at night. If running the beach with a vehicle, keep a list of odometer settings, or use a GPS (Global Positioning System) to mark the locations. A good trick is to put a marker on the dunes. The reflectors used to mark driveways work well. Put them out in the daytime, and as you come to each hole, pick them up. Once you learn a location, finding the holes is easy, but on a foggy, dark night it helps to have good references so you are not groping about.

Looking down a beach from a distance, you will notice points that stand out. But once you arrive at that point, it disappears. Only the bigger, more pronounced points are evident, and even these seem to be little more than bumps once you actually reach them. In low light, you must have marked the points well; otherwise, finding them is difficult. After locating a point, mark it from a distance with a prominent spot along the beach. Then you have a good reference to help find the point.

On heavily fished beaches, look for many footprints and tire tracks in one location. This is a sure indication of a prime fishing spot and one that might have recently provided hot fishing. Lights along a beach also mean action. Neck lights flashing on and off, or a camera flash, are sure hints. Watch what other anglers are doing. Repeated activity by another angler or a group of anglers could be a hint of good fishing.

Watch the bait anglers. They know the best holes and can give clues to what the fish are feeding on. This is all part of **learning the water.** Sometimes you can learn more by observing than by fishing.

Tackle and Flies

A 9-weight is the minimum-size rod for beach fishing. Yes, an 8-weight will work—sometimes. My choice is a 10- or 11-weight outfit with a reel that holds 200 yards of backing. This is big, heavy, hard-running water, with big fish. I want the power of bigger tackle, both for presenting the fly and for landing the fish. Remember, it is not the striper's size or strength that should be considered when choosing tackle. You should select tackle that fits the water conditions, and not the most favorable conditions, either. I have watched good anglers, in rolling surf, labor with a 20-pound striper on heavy spinning gear. In these conditions, what chance would you have with an 8-weight fighting a 30-pound fish? In the surf, use bigger tackle.

Flies

I'm sure that for about half of the surf fishing you encounter, any 4- to 5-inch-long, breathable fly would work. The Snake Fly and Deceiver are my workhorses: all black for low light and discolored water, white for clear water and bright nights. Mix in chartreuse or yellow; both are good colors to imitate sand eels and spearing. In late summer right into fall, small bunker and herring move along the beach. Two- to 5-inch-long, white, wide-sided flies with some flash work well. Also carry some poppers and a few big 6- to 8-inch-long, wide-sided flies and a crab fly.

Fighting and Landing Fish

Fighting and landing a fish in rolling surf poses some problems. In small surf, less than 2 feet, there is little surge, but waves of 4–6 feet have incredible power. You must use that power to help land the fish—don't try to fight the waves. When first hooking a fish, walk up to the beach's crest so you can move with the fish. The height will allow a better fighting angle on the fish and better mobility, and will eliminate any worry about the surf catching you from behind. If the fish runs down the beach, keep pace with it. In heavy water, excess line decreases the pressure and control you can apply to a fish. Keeping a short line also prevents excessive line wear and reduces the chance of weed buildup. On a crowded beach, staying close to the fish also lessens the chance of someone crossing your line.

Once the fish is close, the wash becomes a factor. Getting the fish inside the first wave, between the wash and shore, can be difficult. If a big fish is sideways to the beach or facing away, moving it through rolling white water is nearly impossible; even a small fish will be a chore. The fish must be facing the beach so you can punch it through the roll. The best time to attempt breaching the roll is when the wash moves toward the shore. Try walking down the slope as the wash flows seaward, holding the fish just outside the first wave. As the next wave breaks and begins flowing up the slope, move up the beach ahead of the wave and try to slip the fish through the wave. Using the wave's flow, you can usually pop the fish through the wave, moving it to the beach side of the wash. As the wave recedes, you must give ground, again walking down the slope, but this time, if you have breached the wave with the fish, the fish is on the beach side of the wash. With the next wave, walk up the slope, letting the wave plus rod pressure put the fish on the beach. If the fish is lying on the beach halfway down the slope, just hold tension with the rod and wait for a wave to move the fish farther up the slope. Attempting to retrieve the

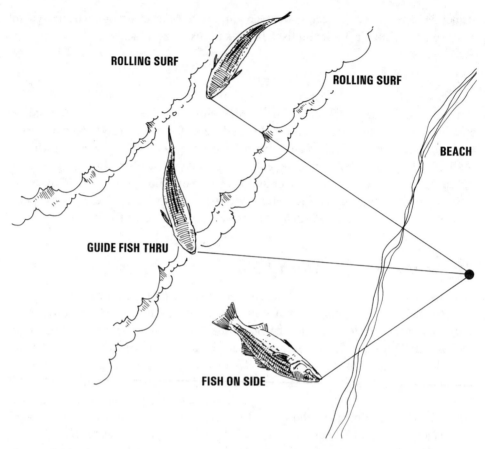

ROLLING SURF

ROLLING SURF

BEACH

GUIDE FISH THRU

FISH ON SIDE

Once a fish is close, near the trough, you must pull the fish headfirst to punch it through the surf line.

fish too far below the break line might be dangerous; you could get hit by a wave when trying to pick up the fish.

Ocean beaches provide prime fishing for the shore angler. Along many beaches, there is good action throughout the season. Both spring and fall can provide hot fishing as stripers feed heavily along their migration routes. This can be good all day long. If there are good concentrations of bait, expect to find fish all summer along some beaches. Warmer-water beaches have less action as the water temperatures reach 70 degrees, and most fishing is at night. In August, periods of low light are usually better even along cold water beaches. Ocean beaches offer a wide variety of fishing. Wave action improves fishing as long as the seas are not too large. With the right conditions along a beach, fly fishing can be outstanding. One of the biggest thrills in angling is watching a striper suspended inside the face of a wave taking a fly.

Driving on a Beach

Many beaches allow four-wheel-drive vehicles to run the shoreline. Some beaches have strict rules and require you to attend a short course to learn the proper way to run a beach. Always carry safety gear, including a jack, a $20'' \times 20'' \times 1''$ jack board, tire gauge, tow rope, shovel, a full-size spare tire, and puncture kit. You should also have at least a half tank of gas, a sound battery, jumper cables, and a cell phone. On isolated beaches where help is a long way off, a winch-like tool called a "come-along" is a good idea.

Never park the car below the high-water mark or in a location where the waves might reach it at high tide. I prefer to run only above the high-water mark; some beaches have rules that require this. Do not run too close to dunes with sharp drop-offs; some areas along a beachfront will have a 4- to 5-foot steep wall of sand in front of a good hole. Run with lights at night, and keep back from the fishing locations when running the beach. When turning around, always back *up* the beach; you can sink a vehicle in the sand by backing down the slope. If you are spinning the tires, stop and either dig out around the car or drop the tire pressure to get the vehicle moving. Remember, there is no bottom to the beach, and spinning the wheels will just bury the car. Keep the speed down, avoid wet or wave-washed sections of beach, and keep in the track—that is, the section of beach with two sets of tire tracks.

Each vehicle and beach will require a different pressure setting for the tires; 14–18 pounds is good for most conditions. If the car is overworking, drop the tire pressure. Wear a seat belt; it will keep you from hitting the roof when you hit a bump. In my vehicle, 15–18 miles per hour is a good comfortable speed.

Running a beach will give you access to excellent fishing and will allow easy travel to anglers who might not otherwise be able to reach some fishing locations. Remember that you are in a hostile and volatile environment, as you are in a boat, so treat it with respect. Unlike driving on a road, when running a beach, you will cause your own peril. Act wisely and running a beach will be fun.

Mixed Rock, Sand, and Gravel Beaches ⑤

*I*t had been nearly 10 years since I had fished this shoreline in Rhode Island. It was a dark morning with light rain and a modest northeast wind. The sea was broken and large, building significantly from the previous day. Even in the darkness, I knew that the water in my original location was too rough to fish. In desperation, I chose this place because I remembered it was sheltered from the swells. Reaching the location that I hoped would hold fish, I was amazed to find it had not changed. After 10 years of storms and pounding surf, the protected pocket was still there, and it still had fish holding in the same places. That morning, half a dozen schoolie fish and one keeper took my fly. The round stones that carpeted the bottom, creating such treacherous walking conditions, also kept this fishing spot from changing. Casting to the white water that rolled over the rocky bar, I fished the hole between the bar and shore. Like a trough along a sandy beach, this spot held fish along the bar. They were taking the fly as it moved from the white water into the drop-off. But unlike a sandy location, a rocky spot will usually remain the same over time. When tide, wind, and water conditions are similar, fishing conditions in such locations will be consistent. Built better than any man-made fortress, many locations with hard structure provide ideal feeding areas for stripers.

Shorelines along our coast offer a variety of fishing opportunities. Beaches—both protected shores and those open to the sea—can have a mixture of bottom covers. Unlike ocean sand beaches, many ocean shorelines with hard, sloping bottoms seldom change, even after bad storms. Sheltered hard shores may remain unchanged for decades, and the pockets that hold fish remain constant. Once learned, these locations

Rocky areas along a beach will hold fish. Here is Jim Bernstein, manager of Eldredge Bros. Fly Shop, with a nice fish.

will be good fishing spots for years. Squibnocket and Stonewall on Martha's Vineyard; the shoreline east of Weakapaug, Rhode Island; and beaches from Greenport to Orient Point, Long Island, are examples of the different kinds of structure-filled beaches. At low tide, they look like rock gardens, with a scattering of different rubble covered with weed. Long Island Sound, Narragansett Bay, and Buzzards Bay have many sheltered locations of mixed structure. There are perhaps more rocky areas than there are smooth locations. This type of water is common from Long Island Sound to Maine. South of Montauk Point, the beaches are mostly sand.

Reading Structure

Places with large rocks help hold the sand. If the rocks are encased in mixed stone, the bottom is very stable and ideal for holding food. Any location with structure has better holding water for bait and fish. Areas with large rocks and deep pockets between them are sanctuaries for baitfish and for bottom baits as well.

A rocky, sheltered shoreline with current is much like the bank of a big river. Along most shorelines, the bottom will be mixed with gravel, hardpan, mussel beds, some sand, and a mixture of different-size rocks. Areas with big rocks offer the best variety. The boulders break the current flow, giving good holding locations for fish, but they are more difficult to wade and tricky to work from a boat.

A large single rock, or a cluster of rocks, provides an ideal holding and feeding location for stripers. Called rockfish because they inhabit areas with structure, bass will remain in rocky areas for long periods. Along a sandy shore, fish move in to feed, then seek deeper water to hold in before feeding again. In large areas of structure, stripers can feed and live without moving very far.

Some shorelines have good structure running for several miles. Only a portion is accessible to the shore angler. The fishing techniques from shore and boat are similar. If there are differences, I will mention them in the boating section. Otherwise, use the same methods for both. Fishing most shorelines, the surf angler must concentrate on wadable locations with deeper water. Look for bars, ledges, and small reefs that give access to holding water. Trying to stumble your way along a slippery, rock-infested shoreline, fishing each section of water as you would a sandy beach, is unwise. Wading rocky locations is a picking game; you must select the better, reachable locations. The boat angler can reach and cover much more water along most rocky shores. The shore angler must choose a wadable place within casting distance of some deeper water. Look for even a small depression, a bar where the water might drop 2–6 feet. Depending on the tidal change, areas with small tides have places that are fishable for a fair portion of the tide. Areas with large tides require more frequent moves, but offer more fishable water. In large-tide locations, the possibility of being trapped by rising water increases drastically. Know the tide, learn the area well, and fish only on a falling tide unless you are completely familiar with a spot.

Pick a High Location

In difficult wading areas, I have places—such as rocks or ledges—that provide good standing and casting platforms for fishing. On the right tides, I select these locations because they allow height and easier casting. Here you are fishing a specific location, waiting for the fish to come to you. When you start learning locations, search for spots that give you an advantage. Height allows a better view, helps casting, and makes line and fly control easier. Once you find a good high perch, be patient and keep fishing; if there are fish in the area, they will find you.

Fishing Around Structure

Sheltered areas without surf will experience wave action only from wind. Without wind, tidal flow is what generates water movement. Usually, moving water produces the best feeding activity. Water flowing around a rock creates an ideal feeding environment for stripers. Work the flow around the rock, allowing the fly to swing

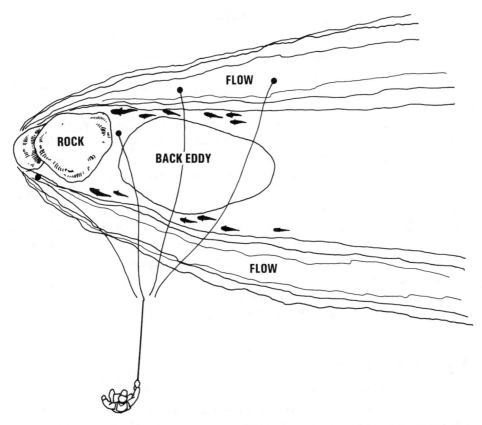

Work the water around a rock carefully, covering the flow both above and below the rock. The feeding lane behind the rock will hold fish.

through both the feeding lane and the pocket behind the rock. In shallow water, when fishing from shore, use an intermediate line, or a floater if you are fishing poppers. When fishing from a boat in deeper locations (more than 10 feet) a Teeny or Depth Charge–style line works well. Try placing the fly ahead of the rock and let it drift just past, then move it quickly so it darts away from the feeding lane. Trout anglers should be old hands at working a rock in a current; trout and stripers are similar in their feeding habits. Wave action enhances the feeding possibilities. With flowing current and surf, keep working the white water and the flow behind the rock. Cast as the wave breaks, and let the fly flow with both movements. If the wave is pushing the fly, use enough retrieve so you can feel the fly.

Ocean beaches with scattered rocks offer the same water movement and conditions as sand beaches with ocean holes and have structure for holding fish as well. Fish the shoreline as you would an ocean beach while working the moving water around the rocks. Keep casting to the rocks' edges. Try to time your cast so the fly lands just after the wave breaks. Casting straight into the surf, try to land the fly to one side of the rock, and retrieve the fly past the rock toward shore. In large surf, to maintain line control, start retrieving before the fly lands. Fish hold on the shore side of the rocks, using them to break the surge. Make the fly swim past the rock, with the white water, into the protected pocket behind the rock. Fish holding around a rock in the surf will feed actively, right in the white water. Getting the fly into the white water at the proper time can be important. On some days, this timing is critical; casting too late or too soon will produce few strikes. If you keep seeing swirls just after the white water rolls, try false casting, holding the cast in the air until the wave breaks. Landing the fly and retrieving it through the white water is often effective.

Even without current or wave action, a large rock or clump of structure will hold fish. Work the fly alongside or over the structure if it is submerged. A Teeny or Depth Charge–style line is effective if there is deeper holding water near the structure. With little or no water movement, retrieve the fly faster, trying a pulsating action, using both short and long pulls. On calm nights or at first light, poppers or surface sliders work well. Surface flies are ideal when trying a new location; they allow fishing even over very shallow spots and prevent hang-ups. Weedless or bendback flies are a good idea to avoid most snags when fishing deep.

Nights Are Productive

At night, or in low light, expect to find fish anywhere. As the light increases, look for fish in the deeper locations and in moving water. In colder locations, or during spring and fall, stripers can feed anytime. Fishing the hot, dog days of summer on late, dark nights can be productive in rocky locations. Long Island Sound and the Rhode Island shores have a steady following of serious fly anglers who patrol the rocky areas at all hours of the night.

Fishing Shallow Bars

Mussel bars, gravel bars, and clumps of mixed stone form rips, as well as acting as passageways to fishable locations. The rips along these locations can have feeding fish. Shallow rocky areas hold fish as flats do, but are much tougher to work. Dark bottoms make spotting fish difficult; you will only see fish that make a surface disturbance. If the flats are very shallow, 1–2 feet deep with no drop-off, use a floating line and buoyant fly to work the very skinny locations. Otherwise, use buoyant flies with an intermediate line. Work the edges of the rips, casting the fly to fish right over the bars. Also try casting along the rip's edge, letting the fly flow with the rip into deeper water. If the rip drops right into deep water, fish as you would a rip. (See Chapter 11, Big Rips and Open Water.)

Along the George River on the Maine coast, there are mussel and oyster bars that form good rips at about half tide down along the river's edge. As the large mud banks empty, they create good water flow over the bars. During one fly-fishing school, we put some students on these bars with good success. The day before, several of the instructors had fished this location. As we eased close to the rip, I told noted Maine guide Pat Keliher to cast a black Snake Fly up on the bar. Pat was into a fish immediately. That afternoon, this one location produced several other fish, all of decent size. Every fish we caught took the fly in 1–3 feet of water. The next day, Pat took some of the students back to wade the bar. One woman hooked a fish of nearly 20 pounds that shook off when Pat had the leader in his hands. There was other action as well, and for this school these rips provided our most productive fishing, although the other water we fished—with big rips, deep holes, and good wave action around structure—looked much better. Small water can bring big dividends. When you are walking out on a bar planning to fish at the end, fish the bar's edge as well.

Fishing the Flow

Fish areas with a large, constant flow by covering the water, casting at different angles to the current using the fan-casting technique. Look at the water in front of you

Cover all the water by casting to different sections. This is called fan casting.

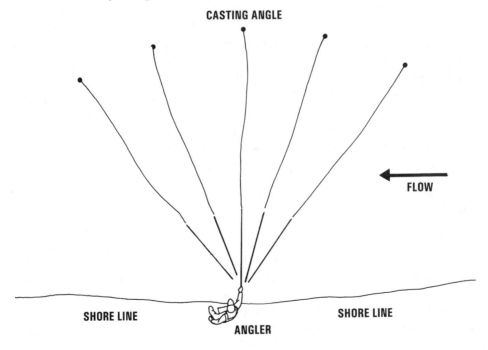

CASTING ANGLE

FLOW

SHORE LINE

SHORE LINE

ANGLER

and imagine that you are painting a fan on the water with the fly and line. Cast straight out, then work the water to a 45-degree angle on both sides of that straight line. If the water is flowing from left to right, try first fishing downcurrent, using both a dead drift and a steady retrieve. Casting left, into the current, will require retrieving to keep in contact with the fly. Here the skilled angler, casting upcurrent, might try dead drifting downstream, letting the fly flow with the current. Maintain contact with the fly by retrieving the slack line; at times, moving the fly faster than the current will not hurt. It is better to move the fly than to lose control of the fly. Try also mending line to alter the fly's speed and position in the flow.

With a current running from left to right, casting to the right requires less attention because the flow helps maintain a tight line. Depending on the flow's speed, a fast retrieve might be necessary. As you fan cast, vary the distance as well as the direction. When fishing a rip line or structure where the current forms a flow that looks like it is boiling, concentrate on the locations with the most water movement. But intermittently, keep working all the water. At times, stripers will move into the flat water to feed.

Boat Fishing

If you are worried about your outboard's propeller, stay clear of these locations. Some good bass hounds who fish rocky areas go through a prop each season. With an electric motor, you will prolong the prop's life. The wise angler uses an aluminum prop in rocky areas to protect the motor's driveshaft. A hard stainless-steel prop striking structure can damage the lower unit.

Learning the water is important for navigation, let alone fishing. Do not run this water at night unless you know it well, **very well.** Move slowly, and keep the motor tilted up; in very shallow areas, use a pole, a paddle, or an electric motor. Large areas of skinny, rocky water are not suited for running an outboard motor. You will only damage equipment and spook all the fish. With any wave action, keep plenty of water under your boat. A boat's usefulness is its mobility, its ability to reach places not accessible from shore. Getting in close is not always a necessity. And do not crowd the shore anglers. Respect their territory; you can fish many locations they can't.

Move Cautiously

Learn by working the outer edges of this water. Fish the outer rocks, getting a feel for the water in the daytime at low tide. When you get to know a place and learn the pockets that hold fish, anchoring works well. Drifting is an effective way to learn a location and to cover large amounts of water. Wind makes drifting difficult if it pushes the boat into shore or downcurrent. A stiff onshore wind requires constant moving and too much outboard noise—electric motors will not fight some winds.

Wind and current flowing in the same direction move the boat too fast to fish some locations. Anchoring helps the beginner because the flow keeps the line tight.

Fishing from an Anchored Boat

Fishing from an anchored boat is like standing on a rock in the middle of a river; both sides can have action. From shore, the most productive water is generally in front of the angler. When positioning a boat, try to anchor so you can cast to fishable water on either side. With two anglers, this will make fishing easier. When there is only one good side, one angler must backcast into the good water, unless the anglers are right-handed and left-handed. When positioning the boat, calculate the wind to make casting easier. From shore, you are at the wind's mercy; use the boat to beat the wind.

Fishing while Drifting

One major difference between boat and shore fly fishing is drifting. Casting from a fixed position, boat or shore, should be the same. Yes, the fishing angle might be different, and you will retrieve upcurrent more often from a boat. However, when drifting, you cast and retrieve while moving downcurrent or downwind.

Casting upcurrent and fishing the fly down the flow works well. This makes the fly look natural, like a baitfish swimming with the flow. Use a steady retrieve to keep in contact with the fly. In a strong current, try making long pulls, getting the fly to bolt through the current. Sometimes pausing between strips can generate a strike. Quick, short strips with a buoyant fly make it dance. Used with a sinking line, the fly will dart to the surface between pauses. Usually when fishing from a boat, you work the fly from shallow to deeper water, or continually work the same depth. This allows more daring retrieves and slower retrieves with a sinking line than when fishing from shore.

When drifting, try casting at different angles around the boat. Work the fly at different angles to the current's or to the wind's direction. With a combination of wind and tide, casting in the same direction as the boat's flow gives the best line penetration. However, this takes more skill to maintain contact with the fly. You must cast a straight line and begin retrieving, sometimes very quickly, as soon as the line lands. Casting uptide will make the fly flow downcurrent, angling with the wind. This is an easier angle to fish and is still very productive. Working into the wind makes casting difficult and gives little penetration into the water if the wind is strong, because the boat's drift is too fast to allow the line time to sink. (See Chapter 11, Big Rips and Open Water, for more information on drift-fishing techniques.)

In some locations, particularly from shore, an angler can lose many flies if not careful. One morning, I watched several novice fly anglers fishing a shallow, stone-filled pocket. They just kept losing flies. I came back to the location at low tide—the rocks in the pocket were littered with flies and looked like a tulip garden. Many rocky areas require constant awareness when working a fly from shore. A boat's height and mobility are distinct advantages in many structure-filled locations.

How to Fight Fish

Fighting fish requires skill and patience. In a boat, if it's safe and necessary, follow the fish, keeping about a fly line's distance behind. Staying close allows you more fighting control and a quicker reaction if the fish tries to tangle the line in structure. Following the fish also permits an angler to land and release the fish faster. Once the fish's first run is over, if you can stay close, landing even a big fish can be routine. The trick is not letting the fish regain its strength. A release float attached to the anchor line provides the fastest pursuit when chasing a fish. (See Chapter 20, Hooking, Fighting, and Landing Techniques.)

One problem you might encounter from a boat is the fish that runs over a shallow area where following is impossible. Then you are in the same predicament as the shore angler.

Keeping pace with running fish along a rocky shoreline presents many problems. If the bottom is mixed rocks and the footing is bad, the fish will quickly carry line over the structure and widen the distance between you. One hundred yards of line flowing through structure will find a place to tangle. You need help from the fish. (When hooking a big fish, be sure to select one that runs only into deep water!) When a fish runs through structure, hold the rod high and try to keep close to the fish. If the line catches around a rock, a full bend in the rod will ease the pressure. A tippet will quickly part under heavy pressure if it is chafing over structure. Holding the rod high gives the best chance of clearing the snags and adds only light pressure to the tippet. This is not the right way to tire a fish, but your first concern is keeping the line clear. Once the fish is clear of the structure, you can start applying pressure. (Follow the information in Chapter 20, Hooking, Fighting, and Landing Techniques.) Just be ready to raise the rod again if the fish works around a rock. Often, a tired fish will find a rock to swim behind as you are working it to shore. When a tippet rubs against any abrasive material and you apply too much force, it will cut through.

Careful Wading

Locations that are difficult to wade demand special consideration, particularly if fishing at night. A wading staff and nonslip footwear will help. Move slowly and plan each step, even shuffling your feet or sliding one foot forward to detect any rocks. When walking too quickly in deeper water, a knee-high rock might send you tumbling. At night, even though it may spook fish, use a light if the wading is bad; don't risk serious injury for a fish. Generally the fish are closer at night, but if you must wade and want to avoid lights, use a wading staff to pick your way. Avoid locations that require wading long distances with poor footing. Choose spots that have deeper water and good pockets near the shoreline. Daytime research is important if you plan to fish rocky areas in low light.

Akin to open beaches, some rocky locations have good runs of migrating fish. Places with concentrations of bait, and areas of structure near estuaries or points, can be key fall hot spots. Some areas attract fish each season, having good populations of resident fish as well as migrating fish. As you keep fishing a location, watch for signs like wind direction or wave action that might gather the fish. It could be a northeast wind in late fall or a moon tide in June that makes fishing better. As with any area you fish, **learning the water** will make fishing easier.

Tackle

In places without heavy current or large waves, an 8- or 9-weight outfit will work. In bigger water, a 10- or 11-weight is a good choice. The shore angler should choose bigger tackle, particularly when fishing in locations with wave action or heavy current. The boat angler can use the outboard to keep pace with the fish, but lifting or turning a fish still requires ample power. For fishing around structure, my preference is a 10-weight; in locations with structure and waves, the 11-weight is even better.

Lines

When fishing from shore, in all but the skinniest water or areas with many shallow rocks, the intermediate fly line will cover most situations. In rock-strewn locations when fishing over structure with little water cover, a floating line helps prevent too many hang-ups. From a boat, the intermediate is a good choice, and in deeper locations the skilled angler might try a Teeny or Depth Charge–style line. A fast-sinking line will get the fly into the deeper sections faster and keep it in the strike zone longer.

Flies

Poppers and other surface flies work well fished over shallow structure with a floating line. In calm water, surface commotion, either a splash or a wake, attracts fish. Also use buoyant flies with any sinking line. This allows the line to rub the bottom or bump a rock without the fly always snagging. Darker flies are effective around structure because there are many small bottom fish here, such as cunners, along with standard baitfish. I like 4- to 7-inch-long, bulky flies to match small bottom fish, eels, or big baitfish that turn dark to blend with their surroundings. When schooling baits are present, try to match these foods with a fly.

Flats and Shallow Water, Mud, and Sand

6

I was surprised at the number of fish landlocked in this small tidal creek in Maine. There could not have been 5 feet of water in the deepest spots, and most of the water was only 2–3 feet deep. Yet there were perhaps fifty stripers, some to 20 pounds, milling about in a 60-foot-wide by 100-yard-long trench.

The tide was rising, but the sea had not reached this location. There was still a slight outgoing flow. The water was low and clear with little movement. A few fish followed our flies, but they were very skittish. Backing away from the water, we waited for the coming tide, hoping that the fish would settle down and start feeding.

As the tide began filling the first hole, the fish lined up along a shallow edge. They started feeding, nosing down and grabbing something from the bottom. I had never seen a group of stripers in such shallow water (at times less than a foot deep) line up and feed in this manner. Their backs were out of the water and their tails were splashing above the surface like those of tailing bonefish.

We could not see the food they were eating, but it was apparently small. Using a small 1-inch-long bonefish fly, we took several small fish, and one that was 6–8 pounds. Almost every fish took the fly off the bottom, or on one hop (when I would move the fly from the bottom, then let it settle back down). If I moved the fly, hopping it several times, the fish would dart away.

There were at times twenty to thirty fish feeding along this edge. Most were small schoolies, but there were a few larger fish mixed in. The bigger fish were very tough to take.

Stripers will venture into shallow water in midday; this is exciting fishing. Here my wife, Barb, is casting to sighted fish.

I have seen numbers of fish in 2–3 feet of water, and an occasional fish that would slip in and out of very shallow water. However, I had never witnessed this many fish feeding for such a long time in such skinny water—there were times when some fish were on their sides in 8 inches. The fish would feed into the current as a group. Each fish would pause, nose down, then move a short distance uptide to feed again.

Our new breed of striper feeds more actively on the flats than did previous generations of fish. Stripers have always fed in shallow water but not in the numbers and with the frequency they do today, particularly in bright daylight. It is probably the dwindling food supply that forces stripers to search out different feeding locations. Whatever the reason, it has created a windfall for the fly rodder, offering excellent sight fishing in light-bottomed, clear-water areas. There is also fine fishing on dark flats and in shallow areas with discolored waters, but instead of spotting the fish, you must look for surface activity to find them. At night, stripers feed actively in shallow water, taking flies much more aggressively than in the daytime.

Flats range from shallow banks along a river, 20 feet wide, to massive flats that can run for several miles. Most northern flats are not like tabletops, as are some bonefish flats that have the same water depth for miles. Northern flats are usually a series of bars with shallow sections. Some locations border sharp drop-offs, with cuts and channels running through the shallow areas. The Monomoy flats off Cape Cod and the waters of Great South Bay on Long Island are examples of large, shallow fishing areas with clear water. In Chesapeake Bay, there are many shallow areas where sight fishing would be good, but the water is usually discolored from heavy rainfall; the discolored water makes sight fishing impossible when fish are in these locations. In clear-water areas, even the smallest locations provide good sight fishing. There are small backwaters in Maine that are dry for half the tide, but can provide good fishing for several hours of the high incoming tide.

Flats Are Different

Many locations you fish will have sections—and in some cases, large areas—of flat, smoothly flowing water. There are no big structures, bars, or deep holes, just relatively flat bottom, or a gently rolling bottom gradually sloping into deeper water. Beaches with gentle slopes are similar to flats and will have slow-flowing water, as will some flats. Flats can develop strong tidal flows unless they are blocked by a large landmass. Reading this water is difficult because there are no dominant features. Daytime sight fishing is the best method to use, but blind casting works well at night once you locate the fish. On big flats, the fish might be in only one location. Without a rip line or structure to concentrate the fish, you must find the hot feeding area.

All flats are not the same, even though they look alike. Shallows in the vicinity of big estuary systems will have big baits nearby. The larger baits may not move onto the flats, but the fish are programmed to feed on big baits at certain times of the year. A large fly might trigger a fish to strike even if there are no big baits on the flat. In locations with only small baits, large flies usually spook fish. Small fly patterns like sand eels, shrimp, and crabs are effective in most shallow-water areas. The smaller patterns should be the first flies you try, but experiment. When learning a flat, finding fish is only half the battle—determining what fly the stripers will take and how to fish it are equally important.

Tide size, water temperature, and time of the year, as well as weather conditions, all affect shallow-water fishing. Fish activity on flats in warm water locations might diminish in the summer if the temperatures get too high, but in cold water areas of Cape Cod and northward, it could be the best time to fish. Water warmer than 70 degrees will have less activity. Flats located near major feeding areas like big rips, river mouths, and ocean beaches will be influenced by feeding conditions in these places. If large amounts of food move into the deeper, easy-to-feed locations, activity on the flats will suffer. However, if that food source suddenly disappears, fish activity in the shallows will explode.

Tide size and water movement influence how you fish a location. A 2½-foot change in tide might allow fishing at any time. A 10-foot tide makes timing in some areas critical, allowing only a small window—perhaps an hour—of prime fishing. In areas with big tides, fish must move constantly, particularly on a falling tide; in places with small tides, fish can sometimes hold in one location, even at low water.

As we discuss different types of flats, you will discover that even these shallow locations take research and time to learn, and that on one flat fish will charge a certain fly pattern while on another they will run from it. Flats are like any other water type—**learning the water** is the key to success.

Sight Fishing

Smaller waters offer good fishing for the wading angler. Some places are too small for boats—you will just spook fish. Unless fishing with a skilled guide, most anglers will find wading easier than boat fishing. Wading gives the angler more time and allows sideways movement to adjust for a cast. And you can get closer to the fish. When wading, the unskilled angler will spot fish much better because only the fish is moving. From a moving boat, everything is in motion. Anchoring the boat works well for the novice, because the boat's height allows a better view for spotting fish.

Using a boat, you cover much more water and can fish large flats on an incoming tide. In big-tide locations, you will miss some of the best fishing without a boat, because as the water begins rising, you must head for shore. Flats-fishing opportunities are everywhere, but choosing the right one takes some research.

Small Flats

Pocket-size flats can offer big dividends. Some are only the size of a tennis court, but at the right time they will have a constant flow of fish. Football-field-size flats are still considered small. When sight fishing, post off to one corner of the flat and let the fish come to you. Usually the fish move into the tide, but expect some fish to cruise downcurrent as well. If the flat is very small, put your back to the shallow side of the flat and concentrate mostly on the edges. Look for the fish to come from the deeper water onto the flat. On a flat with some wading room, the rising tide makes the fish bolder, and they will work well onto the flat; on a falling tide, keep watching the edges.

The best small flats are located near deep water in a protected location. A pure saltwater estuary may have many wadable, pocket-size flats. Some, however, are reachable only by boat. Canoes and sea kayaks can open up many fishing opportunities for the adventurous angler.

Spotting the Fish

When wading a small flat, posting off, and just looking for fish, the key is seeing the fish with enough time to make a cast. And the cast must be close enough to entice the fish without spooking it.

Spotting the fish is the main concern. Yes, when looking at a striper, the novice would think it should be easy to see. Those shiny sides and those dark stripes must stand out like a big diamond in a goat's backside. But that same silvery side turns a striper into a ghost, blending into the bottom. Those dark stripes and green back turn to a light beige olive, and some fish have little color. Any shiny-sided fish—this is very true of bonefish—reflects the bottom, blending into its environment as a mirrored wall blends into a room. Seeing movement, looking for shadows, and looking for parts of a fish like an eye or tail are the secrets to spotting fish in shallow water. The biggest mistake is to look for "a fish." This is the reason that holding in a stationary position is better for the beginner. The angler notices movement much better when standing still. With good overhead sun, look for the fish's shadow, plus anything that moves. Distinguishing a fish from the bottom in a moving boat takes practice and skill.

If the flat is big enough to move about, wade slowly, stopping frequently to check for movement. Walk quietly. Do not splash, crunch the bottom, or lift your feet when walking. A slow shuffle, sliding your feet along the bottom, works best. You are hunting, searching for fish in an environment that makes them uneasy. Noises or movements that would never alarm stripers in deeper locations will send them screaming from skinny water. Stalk as you would when leaving your house at 3 o'clock in the morning—think about every movement and every noise you make. Wading larger flats might mean walking quickly through less productive water to reach a prime area. However, expect to see fish anywhere.

Last year I walked out on a flat at midday at low tide to check out the bottom, planning to fish along the drop-off. I was moving carelessly because the water was so clear and shallow—a foot to 18 inches. There was a striper of perhaps 12 pounds cruising in this thin water, 100 yards from the drop-off. I never had time to raise the rod before it bolted to safety.

On flats that are big enough to walk, work the edges on the last part of the outgoing and the first part of the incoming tide. Stay about a cast and a half from the deeper water. This gives you enough time to spot the fish and cast before the fish drops off the flat. At lower tides, most fish will be reluctant to venture any distance onto the flat. You must get the fly to them quickly, while they are still moving onto the flat. Casting as a fish fades back off the flat usually spooks them, because the fly generally moves toward the fish.

Casting to Sighted Fish

If your casting doesn't go to hell the first time you see a big fish, take up golf—you're not getting any thrill from the sport. Casting to cruising fish in shallows is the most exciting form of fly fishing there is. It's you against the fish with, at times, just several seconds to make a tough cast. I should say, Try to be calm, but you won't be. Even very good casters have off days; don't be discouraged by a bad outing. Look at a $10-million-a-year basketball player who misses one free throw after another. What causes problems for most anglers is trying to rush, trying to cast too fast, or casting at a fish that is too far away. Set up and wait for the better, easier shot. Go slowly. If making that extra backcast helps you get the fly to the fish, use it. You might miss some chances, but if taking more time improves your casting, use an extra backcast. If you rush and never make a good cast, it will be a long, frustrating day.

Go at a pace that you can handle. Some opportunities are beyond the skill of many anglers. Let them pass, but remain ready for the next chance. Flailing after a long shot might cause you to miss the best chance of the day.

Practice a routine, a system that you can use without thinking. There are several ways to cast to a sighted fish. Stand with 15–20 feet of fly line beyond the rod tip, holding the fly in your noncasting hand. The extra fly line should be coiled neatly in a stripping basket—I use a basket even in a boat. This prevents any problems with line management. Fly lines catching on snags around the boat and standing on the line cause perhaps half the miscues when sight casting. If you prefer to sight fish without a basket, be sure to place the coils of fly line in a location that is snag-free and not underfoot. My advice is to use a stripping basket or suffer.

Hold the fly with the hook pointing away from your body, between the thumb and first finger. **Do not drop the fly.** Hold the fly lightly and allow the cast to pull it from your fingers. Dropping the fly before the line pulls it from your fingers will leave it loose around your legs. You might hook yourself instead of the fish.

Hold the fly line in the casting hand between the first and middle fingers, like someone holding a cigarette. Do not pinch the line to the rod, or it will be too hard to grab when you begin casting. This makes the line easier to grab once the fly is in the air. I prefer to make a forward roll cast, because it helps get the line out quicker, but some anglers make a swiping backcast, then begin casting. Choose the system that works for you. Making a roll cast first, then shooting some line on your backcast, allows a quick cast to a fish at 40–60 feet. When casting more than 60 feet, use an extra backcast. At that distance, you should have enough time to make the extra cast—if you don't, accuracy at the 70- to 80-foot range will be difficult.

Attempts of more than 70 feet are low-percentage casts, even for very good casters. Too much can go wrong at that distance; 30–50 feet is the ideal range. Del Brown, the

Pip Winslow with a nice striper that took the fly in the shallows; fly placement is important.

world's most successful permit angler, fishes only 50 feet of fly line. Del has landed more than 400 permit on a fly. Need I say more?

Once you develop one system, practice the other as well. On a calm day, if a fish is close, the noise of a forward roll cast can spook it. In these conditions, I make a short, quick backcast, then cast to the fish.

Unlike wing shooting, where you are trying to hit a small target, most sight casting involves throwing to a zone, a location where the fly intercepts the fish. There are many variables, such as current flow, the fish's speed, water depth, and perhaps wind. The precise fly placement required in some dry-fly fishing is impossible and unnecessary. Look ahead of the fish, pick a 5-foot patch, and place the fly in that zone. Deeper water, stronger current, and faster-moving fish require more lead; putting all of these conditions together means more guesswork than skill at times. Test each location for the best lead before actually casting to a fish to determine the water flow and depth. Casting to locations on the bottom helps warm up and refine your casting skills. Constant practice is the only way to improve your sight casting.

Fly Placement

There are times on the flats when fish feed aggressively, when a fly landing in the path of a fish brings an immediate response, a rush to eat the fly—particularly when you are casting to groups of fish competing with each other for food. These are great days, times you should cherish, because this is not the norm. Most of the time with overhead sun, in clear water of 3 feet or less, bass are tough to take. In 18 inches of water, one 10-pound bass will make your day's fishing. It can be that tough, yet that rewarding. My most memorable days on the flats have involved taking a few tough fish, because you earn each one in an environment where they have all the advantages.

Normally, fly placement is critical when fishing shallow water. You do not need to hit pie plates, but placing the fly at the proper angle to the fish is important. A fly that moves toward a fish in the shallows looks unnatural. A baitfish, crab, or shrimp **never** attacks a gamefish.

Food in the shallows usually tries to hide. If the fish aggressively attack the fly, retrieving works well. On certain days, and later in the summer when heavy fishing pressure has made the fish spooky, letting the fly settle to the bottom is the best technique to entice a striper in shallow water. Cast well ahead of the fish, and let the fly drift to the bottom without movement. There are times when even one strip, a 6-inch movement, will spook the fish. This is particularly true with small fly patterns, such as sand eels, shrimp, or crab. A bigger bait—one that cannot hide—might try to outrun the fish, but will never swim toward it.

Getting the fly in front of the fish is important. Waiting for the proper casting angle and time is also critical.

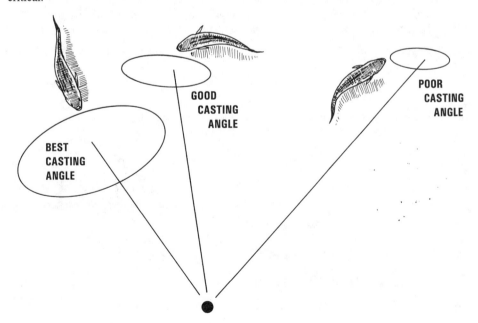

GOOD
CASTING
ANGLE

POOR
CASTING
ANGLE

BEST
CASTING
ANGLE

A fish swimming directly toward the angler offers the best casting angle. If you cast short, let the fly settle and try giving it one small hop as the fish approaches. If the cast is long, try stripping the fly before the fish sees it, and then let it sink. Hitting the fish on the head will end any hope. With a head-on cast, the fly can land perhaps 4 feet to either side of the fish, and the fish will probably see it.

Any cast to a departing fish is a "Hail Mary," not a good choice. This low-percentage cast seldom works. The smart decision is to let the fish go, hoping that it turns or drops off the flat and comes back.

A fish moving at right angles to the angler demands more discipline than a fish coming head on. There are many variables depending on water depth, sink rate of fly, the speed of the fish, and current flow (if any). If the cast is too long, you can adjust the distance by stripping until the fly reaches the fish's vision. But if the fish detects any encroachment from the fly, it will spook. In 2–3 feet of water, 15 feet is not too long a lead. If the fly lands too long or too short but is settling near the fish, don't move the fly. The fish will alter its path if it sees and wants the fly. The secret is getting the fly into the fish's sight window while it is falling. Then the fish will move to the fly without the angler adjusting the distance. And once the fish heads toward the fly, **do not move it.** If the fish speeds up, becomes brighter in color, wiggles, or does anything that appears different, watch and wait. When the fish nears the fly, it will either tip up on its nose or turn sideways to take the fly. Pause for a two count, then strike by using several overhand strips with two hands, or a long strip if striking with one hand. If you feel weight, keep retrieving until the line tightens, then drive the hook home. If you feel no resistance, drop the fly and watch the fish. If the fish bolts in the direction of the fly, wait longer before strip striking to hook the fish.

Watching the fish's body language is key. With enough experience, hooking fish becomes second nature. However, this will frustrate the beginner, as bonefishing

Stripers will either tip nose-down or turn on their sides to take the fly from the bottom.

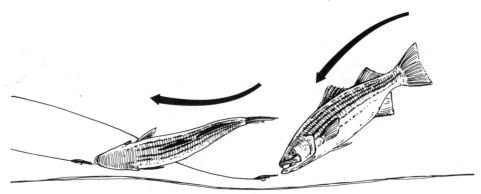

does. At first, you need help from the fish. We all learn the same way: by finding some aggressive fish to cast to.

Casting to pods and schools of fish is much easier. Competing fish are less wary. Casting the fly so it lands in the range of several fish increases your odds. When you drop the fly in front of a group of fish, one or several will spot it. If several fish bolt for the fly, one will take. Smaller fish feeding in groups are usually more aggressive.

Learn the Fly's Sink Rate

Test a fly pattern to determine the sink rate, and keep it wet so it sinks upon landing. Usually the fish are looking down. A fly cast too close to a fish might not get its attention. I have had fish swim right by a fly because it was above their line of sight, over their heads. The deeper the water, the farther the fly should land in front of the fish. This is also true on calm days when the noise of a fly landing might startle a fish. I have watched a striper swim 15 feet for a fly when it landed in the proper location. If the fly lands beyond the fish's range, pick up quietly and cast again. If you cast too close, the fish will spook. Working along an edge, where fish keep moving back and forth, continually feeding, be careful with your casts. Once you chase that fish, or group of fish, they are gone.

One time that you should cast directly onto a fish is when it is tailing. Stripers will sometimes feed nose-down to grub food out from the bottom. Unlike bonefish, stripers will stand vertically on their heads to feed; many times their tails wave above the surface and splash water. They are most often feeding on seed eels that burrow into the sand or gravel, but they will also nose out crabs over mussel bars. This can occur at any time, but I have witnessed it mostly at night or at first light. The face of a grubbing fish will be red from rubbing the bottom; if fish have red, scuffed-up faces, it's a sign that they are feeding on the bottom, and fish feeding like this should take a fly aggressively.

Cast with a sinking line or a weighted fly so that the fly bumps close to the fish along the bottom. Bounce the fly in short hops, letting it pause between pulls. There is little chance of hanging up along a sand or gravel bottom, but when casting over a mussel bottom, keep the fly moving so it does not catch. It might be hard to do at first, but take your time and cast to the bigger fish.

Low Light

Shallow-water locations are ideal for fly tackle. In low light and at night, stripers move up onto flats, feeding aggressively. Places with good tidal flow will always have bait. Sand eels and spearing, as well as bottom baits like crabs and shrimp, are important food sources throughout the season, along with small bunker, herring, and snapper blues, which appear in the late summer and early fall. Seldom do big baits like adult menhaden, herring, mackerel, or squid venture onto the flats. However, look for these big baits along the edges in deeper water.

The combination of small baits and shallow water makes the flats prime territory for the novice fly angler at night. Some areas offer easy wading without severe drop-offs. On a falling tide, with a good bait supply, fishing can be hot for hours. Here the angler can just cover water without worrying about getting the fly down or controlling the fly in the wash. And the fish can be anywhere. Also, on a falling tide there is no danger of being stranded by rising water.

When working a flat at night, casting angle is the main concern. The angler must keep in touch with the fly. Casting up or across current requires a trained hand; feeling strikes is difficult, even for the veteran. With even a light flow, work the line quartering downcurrent. In a strong current, use a dead drift, shaking the rod or pulling the line without retrieving to pulsate the fly. Use a faster retrieve if casting up or across the flow. Without flow, keep casting to locations in every direction, even behind you.

Locations with sand eels offer interesting fishing at night. As a beginning marine fly rodder, I found out that fish will follow a wading angler, feeding on the sand eels that the angler kicks up. One night, while wading, I left the line trailing perhaps 15 feet behind me. The flat's sandy bottom was filled with sand eels that burrow into the sand at night to hide. The small baits kept popping out as I walked. On two occasions I took fish while walking, or "foot trolling." The fish, feeding on the sand eels I was kicking up, took the fly trailing behind me. I started walking some distance while shuffling my feet, then cast behind me and found it worked fairly well. The discolored water concealed my presence—in clear water, even at night, stripers will seldom get that close to a moving angler.

However, at night, if you move slowly and quietly, fish will still take a fly near the angler. On still nights, noises like the fly line ripping from the water's surface will alarm fish. Even though it's dark, fish in shallow water are never at ease; they will flee from any disturbance, particularly big fish.

When wading, if you begin to walk up onto a bar, start casting before you actually reach the top. Fish will hold behind a bar, particularly in flowing water, where they can hide and attack bait as it moves with the tide. As you walk up the bar, fan cast in all directions, make a few steps, then repeat the casting pattern.

On still nights, surface sliders that make a wake work well. A popper—worked slowly by popping and then stopping the bug for several seconds—will draw fish from some distance. Also, when the water is calm, fish activity will show on all but the blackest nights—keep listening for sounds of feeding fish. On still nights, you can stalk fish when they are showing on the surface, at times casting to individual swirls. Unlike most daytime flats fishing, usually at night a fish rushes the fly.

Even at night, fishing on a flat requires hunting. On bigger flats, fish keep roaming until they find bait. A coming tide brings stripers up from deeper channels and cuts searching for food. At low incoming and on the last of the dropping tide, look for them along the edges. In some locations, the lower tide concentrates the fish, making the edges very productive.

On flats that do not empty, look for fish to hold in pockets between the bars at low water. Many times fish remain in these deeper sections until the flat begins to flood, then spread out on the flat to feed. I've found fish in these areas even in the daytime—at night expect to find fish anywhere.

As the shallows fill, begin working the whole flat, concentrating on the rips that form along the bars. The edges of bars are ideal locations as well. Keep these places in mind on a falling tide, because moving water holds fish.

Only along the edges, at colder times of the year, would you need a fast-sinking line. Floating or clear sink-tip fly line works well, especially when fishing surface patterns. Most fish take the fly in less than 3 feet of water. If you plan to fish surface flies, choose a floating line. But an intermediate line will cover most conditions, except when fishing sliders on top. Except at the edges of drop-offs, most fish taken while wading a flat strike the fly near the surface.

Mixed Grass and Sand Flats

Locations with good current flow form areas of mixed grass and sand. Most of the mixed flats I have fished are in small-tide locations. The grass patches hold the sand while forming sidewalk-size paths with white holes in between. The paths give the angler access to deeper water, plus an elevated platform for sighting fish. As the tide drops, these areas offer great sight fishing. The fish work up on the grassy areas, nosing through the weed. They will also cruise into the light-colored pockets. If the fish remain on the grass for a while, they turn bright green. They literally appear to glow, and their features stand out. Sometimes, however, when fish first move onto the grass, they are difficult to spot. Look for a fin, a tail, or a wake as the fish grubs out food from the grass. When the fish move from the grass over the light sand, they show up like green torpedoes. Coming off the dark green weed, the fish might still be very dark and are hard to miss. One place I fished produced best on the last of low tide; just as the flow turned east, fish started feeding. The fish were spooky, but I did fairly well with a 2½-inch-long, sparse sand eel fly and took one fish on a crab pattern. But just seeing the fish nosing up on the grass patches made my day.

Unlike a level flat, or one where the depth changes gradually, the drop-offs along some of the grass sections were sharp. You would not drown, but you could fill your waders with a misstep. Some of the grass patches were large enough to post off, so you could hold in one location, watching both the patch and the light sand to either side. Spotting fish over the dark bottom was difficult. I found that moving slowly and stopping frequently worked best. At the right time of the tide, holding in one place worked well. A floating line worked best when the fish were feeding in 1 foot of water. When the fish were holding in pockets at higher tides, an intermediate line was more effective. At low water, this was some of the most exciting sight fishing I have ever witnessed, because the fish would emerge out of nowhere, slipping out of a hole up into 1 foot of water. Fish would just appear before your eyes. Quick, accurate casting was a must when the fish were on the grass. Fish in the lighter pockets between the grass patches offered the best opportunities because they showed up so well, and the water was not as skinny.

Boat Fishing

The classic way to sight fish in shallow water with a boat is to pole along, hunting for fish. A common practice in the tropics, it is now becoming popular in the Northeast. The number of shallow-water guides and flats boats in the Northeast nowadays is surprising. Anglers and guides have fished the Northeast flats for many years, but not with the intensity and dedication that have developed recently.

A guided flats trip usually means the angler stands in the bow of a boat while the guide poles along in shallow water looking for fish. Action can happen quickly. Some shallow-water locations have good current flow. This makes poling tough and stopping the boat particularly difficult, if not impossible, when moving downcurrent. When you're drifting quickly, any fish you spot downcurrent of the boat requires a fast cast. If the fish are swimming uptide and the boat is moving downtide, you close on the fish in several seconds. If you don't present the fly quickly at a long distance, the boat will spook the fish. Even for the veteran flats angler, this is a difficult situation; it is beyond the skills of many beginning fly rodders. Spotting the fish, clearing the line, and making the cast take practice and experience even under normal conditions. In places with heavy current, or if anglers are not skilled at sight fishing, fishing from a stationary boat is best. Even with a good guide who can handle a boat well, most fly rodders will have better success posting off and letting the fish come to them. In locations with light current, poling or drifting is effective as long as the wind is not strong. But anytime the boat moves too quickly, sight casting to fish becomes even harder.

If you plan to post off on a flat, position the boat near an edge or a trough. Hold about 40 feet away from the deeper water so you have a good casting angle at fish moving along the edge, and so you can still react to fish that swim from the deeper water onto the flat.

One sandbar where I sight fish has a drop-off on one side of about 18 inches with a dark bottom. The other side is a light sand bottom that gradually slopes into deeper

Many anglers now use southern-style flats boats to pursue stripers in shallow areas.

water. I like to anchor in about 3 feet of water so I can cast just over the bar into the dark-bottomed depression. Fish sometimes run from the depression up onto the bar, but mostly they run just along the bar in 2 feet of water. These seem to be ideal depths for sight fishing for stripers. In water much deeper than 3 feet, it is harder to spot fish and to get the fly down quickly. Two to 2½ feet is the ideal depth. You will not usually find many fish in very thin water unless it is right along a bank.

Learning locations is the key to success. There are certain places that funnel fish at different tides. The key is learning where to post off at the right tide. This is why poling the boat over large areas helps to determine the hot spots or to cover large locations quickly. Some locations have fish scattered all over, and poling is the best way to find them.

Along with poling, an electric motor works well to move a boat quietly. They are very effective in deeper locations—4 to 7 feet—when you are moving along an edge looking into the shallows for fish. Some edges are impossible to work from the inside; there is not enough room, and the boat spooks too many fish. A shallow bank right off a dry shoreline can hold many fish. Sometimes these small flats, 10–20 feet wide, offer hot action. Other than casting from shore, which is the ideal way to fish a flat along a bank, using an electric motor to work along a shoreline is an effective way to fish.

Other than the mobility and height of a boat, sight fishing is basically the same as when wading. You are casting to a sighted fish, trying to place the fly so the fish sees it. Usually you can see the fish well and watch its reactions; you can see when it takes the fly. The basic fishing techniques are similar to wading. The major difference is that you are above the water's surface, presenting a taller profile to the fish. When wading, you can sometimes get very close to fish; from a boat, you must cast while the fish are a greater distance away. When fishing large flats, boats allow better water coverage and give access to locations unreachable by wading.

Soft Flats and Dark Flats

Wading soft flats, particularly at night, is uncomfortable and at times unwise. When walking in large areas of soft mud, you will eventually find a spot with deep mud or with no bottom at all. Unless you know the location well, use some sort of craft to fish soft, shallow areas. Most sand or light-colored flats are hard. The dark flats might be firm, but most are soft, particularly in and around estuaries.

A strong tidal flow over a flat, or a light-colored flat, generally means it is hard. The only exception to this rule is the mouths of estuaries located along a beach with fine sand. If the outflow is strong, the sand might be unstable right near the mouth. If you wade at the edge of a bar in a strong current, the bottom might slip right from under you. And at low tide, you could wade into mushy spots, but they are seldom more than calf deep.

Fish most dark flats by blind casting using a small popper or surface fly. Try a slow retrieve, letting the popper or fly sit for several seconds before moving it. If there is good current and a wind chop, fish an intermediate line, working the fly at different angles to the flow. You are covering water, even during the day, as you would when night fishing. On soft, dark flats, use a boat to drift along, casting to cover as much water as possible. On an incoming tide, fish move up looking for food; this is particularly true in northern areas, where the flats have calming activity at low water. The fish seek the dug-up areas looking for food. Many clam flats in Maine are active feeding areas on a rising tide. On a falling tide, watch out in locations with big mud flats that dry out—you will sit for a long time waiting for the tide. Move while there is still enough water to reach the channels.

When working dark flats, sight fishing is difficult in all but the best conditions. For the best sight-casting opportunities, fish must be showing on the surface; spotting fish over a dark bottom is tough. Calm days are ideal; look for any surface activity, such as a wake, fin, or tail that would offer the hint of a fish. Many anglers ignore mud flats because they are not ideal sight-fishing areas. But they are worth a try on a bright, clear day in very skinny water. Concentrate on the water close to the boat, within 50 feet. Cast to any shadow, and look for a tail, an eye, or the flash of the fish's side. There are days when you can spot fish, but this is only for the seasoned angler. On a dark flat, fish are usually less spooky, so you can cast closer to the fish, but not over them.

One technique to to entice a fish in shallow water is to use a fast-sinking line with a buoyant fly. If fish are picky, sometimes a fast-moving, larger fly that darts along the bottom will produce action. The line runs right on the bottom, while the buoyant fly holds just above. Using a short pull and pause with a fast retrieve makes the fly dance up and down along the bottom. This works best in snag-free locations on both mud and sand bottoms.

Walk Softly and Carry a Big Stick

If you plan to fish soft areas or flats with potential soft spots, check the location at low tide in daylight. Some areas might be soft just on the edges, leaving the main flat areas firm enough to walk. I know some flats inside marshes that are tricky to enter but very hard once you get onto them. You must enter and leave these places in fixed locations, or wading is difficult. Places with strong tidal flow in both directions should be hard, but watch the backsides of bars and other areas that block the flow from one side of the tide. These locations collect mud, creating soft pockets with severe drop-offs. Beware of gullies that drain flats or creeks at the end of the tide. These locations collect mud while eroding the hard bottom. A wading staff will help to locate the soft areas; keep probing to be sure that the footing is sound. Never take big steps. If you are not a good swimmer, wear a life vest.

Shallow water offers ideal light-tackle fishing. Eight- and 9-weight rods work well, and unless the flow is strong and runs for a long distance, large reels are unnecessary. Most sight casters like 8-weights unless the wind picks up. Clear sink-tips or floaters work well, but an intermediate line is also an excellent choice if you plan to work the drop-offs. Sight fishing usually requires small flies like crabs, shrimp, and small, precise baitfish patterns. In clear, calm water, on bright days you might need leaders longer than 9 feet; fluorocarbon is my choice for tippet material.

Shallow areas seldom stack in with large numbers of migratory fish. Flats inside estuaries might have runs of big fish in the spring looking for the big baits, but this is short lived. In the spring, look for the early fish that flood the flat; they will rush the fly. In the fall, look along outer, shallow ocean beaches on calm days for large groups of fish that are on the feed. From late spring to early fall, the flats usually have small runs of fish, plus fish that reside for the season. These are the tough fish, the ones that you earn, one at a time.

Cliff Fishing 7

I have Herb Chase and Ray Smith to thank for my love of cliff fishing. Both Rhode Island anglers developed this fishing in the early 1970s off the rocks at Newport. Now as I fish a section of cliffs along southern Maine many years later, I still remember their basic advice: Let the fly and line flow with the moving water.

The section of rocky shoreline they fished had one good deep section of water after another. The seas were not large—2 to 3 feet—but the cliff's shape and wave direction gave the water excellent movement. In smaller surf, you could get close to the water's edge and work each section of crystal-clear water. This was finesse fishing, throwing short casts and mending the line to work each pocket with the fly. I used only 30 feet of fly line, letting the fly flirt with the rocks. Some fish took only inches from the rocks' edge, rising up and sipping the fly like a trout feeding along a ledge. The best fish were the ones that slipped up behind the fly, taking as you lifted it from the water. Sometimes you could see the fish coming, darting from the deep blue water to inhale the fly before it escaped. Other times, the fish took in the flowing white water, crushing the fly with a hard jolt. This particular day, the fish were not large—5 to 8 pounds—but most fish hit close, and you could watch many fish take the fly. This was a banner day to learn cliff fishing, because it was safe and the fish were active. At times of moderate surf and clear water, only sight fishing in the shallows offers a better study of how a striper feeds than cliff fishing does. And from the cliff's height, it almost seemed that you could grab some fish with your hands.

Fishing rocky cliffs has become one of my favorite types of fly fishing. It is daytime fishing, and in some locations the action is hot all summer long. North of Cape Cod, the cold water makes this a great summertime fishery. In Rhode Island, it may turn to low-light fishing in the hot weather. Fly patterns are usually simple. Most of the time I use two flies: a 4- to 6-inch-long Snake Fly in all-black, black and orange, or all-olive; or a 5- to 8-inch-long Deceiver tied like a flat-sided baitfish, white with a dark top and some flash. Small lobsters are the staple food source along the cliffs, but expect to find numerous baitfish of many types along the rocks. There are also many small bottom fish that live around the rocks and kelp. Miles of this structure exist in New England, and many days I have a fishery to myself.

Just standing on those rocks with the sea pounding at your feet, the white water cascading up and mixing with the deep blue ocean, is exciting enough. It is the same rush some people must get when standing on a peak hundreds of feet in the air—you are just a step away from danger. To think that a fish could even survive, let alone feed in this water must astonish the newcomer. When the surf is big, when it thunders against the rocks, there are only certain fishable, safe places. Big seas bring the stripers in to feed, but the heavy surf demands skill and experience, and this is not the time to learn.

The rugged coast of Maine offers more opportunities for cliff fishing than any other striper destination. Massachusetts has good sections of this water at Cape Ann and north and south of Boston. The cliffs at Newport, Rhode Island, were pioneering grounds, but you will also find good structure from Sakonnet Point to Black Point, near Point Judith.

First, look for a good section, at least several hundred yards long, of rocky shoreline that has deep water right at the base of the structure. Small sections are good, but might not offer enough variety in different water conditions. Choosing the best locations to fish depends on several things, but the sea's size must always be the first consideration. Bigger seas restrict your fishing locations. Eight- to 10-foot swells make most places too dangerous and too difficult to fish. At times of big seas, the only accessible places are the high perches with deep water right near the cliff's base. Some locations will have 15- to 20-foot holes right at the cliff's edge. If there is a high, safe perch within casting range of deeper water, these places are good fishing locations, even in heavy seas.

If the sea is not too large, 2–3 feet, you can work many locations along a ledge. Small surf allows access to any shelf, and water depths of more than 5 feet offer protection so a striper can move freely into many places—and so can you.

On calm sunny days, walk the structure looking for deep water, places where the ledge drops straight down. In areas with large tides, low water gives the best perspective if walking is safe. Avoid smooth rocks with dark slime and weed-covered areas; stay on the barnacles or the clean sections of the ledges. Some areas are too dangerous to walk or fish at lower tides.

While assembling your tackle, spend time watching the water to be sure it's safe.

Never fish these areas at night if there is a sea running. Even on calm nights, walking along some structures is treacherous and is only for veteran anglers. Fishing in the darkness is risky when a small swell is running; in a big sea, it is suicide. I enjoy cliff fishing because it offers daytime action from shore. Fishing the cliffs with a boat is for seasoned guides only; I will mention how to work some of the safer locations later in the chapter, but this will be brief and accompanied by many warnings.

Walking the rocks is the best way to locate the deep pockets and undercut ledges and find potential landing areas. While finding the deep, sharp drop-offs along the cliffs, look as well for cracks or gullies in the ledges where you can land a fish. Any crack in the ledge large enough to slip a fish through might be a potential fish-landing spot if it leads to a safe resting place.

Look for White Water

The keys to cliff fishing are wave movement and white water. The white water draws fish into the cliffs, congregating them in the places with the best water movement. I

The mushroomlike cloud of white water is an ideal feeding location along a cliff.

always thought that the waves in the 6- to 10-foot range created the best fishing, and in some places this is true. However, in many places, smaller surf permits better access to more water and concentrates the fish in certain areas. Depending on the wave direction and size, some sections of structure will have wave action in just a few locations. This draws stripers to a handful of prime spots; bigger surf spreads the fish out, allowing feeding in many locations. In smaller surf, look for places with the best white water and concentrate your efforts there. Along large sections of cliffs the better places will stand out, because the white water shows up well, particularly in early-morning sunlight.

The waves' direction, size, and speed all influence the type of movement that is created along structure. One place might have good working water with a quartering swell, while another spot is better with a straight-on swell. I know places that are excellent in big seas; it is the only time they have good white water. Most locations have fish in all water conditions, but the fish will move depending on how the water is working along the cliff. Learning to read white water is the key to finding fish.

The places that form billowing clouds of white water that rush out into deeper water are the prime feeding locations. This cloud is usually mushroom shaped, looking like a classic atomic explosion. With the right wave action, certain sections along the cliffs will keep forming this flowing water. Along some cliffs there will be a number of prime spots. Always look for these clouds first; they are the places to fish hard. Then, work the water around these places. If there are several good flows in one spot, keep moving back and forth, fishing each one until you find fish.

Locations change in appearance with varying sea conditions. The big classic holes with very deep water should remain stable in most seas. It is the shallower pockets that change constantly; one wave direction and size will offer exceptional fishing, but with different sea conditions, the same spot might be unfishable. **Learning the water** is the key to fishing any location. Once you understand cliff fishing, reading the water will be easier; the skilled anglers will spot the better water in any sea condition. But at first, research locations in calm water or with small waves. In small surf, plan to fish while **learning the water.**

Fishing Small Surf

Waves of less than 3 feet allow the angler to move about, fishing most locations. There are two ways to fish structure like this in small seas. Let's say there is some white water, surf from 2 to 3 feet, flowing around one section of rocks. The sun is overhead, the water is clear, the tide is falling, and the footing is good, making for easy walking. In small surf, an intermediate or clear-tip fly line works well, using 4- to 6-inch-long, dark attractor patterns. Concentrate on the sections with the best white water. The waves' force will dislodge foods like crabs and lobsters from the rocks and pull baitfish from their protected lies. White water is the telltale sign of good water movement and makes feeding easier for stripers. Even if there is little white water, fish the moving water along the rock's edges, working the swirling water. Fish these small flows as you would a rip, letting the fly swing with the flow, then retrieving the fly at the flow's end. Cast across the flow, mending line up into the flow to keep the fly from swinging too quickly or to allow the fly to hold in one location like a confused baitfish. Work the fly near the rocks and flowing kelp, using mends, or throw slack line to allow the fly to hold along the structure. Use short casts, fishing the water near your feet. Keep moving so you present the fly from different angles. In bigger surf, there are only certain safe places to fish from; when you can move freely on the rocks, cover the water by walking from spot to spot, using a short line. Fishing with a stripping basket lets you move freely without worrying about loose line.

Keep focused on the water you are fishing. Many times a fish will follow and not take. Wait several minutes for the fish to settle down, or come back to the fish after working another location. Usually fish will hold in one location and, given a rest, the fish will take on the next cast. In the white water, look for a shadow in the vicinity of your fly. On bright days, a fish will show up as a blue blob in the sparkling white

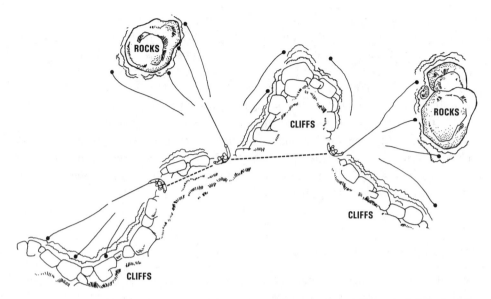

Cast to each small pocket of water along the rocks and keep moving until you find fish. On calm days, this is like fishing pocket water for trout.

foam. It looks like a blue flashbulb going off. Again, give the fish time to rest, and try another cast. In small surf, with clear water you can spot many fish, but you must keep watching.

After working the moving water near the rocks, try getting the fly down, fishing the deeper sections along or away from the cliff's edge. If there are deep drop-offs right at your feet, use a fast-sinking line, casting over the hole and letting the line sink. Use a countdown system, allowing the line to descend for, say, a ten count before retrieving. Use a fast retrieve, working the fly in long pulls toward the structure. This technique works well on calm days when you might find fish cruising along the structure. There are times when fish will feed along structure without wave action, but white water makes stripers feed more aggressively in these locations.

Make the fly swim through the cuts and over the smaller pockets. Try fishing a popper to work the edges of drop-offs or shallow areas with pockets of deep water. Cast the popper around the pinnacles of structure, working it into the drop-offs. Poppers or surface flies work well in areas with small sections of deep water surrounded by subsurface snags.

Focus on any of the better flows of white water that rush off the structure. Watch the white water as it flows from the rock. After a wave or a set of waves breaks against structure, it will flow off the rocks back into deeper water. In bigger surf, timing is tough. You usually need to plan the cast for the right moment and then slip loose line to allow the fly to reach the flow's outer edge. In small surf, cast and let the line and fly swing out with the flowing white water. If the fly swings too quickly, or does not reach the slower water beyond the flow's edge, you need to feed some line as the white water drifts out. This is similar to feeding fly line when fishing a steep beach. You are slipping loose line from your basket to allow the line and fly to move naturally with the flow and to fish the outer fringes of the white water. Near the end of the flow, begin softly pinching the line, tapping your thumb and forefinger together as the fly line slips through your hand. As when slipping line on a steep beach, pinching the line while cliff fishing will help detect strikes as the fly drops back. In larger surf, feeding line is an essential technique; learning while fishing smaller waves will help develop this skill.

Fishing Big Surf—Safety First

There is only one important consideration when fishing the cliffs during big surf: safety. Never fish a location where you must climb back up to escape an oncoming wave. Choose a high fishing spot with a flat route back to safe ground. Never climb down to retrieve a fly or a fish, and never turn your back to the sea. I move away from the water's edge to change flies. Do not walk across low sections of structure to reach a high fishing spot on an incoming tide. Most of all, don't take chances. With that said, I do not know a fly rodder who has been seriously hurt while cliff fishing. I have a good friend who had a close call though, and here is his story.

I will call him Fred; he asked me to hide his identity because if his wife knew the story, he would be forbidden to fish the sea. Fred walked out on a section of structure without first watching it to see if it was safe. (Always stand back and let a big set of waves pass to see if your location is safe.) Fred was not watching the sea; he was too busy fishing to even notice the big wave that walled up and knocked him off the cliff. Just before the wave hit, his friend yelled, but it was too late. The wave dragged Fred down the steep wall, and he clung to some kelp. Miraculously, the next wave pushed him up the rocky wall, and his fishing partner pulled him to safety. Luckily, the next wave was small and did not pound him into the wall. It was equally fortunate that Fred's partner could grab him before being sucked into another incoming wave. Fred lost some tackle and some chunks of flesh, but he's alive. And Fred said, "Those long few seconds that I spent in the grips of the sea were terrifying."

The power of a 10-foot wave would tumble a tractor trailer. I'm a surfer; I've been hit by waves. Unless you have experienced—firsthand—the force of a wave, you cannot imagine how strong it is. You cannot hold on or swim against this force. A wave will throw you about like a garbage can in a hurricane. If you respect the sea and are careful, fishing the cliffs is safer than driving a car. If you are careless, it's like driving drunk.

Look for a landing location—a gully or crack in the rocks—to land the fish.

Choosing a Location in Big Surf

First look for that mushroom cloud of white water flowing back from the rocks into deeper water. Then find a high perch with deep water at the base of the cliff. To fish properly in big surf, there must be deep water right at the angler's feet. If the waves break before reaching the rocks, line control is impossible. If the spot looks good, search for a landing area—a gully or a section of water where you can lead a fish away from the force of the waves. Finding good, safe fishing locations along structure with big surf takes time and research. But once you find them, they will never change—they will be lifelong, predictable fishing spots.

Reading the Surf

After fishing big surf a few times, it will become less intimidating. Once you begin to learn some good locations and know how to fish them, the technique is not difficult.

The keys are fishing small sections of water and learning to read the waves. There are two types of waves: wind-blown waves and ocean waves. Wind-blown waves are formed by onshore winds; these waves are generally broken. Wind-blown waves have no shape, no rhythm, breaking sometimes one after another. There is no way to predict how wind-blown waves will break; the big seas are hard to fish. A strong off-shore wind will add shape to wind-blown waves, forming them into sets of waves. This makes the waves more predictable, giving them shape, and forms them into sets as they move to land. This is the way an ocean wave or swell moves. Ocean waves develop many miles from land, formed by large, low-pressure weather systems. A hurricane a thousand miles from shore will pump large swells in for several days; a big thunderstorm might send swells against the shore for a tide. Ocean waves move to shore in sets of threes or eights; usually the last wave is the largest.

When big sets of waves are rolling in, they begin to build—or wall up—outside the structure. Watch to see how they react, where the peak is, and how many are in the set. Watch each wave or series of waves to see what happens to water flowing in the hole. Locations along some cliffs develop a rhythm, a pattern, and by watching the waves you know when the holes will work properly.

There are days when I watch a hole for 15 minutes to get a feel for the water's movement. Look for signs of feeding fish, such as tails, fins, or boils in the white water or just on the edges of the darker water. When you can see where the fish are hold-

Oceans swells that form sets produce the most predictable water along a cliff.

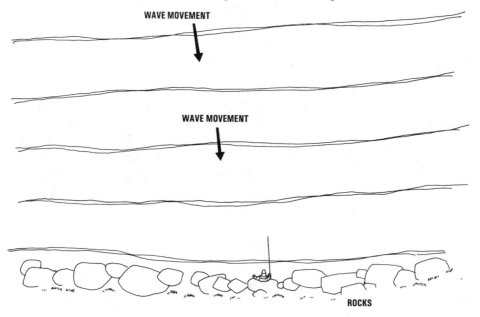

WAVE MOVEMENT

WAVE MOVEMENT

ROCKS

ing, keep presenting the fly so it flows into the feeding zone. Sometimes the fish feed only after the white water has stopped flowing. Here a popper might work if you cast as the flow slows, then work the popper right across the feeding zone. Most of the time fish will not show, but expect them to be there on every cast. Also use this time to look for weed in the water. Onshore wind will push baitfish into the rocks, but it also piles up weed in some holes. Look for clean fishing locations before you make a long walk over slippery rocks.

Learning to read and predict the waves is a must when fishing big surf. A series of waves that break against the rocks will build up thousands of gallons of water. The waves' force pushes and holds this water, for several seconds, above the level of the sea. When gravity takes over, the water rushes downhill back into the sea. Timing is critical. You must plan the cast, catching this flow of white water as it drains back into deep water. Casting in the middle of a set of waves might force the line up onto the structure or to the wrong side of the flow. The cast should land on the ocean side of the flow. There are times when I false cast, holding the line in the air, waiting for water to build up.

Some of this is certainly trial and error, requiring ten casts to get one that is right. When the surf is broken, keep casting, testing the flow to find the right one. Even in good surf, some holes will be tough to fish. If the footing permits, try to get to the side of the flow so you can cast across, and let the line and fly swing across and down

When the surf gets big, there are fewer fishable locations along rocky cliffs.

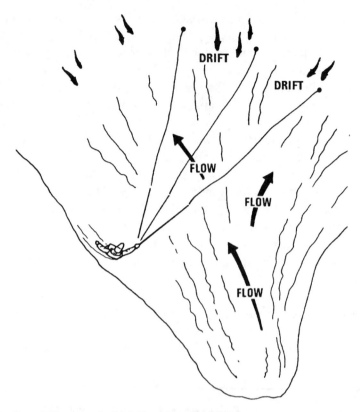

Timing is important. Try to catch the flow at the right moment, so the fly flows out with the water rushing from the cliff and holds just at the edge of the white water.

with the flow. Casting from directly behind the flow is difficult in big surf. After the cast lands, you must feed line immediately to get the fly to look like a natural bait. If the force is too strong or the flow is too long, the fly will not reach the outer edge of the flow. A fly that stops in the middle of this flow or swims up through the flow looks unnatural.

Fishing from the side of the flow allows more line control. Here you can shorten the cast to fish just one side of the flow, or mend line into the flow to slow up the swing. Try casting at different angles to the flow, and experiment with different mends to work as much water as possible. Most of the time in big surf, you are dead drifting and swinging the line so the fly comes to rest in the slower water at the flow's edge. Stripers usually take the fly along the outer edges of the white water. This area has less force, so they can feed with little effort. And here is where any food washed from the rocks will be deposited. Keep working the outer edge of the white water, letting the fly swim through this section at different angles.

As the white water's force diminishes, retrieve the fly to work the slack water before the next wave catches the line. Sometimes, immediately after the flow stops, another wave walls up. Before the next wave catches the line, either retrieve or pick up the line and prepare for the next set of waves. In some cases, you must react quickly to prevent the line or fly from snagging the bottom.

Fishing from a Boat

My advice is to leave the boat fishing to the guides. If you want to roll the dice, here are a few helpful hints.

On a calm day or when the waves are small, fishing from a boat will not present serious problems for most anglers (although you might bang up the boat or the outboard motor). In small surf, I think wading is a more effective way to fish. You can cover the water better without making noise.

Waves in the 3- to 5-foot range start to have power. Bigger ones not only have hitting power, they also have tremendous pulling force. One minute you might be sitting 70 feet from a ledge on a 15-foot shelf, and the next minute you are being driven into the ledge. One big wave will literally suck the water from under your boat, and the next one will pile-drive you into the rocks.

If you are a skilled boater, fish only along the edges of the rocks where a wave cannot push you into the structure. Fish the backside of structure where the waves' force will push you away from the rocks. There are many pinnacles of structure that rise up from deep locations. The smaller ones are fairly safe to fish, because you can always work them from the backside. Keep the motor running, having one angler fish while the other runs the boat. Never anchor, never fish by yourself, and never fish in close if the wind is blowing toward structure. Engine failure might be disastrous.

Work the water the same way you would when fishing from shore, working the flows from the side. Concentrate on the white water, fishing the moving water as it flows from the rocks. When casting across the flowing water from a boat, you can usually work the fly deeper than you could from shore. Whenever you can, get the fly to fish along the structure's edge or along the edge of the white water. From a boat, you have many more opportunities to fish the fly for most of the cast. From shore, you might only fish the fly a few feet before a wave makes you pick up and cast again.

Because the flow is usually moving toward the boat, you must retrieve to maintain line control. Many times you will cast straight into the structure, with the flow moving quickly toward the boat, just the opposite of fishing from shore. With the water flowing toward the boat, a fast retrieve is the only way to control the line and fly. Try making some casts to catch the waves breaking onto the cliffs. Time the cast to catch the wave just before it hits the structure. There will be some slack water briefly after the wave breaks when you can work the fly along the structure before it spills back into the sea. Also, cast between the waves when the water level along the structure is down and the water is slack. Get the fly in tight to the structure, moving it along in the clear water. Like fishing from shore, this is trial and error, trying to time the wave to make the fly look real. The major difference when fishing from a boat is using the retrieve to adjust the fly's movement rather than feeding line to make the fly look like a natural bait.

Get the Fly Tight and Let It Sink

Cast the fly into white water, trying to land it within inches of the rocks. Getting the fly in tight is key when fishing some locations. Fishing most rocky locations is like fishing against a bridge abutment; the water depth drops quickly. At times, let the line sink so the fly will work down the slot, away from the rocks. A fast-sinking line is the best choice when fishing from a boat. Keep casting to different locations along the rocks, working the fly with long quick pulls. In the deeper pockets, let the line sink, counting to ten or more. Fishing deep can be very effective. In most cases, it is impossible to work the deep sections from shore; a boat allows access to the deeper holes.

Fishing from a boat is much easier than shore fishing because you are simply covering water. Cast in tight and retrieve quickly back to the boat. There is little finesse, because the flow is usually moving toward the angler. That is why a fast retrieve works better—to keep a tight line and positive fly control. Remember, fish as deep as you dare.

Tides

Cliffs with good footing are fishable at all tides. If there is good water movement, the tide is not significant. Some ledges in Maine have clean, shale-type rock that offers good traction. Even some weed-covered rocks allow walking at low tide if the sun dries them. The worst walking is on the black, smooth, slime-covered rocks. Avoid these locations at lower tides. There are places in Rhode Island I would fish only at higher tides. In big-tide locations like Maine, falling water keeps offering new fishing areas as the level drops. You can wait for a lull in the waves and reach a spot that would be dangerous to fish on the coming tide. With a rising tide, avoid any location that requires crossing low terrain to reach. Smaller surf usually allows better access on lower tides. Some ledges flatten out; here you cannot reach fishable water in big surf. Once you learn an area well, you can predict the right tides. Start fishing a new place at high tide, and you will never get into trouble.

Hooking Fish

When you're fishing from shore, the fish will often hook themselves. When a fish takes at the end of the swing, the line is straight and the strike is positive. Remember, it is important to keep the rod low and pointed at the line to maintain direct contact with the fly. During the swing, follow the moving line with the rod. If there is a large bow in the line when the fish takes, keep retrieving until the line is tight. Even with a bow in the line, most times the hook-set will be positive because there is such force on the line from the waves. When roll-casting a short line, I will hook fish with the rod, but only if I have to. For information on hooking fish from a boat with a sinking line, see Chapter 20, Hooking, Fighting, and Landing Techniques.

Preventing Hang-ups

Some hang-ups are unavoidable because you need to cast and work the fly close to the rocks. Hang-ups occur from shore when you cast too soon, before the flow is ready to move seaward, or when you try to fish too long after the cast has stopped. You must wait for the wave to begin flushing into the sea before casting. If you cast too soon, try picking the line up, casting again or waiting for the next wave. When there are long spaces between sets, there is time to fish out the cast. There are days when you can, at the end of the flow, retrieve a good distance back to the structure. Deep locations allow long retrieves as well. However, there are times and places that demand quick action to prevent a lost fly or line. Until you know an area well, pick up the line if it looks like a wave is walling up ready to break.

If you hang up, try letting a wave pull the fly free. As the wave surges away, feed some slack, forming a bow in the line, and with luck the wave's force will free the fly. Most of the time when you snag kelp or weed, the fly will pull free.

If a big wave forces you to flee the fishing perch while you are presenting the fly, pick up the line and cast it back over the rocks in the direction you are moving. This will save the fly line and make your departure quicker. Trying to retrieve the line before moving could get you in trouble.

You need to use special fighting techniques when fishing the cliffs. (See Chapter 20, Hooking, Fighting, and Landing Techniques, for details.)

Special Tackle

This obviously is not 7-weight country. I use 10- and 11-weight rods even when the surf is small. I want lifting and holding power, as well as the longer power stroke that the bigger rods offer. These fish seldom run, so they do not tire easily. A bigger fish from shore in heavy water can be a tough foe; in big surf, they have all the advantages. I want at least a fighting chance to land the fish.

I use 20-pound-test Orvis Mirage fluorocarbon tippet material. Fluorocarbon is very tough and abrasion resistant, much more so than monofilament. It is ideal for fishing around structure. In most fishing conditions, 16-pound tippet is ample for stripers, but use 20-pound when fishing the cliffs. Plan that the leader will take a beating, perhaps losing half its strength.

If I had just one fly to fish, it would a dark Snake Fly, 5 inches long. My second choice would be a herring-type fly in white with some flash, 6–7 inches long. These two flies make up 90 percent of my cliff-fishing arsenal.

On a bright sunny day with a mild surf, try cliff fishing and see what it's like to watch a big striper rise up from 15 feet of water and take a fly at your feet while you're fishing from shore.

Jetties 8

I had already fished the jetty hard for several hours, starting well before first light. There was a flurry of small fish at dawn, but not what I had expected. The conditions were right, with a quartering wind blowing over the jetty and modest wave action. The water worked nicely over the outer bars, and there was a good flow along the jetty's edge that ran out to sea. I expected big fish to be feeding along the jetty this morning.

After waiting for a while, I finally started back to the beach, stopping to search for fish every 50 feet. It was low incoming tide, and I had found fish here before, after sunup, on this tide. It was late in the season, the conditions were right, and I hated to leave. I stopped where the jetty meets the beach and sat down.

The first thing to appear was a fin cutting through the white water. Then a small swirl broke the surface. In a few minutes, a group of small stripers started feeding in the pocket between the beach and the jetty. Even though the fish were small, I hungered for action and slipped down the steep rocks to the beach. It did not take long to hook a fish, and in a few minutes I had several. On the next cast, I let the fly sink and tried bumping the bottom. The water was only about 3 or 4 feet deep. When the fly stopped, the take was too solid, and I thought I had hung the bottom. Then the water in front of me erupted, and a big tail waved back and forth in the air like an alligator with its head stuck in the sand. When the run started, it was fast, with the fish heading down the beach. I gave chase, getting as much distance from the jetty as I could. The fish ran about 150 yards up the beach, but stayed close to shore. When the run stopped, I had only 50 yards to gain. I had the fish on the beach quickly, so it never had time to regain its strength. Looking at the fish's size, I was shocked. Here was a striper of perhaps 40 pounds, feeding in 3 feet of water right next to the jetty, only 25 feet from shore. Jetties can offer an opportunity for big fish right at the angler's feet.

Most jetties are retaining walls built to protect a beach or harbor mouth from erosion. Wooden jetties are uncommon and usually found in very sheltered areas. Most jetties are built with large stones; along open shorelines, only rock jetties can withstand the pounding from waves, and even these deteriorate over time. Jetties with carefully laid stones are easy to walk, but those that are rough set require the agility of a mountain goat. Some rough-set jetties or jetties that have collapsed over time are dangerous. Not only are they difficult to walk, there are holes and pitfalls throughout the structure. Either slipping off the edge or falling into a big hole can be fatal. If you are alone, slip into a hole at low water, and cannot move, the tide might cover you— not a good thought. Fish tough jetties with a partner, and carry a length of rope, a flare gun, and a cell phone. Most of the jetties I fish offer easy walking, and even the rough-set ones do not have large pitfalls.

All harbor openings and many estuary entrances need jetties to keep them from filling with sand. If these entrances flow into the open ocean, the jetty is usually large. You will find smaller rock jetties at the mouths of many estuaries and harbors in sheltered water. All of these locations provide excellent fishing. The beaches of New Jersey are famous for their jetties. There are some anglers who fish only jetties because the fishing is so consistent.

Obviously, finding jetties is easy; just look on a nautical chart for any opening that flows into open water. Along open beaches, the larger ones are marked on a chart by a black line jutting into the sea. Some jetties have beacons to mark the entrance to a harbor, and these should also be marked on a nautical chart. I prefer fishing larger jetties when there is wave action to create water movement. Jetties are good places to hide on windy days and give access to water along beaches that would be unfishable with fly tackle on some days. When a beach is too rough to fly fish, a jetty lets you get beyond the heavy water. It will also draw stripers in rough water, because there is easy feeding along the structure.

Jetties always have food sources living in and around them. Because many jetties guard the mouths of estuaries, they have a constant flow of food holding along their rocky edges. The rocks themselves hold food like crabs, lobsters, and small fish. From late summer to the season's end, schools of spearing, anchovies, and numerous flat-sided baitfish will congregate along these structures.

Working smaller structures at the mouths of estuaries is like fishing a natural rocky area with a flow. You are fishing an outflow. (For fishing information, see Chapter 9, Outflows.)

Jetty fishing involves working along the structure, fishing the fly around the rocks or the flowing water that surrounds a jetty. This is pure surf fishing; fishing a jetty from a boat is dangerous and not very effective. If there is wave action, getting close enough to fish properly is difficult, and running the motor will drive fish off. Standing on the jetty you can fish slowly, working the water properly. I do not recommend using a boat near jetties that have beach access. Leave these areas to the surf anglers. Big breakwaters, with no connection to shore, are very similar to offshore structure. Use the same techniques to fish breakwaters from a boat as you would use fishing the cliffs or fishing a steep ledge. (See Chapters 7, Cliff Fishing, and 10, Estuaries.)

Jetties offer access to water that might otherwise be unreachable for both boat and shore anglers. If there are waves breaking around a jetty, a shore angler can still walk the length of the jetty and fish the water. The only exception would be in huge surf. Reaching that same water would be impossible without using the safe environment of that jetty. Think of a jetty as an anchored barge that you can walk on and fish. Long jetties give access to deeper water, much like cliffs, but the walking is usually better.

Research a jetty as you would any other piece of water. At low tide, look for bars that run along the beach near a jetty; many have a series of sandbars that run perpendicular to the structure. Usually the bars end before reaching the jetty, leaving a gully right along the structure. With wave action, the ends of the bars will have working water. Look for piles of stone and gravel or holes along the structure. Places where some of the structure has fallen along the jetty create good holding and feeding locations for stripers. Find fishing perches—locations with good footing—along the side of the jetty. In big-tide areas, you will need to plan for both high and low water.

How to Fish a Jetty

Let's discuss researching and fishing a big, open-water jetty in a location with large tides that fluctuate 10–12 feet. There is a wind quartering from left to right at 20 knots, creating 3- to 5-foot seas. This is just what I want when fishing a jetty. (While I am discussing these fishing techniques, I will offer advice for other conditions as well.)

It's unnecessary to have a tremendous amount of water around a jetty to hold fish. I usually fish the lee side in water 3–10 feet deep. With wave action around the structure, I like to fish just outside the break line. Many times a flow forms along the structure from breaking waves that build up along the inside bar. In this case, the current is running from right to left, and the water is flowing from the shore out to sea.

Usually, all currents along a jetty flow out to sea. This flow is a feeding trough, pushing bait from the shoreline out along the jetty. Generally the flow runs close to the structure. On a falling tide, any baitfish along the shore will be forced to move out in this flow as the water drops. As the tide rises or drops, this flow moves, adjusting to the water level. If the shoreline is weedy, this first flow might be dirty. The next flow out along the jetty should have cleaner water.

There are flows around the outer bars as well, but they will not be as large. In bigger surf, good flows form around the bar's end, but often some distance from the jetty. This flow is enhanced when good-size waves break over the bars. The combination of breaking surf and flowing water also makes the bars ideal feeding locations.

Where the Beach Meets the Jetty

This first pocket of water can provide hot fishing, particularly on low incoming tide, as long as the surf is not too heavy. At lower tides, fish this spot from the beach, wading out next to the structure. Cast into the pocket, and retrieve to feel what type of flow there is and how the water is moving. The water in this location can move in several directions at once. Use a steady retrieve to keep pace with the fly, but if you feel any flow pulling on the line, hold tight and allow the fly to hang in the current.

Where the beach meets the jetty is a good location, especially on low incoming tide.

There might be some surge from the surf, but if the water appears slack, fish it the way you would work open water along a beach; just cover the water by casting and retrieving. Do not spend too much time, and be ready on the first cast. You will know right away if there are fish in this pocket.

When you fish this location at high tide, cover the water for 100 feet on both sides of the jetty. Wave size, wave direction, wind direction, and the jetty's location will all determine if this water is fishable. Water away from the jetty will be more productive on days with less wave action. Good water movement generally draws fish to the structure.

Jetties along ocean beaches can have good holes well away from the structure. However, stripers love structure, and if both the jetty and the holes have good supplies of food, the jetty should be more productive. I once heard an angler joke that if you dropped a cement block along a south New Jersey beach, there would be a dozen boats fishing it—structure is that important to stripers.

The First Section of Moving Water

The flowing water, both on the inside and along the bars, is the place to focus your efforts. Fish the inside flow first. Use short casts, 20–40 feet, and let the fly hold next to the jetty at the cast's end. Feeling the fly and detecting strikes is tough, because you are usually well above the water's surface. Also, when fishing from the side of a jetty,

Work the water behind and along the bars, getting the fly to move with the flow. Try different-length casts and different retrieves to remain in contact with the fly.

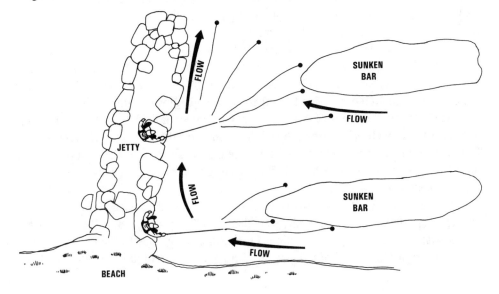

you have waves rolling past you; when you fish from the beach, they roll toward or away from you. Because water levels keep changing from wave action and the flow from the inner bar keeps fluctuating, this water will have little rhythm.

At night, fish only as much line as you can feel, casting at a quartering angle down-current. The casting angle should be about 45 degrees from the jetty. This gives a good swing but will keep a tight line most of the time. Keep the rod low and pointed toward the fly. In darkness, look for bubbles—the white foam from breaking waves—as they flow along the surface. They indicate the speed and direction of the flow. From the jetty's height, foam will be visible on all but the darkest nights.

In daylight, the flow is easy to follow. Cast across the flow and mend some line up- or downcurrent to change the fly's pace. An upcurrent mend will let the fly settle deeper and works well in stronger flows. When positioned near the end of the flow, cast, mend upcurrent, and let the fly settle. As the fly nears the slower water, when you feel less pull on the line, begin to retrieve. This will turn the fly quickly into the current and bring it toward the surface like a fleeing baitfish. Try doing this in differ-ent locations in the flow. Mending downcurrent increases the fly's speed during the swing, which works well in a slower flow because it gives a positive feel when a fish takes at the end of the swing. A fish usually takes as the fly turns upcurrent. Even if the fly is traveling downtide, if it is traveling quickly, the strike is easier to feel. It is when a fly travels slowly downcurrent that strikes are difficult to detect.

Moving farther out on the jetty, fish the water that flows around the bars. Try posi-tioning yourself to swing the fly along the inside corner of the bar. With the flow moving right to left, the best casting position along the jetty is below the bar, so your cast lands on the beach side of the bar and swings out to sea, sweeping along the in-side edge. Casting at a quartering angle from the jetty gives a more positive feel to the fly and better strike detection. If casting straight out to the bar, begin retrieving when the fly lands, or you will not feel the strikes.

Try different casting angles and mends to cover the water. Focus on the flow around the bar, and work the white water as well. This is like fishing water rolling over a bar in an ocean hole, but you are casting from the side. Waves breaking over the bar sweep the line to the side first, then the flow begins pushing toward you after the line flows into the drop-off. Watch as waves break over the bar, and time your cast to land as the wave breaks, letting the white water carry the line. You will feel tension from the white water pulling the line, and once that tension lessens, you must retrieve quickly to maintain fly control. If the flow rushing toward you is strong, use a fast re-trieve to keep in contact with the fly.

As you move out on the jetty, the water depth should increase. Depending on the wa-ter depth and flow speed, I generally start fishing with an intermediate line unless the seas are large. With heavy wave action, I use fast-sinking lines for better line control and penetration. Only on a calm day when fishing poppers would I use a floating line.

Keep moving out, working each bar as you head to the jetty's end. With a heavy swell, the very tip of the jetty will probably be too dangerous to fish. Creep as close to the end as the surf allows, and fish the white water. With waves higher than 3 feet, look for good white water and a strong, short flow of water just at the jetty's corner. This flow should roll, left to right, from the jetty's corner angling toward the beach, opposite the other flows along the jetty. This is a tricky little piece of water, because the flow angles toward you unless it is safe to stand right near the flow. Cast as the wave breaks, and let the line and fly swing in the white water. Keep working this water using short casts, and fish the fly slowly after the drift stops. While the fly drifts, add short pulls, making it dart. This action also helps to detect strikes and keep in contact with the fly. Try casting over the white water and retrieving through the flow, varying the retrieve's speed and the length of the pulls to work the white water. Of course, while working water along the jetty, try retrieving immediately after the fly hits the water.

Fish Close to the Structure

In the lulls between waves, cast right along the structure, beyond the jetty's end, working the fly right along the rocks. When fishing the jetty's length, keep working the fly close and make some casts alongside the structure. Whenever the fly swings

Feeding stripers will sometimes push baitfish right onto the rocky wall of a jetty.

against the rocks, let it rest there for several seconds. I once had a 46-pound striper take the fly as I lifted it from the water. The big striper grabbed the fly with just the leader outside the rod tip. I thought the fly had hung up on the rocks. If I had picked the fly up before it reached the jetty, I never would have known that trophy fish was there.

Pick a Good Spot and Hang In

Some jetties have limited access; on a given tide, there may be only a few good fishing perches. I like to keep moving to find ideal water with good movement, but this is not always possible. If the footing is bad, choose a good standing location and fish hard. Stripers seldom hold for a long time along a jetty; they circle, looking for food. If you keep fishing one good location, the fish will find you, unless there is a heavy concentration of bait to hold fish in another area along the structure. Take time to research the water along a jetty to determine the key, safe spots to stand at different tides. The secret is **learning the water** so you know where the bait will hold on a given tide and which locations have the best water movement on that tide.

Harbor-mouth Jetties

Big jetties at the mouths of harbors have a combination of different waters. The shoreline side is usually similar to a jetty on an open beach, needing wave action to add water movement. The harbor entrance wall of the jetty will have flowing water alongside it. At their ends, and in the deep water alongside the structure, these jetties can hold fish. Fish the structure as you would an outflow, with short casts, working the fly right to the rocks. At the jetty's end, fish the flow in either direction. The flow might combine with wave action, so fish the white water as it mixes with the flow. Use the methods previously mentioned, because this water will resemble the wave-battered front section of a beach jetty. I fish both beach and harbor jetties with similar techniques.

The problem with fishing the inside or the end of a harbor jetty is landing fish. Along the beachside wall of a jetty, the fish usually runs straight out, away from the structure, giving you time to reach the shoreline and walk the fish onto the beach. Often there is nowhere to beach the fish, so you must land it along the structure. With big fish, this is difficult and dangerous when surf batters the rocks. Look at big jetties first to see if there is a good landing spot. If there is none, it would be wise to find locations with landing areas, or just fish the beach side. Small fish are not difficult; just lift them up with the tippet. The big fish will give you fits.

Flat Water Around a Jetty

Unless I'm sight fishing, I seldom fish jetties on flat days, except when they guard the mouth of an estuary where water movement comes from within. I believe that wave action draws fish to the jetty; I have less confidence without it.

On calm days, cover as much water as you can by casting and moving around the jetty. I prefer a sinking line, moving the fly quickly, or fishing poppers in low light to draw fish from surrounding water. Poppers attract fish from great distances in calm water, exciting them to strike. On a calm night, try fishing a floating line with a big surface fly that leaves a wake. Use different retrieves; sometimes a fast-moving fly might excite fish, even at night. On a calm, bright, sunny day, use the jetty's height to sight fish.

A jetty having shallow sand flats alongside is a good place to look for stripers on low incoming tide. The jetty's high platform makes both spotting and stalking fish easier. Use the same fly presentation techniques mentioned in the sight-fishing section (see Chapter 6, Flats and Shallow Water, Mud, and Sand). Remember to make some practice casts first, because the height will affect your distance judgment.

A Great Place to Hide from the Wind

When the wind begins to rip, there is no better fishing location than the lee side of a jetty. Many jetties offer a sanctuary in the wind, unless of course the water becomes so riled that the fish move offshore. Big jetties have high, steep walls that break the wind, offering a sheltered side in many weather conditions. The lee side of a big jetty will be one of the few fishable locations in 40-mile-per-hour winds. I have spent some cold, tough mornings hidden from the wind in a jetty's rocky pocket.

There are several reasons why I fish jetties in strong winds. First, jetties offer protection from the cutting wind, and the fish are close, so casting is no problem. In most cases, you need only a short roll cast to reach fish. Also, wind blowing over the structure actually improves your casting distance because it carries the line. You need only roll the line into the air to make a cast. It's great to feel the wind ripping at your rod tip when casting, while you are below the rocks protected from most of it.

Furthermore, the lee side of a jetty offers protection for schools of baitfish. Many times, bait holding along a section of beach will pack against the sheltering structure during a hard blow. You can be sure that where the bait congregates, the stripers are not far behind.

What Side to Fish

The weather, mainly wind, governs which side is better to fish. On a calm day, the whole jetty should be open for fishing. In daylight, walk out looking for any activity like bait, feeding fish, or water movement that looks inviting. During a heavy blow, weed builds up quickly on the windward side, making fishing difficult. As the wind begins to build, bait will move to the lee side for protection. Once the wind begins to build and waves or ocean swells are hitting the jetty, fish only on the lee side. With a large swell and strong wind, the only fishable water is on the protected side. In a straight-on wind, pick the side with some shelter, such as a bend in the jetty, or look for a bar or other structure that offers some protected water. When the wind is blowing straight along the jetty's side, both sides weed up quickly, oftentimes making fishing impossible.

Landing Fish

Never attempt to land a big fish from the jetty if you can walk the fish to a nearby beach. After hooking a big fish, let it run with only slight tension to get it away from the jetty. Once the fish is heading away from the structure, begin walking to shore.

With an onshore wind quartering away from the jetty's side, or even an onshore wind along the structure, hold the rod high to create a bow in the line. This leads and pushes the fish toward shore. Unless you are running out of line, keep moving toward the beach. Walk slowly, looking down to avoid a tumble. Even if you lose line, keep moving to the shoreline, climb down to the beach, and begin walking quickly away

When landing a big fish from a jetty, it is important to reach shore while the fish is some distance from the structure.

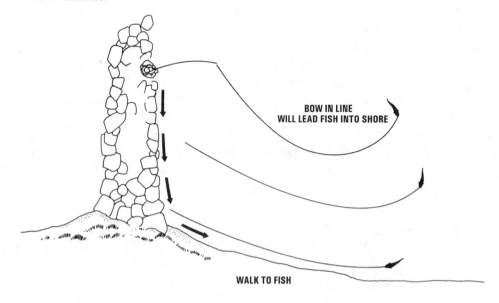

**BOW IN LINE
WILL LEAD FISH INTO SHORE**

WALK TO FISH

from the jetty. Walking toward the fish, you will gain line back easily. Usually, the fish is beat just from fighting the wind dragging the fly line and backing. At times you might have 200 yards of line out. On a long jetty, the fish could hold off the beach, not moving to shore. As you walk toward the beach, line will keep slipping from the reel because the distance between you and the fish widens even though the fish has stopped running. But you will gain this line back easily once you start walking up the beach toward the fish.

The key is gaining distance from the jetty, because if the fish has any power left, it will head back toward the structure. Once on the beach, walk toward the fish, gaining line, and keep walking until the fish is straight out from your position along the shoreline. Stay on dry ground and fight the fish, using the waves to your advantage.

Gear

Aluminum-studded foot gear or chains that strap onto the wader's boot make walking safer. Felt soles are false security; on some rocks, they are more slippery than rubber cleats, because they have no tread to catch the creases in the rocks. Walking the rock on a jetty is similar to cliff fishing. Avoid rocks with black or green slime, stay on barnacle-covered rocks, and do not stand or walk on rocks that slope toward a pitfall or into the sea.

Fish without a stripping basket and you will lose a fly line. Even on flat jetties, there are too many snags to catch the line, or holes where the line will slip and perhaps tangle, beyond reach, under your feet. Once the line slips into a crack and the waves wash around it, the line is gone.

Match flies to foods around the jetty. If there are no schooling baits, try dark, short, chunky patterns 3–5 inches long to match foods like small lobsters, blackfish, mummies, and cunners, which are mainstays along a jetty. Yellow, chartreuse, or black Deceivers, Snake Flies, and Clousers are also effective. In spring, squid will be active around harbor jetties. In fall, look for spearing, sand eels, anchovies, and small, flat-sided, herring-type baitfish along the structure.

When the seas are big, use 10- and 11-weight outfits and 16- to 20-pound fluorocarbon tippets in case the fish drags the leader along the rocks. When fishing big jetties, I want more than 200 yards of backing. Line selection is clear-cut: Use an intermediate or fast-sinking line when the water is rolling, and add a floating line for calm days. With a little stretching, an intermediate line will cover most fishing conditions. If you grease an intermediate line, it will fish poppers and work as a sight-fishing line as well.

I use jetties as sanctuaries in foul weather, but they offer good fishing on many occasions and put fish right at the angler's feet. Jetties hold migrating fish in the spring and fall and are good summertime locations at night and in rough weather. They offer perhaps the best opportunities for the fly rodder to hook a big striper from the surf.

Outflows 9

*T*hough there are times when following your nose, instead of knowing where you are going, can get you in trouble, I've been lucky now and then. I had not followed my own advice of checking a fishing location the day before. It was an early morning in September on Martha's Vineyard, Massachusetts, and I was looking for an outflow that I had never fished before. Following some crude directions, I happened upon the right sand road and came to a beach with a beautiful outflow lined by jetties on both sides.

It was past first light. I'd gotten lost twice and had wanted to be fishing before it got light. Still, I was surprised to be alone and quickly headed for the end of the small, flat jetty at the mouth of the outlet. The tide was rushing in, forming a nice rip along the front of the jetty. Near the car, I had stretched out the full fly line, which now lay in my basket waiting for the first cast. After walking to the outflow's end, before even casting, I reeled in most of the line; there were fish breaking all over the rip, right at my feet. After a dozen fruitless casts, I needed to make a tackle change to cope with a basic problem: The fish were feeding on thick schools of sand eels, and the only way to make them notice my fly was to fish deep. I quickly switched to a sinking line, a sand eel fly, and a slow dead drift downcurrent. Casting a short line upcurrent, I let it sink, utilizing that old nymph-fishing trick of dead drifting using the rod, swinging it with the current flow while watching the line to detect the strike.

This technique works well once you get the feel, and gauge the speed of the drift. After casting upcurrent, reach the rod in the direction of the cast, and let the line and fly sink while stripping in the loose line to eliminate slack at the rod tip. Try counting to about ten, and begin sweeping the rod downcurrent, keeping pace with the moving line. Swinging the rod at the same speed as the current forms a bow in the line between the rod tip and the water. Once you get a routine down, a bow of the same angle forms every time. Watch the bow. If it moves upcurrent, stops, or jumps, strike by lifting the rod.

In this case, the technique simulates a dead sand eel drifting with the tide. With the sand eels so thick, only a fly presented below the thick baits would attract attention. It was tough fishing, but I did well that morning until bluefish moved in and started eating flies like popcorn. It was a typical morning around an outflow. I had never fished this location before, but at any outflow there is always a good chance for fish if there is water movement.

Outflows, also called inlets, breachways, or river mouths (smaller ones are called creeks), are places where the changing levels of the sea create water flow. Any opening along a shoreline that connects open water to a section of protected water will have good water flows as the tide rises and falls. They range in size from several feet across to large openings, like the mouth where Cape Cod's Pleasant Bay enters the Atlantic Ocean. Any opening, or the protected water up inside, is a good location to find fish.

In heavy concentrations of bait, you sometimes need to get below the bait, where the stripers will single out your fly.

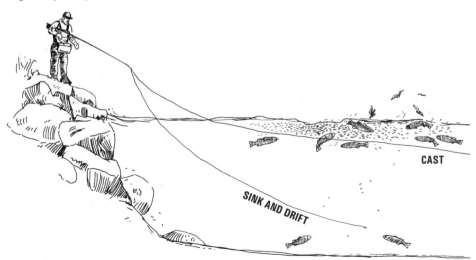

CAST

SINK AND DRIFT

Any backwater that empties into open water, or a creek that flows into a main flow, is an ideal feeding place for stripers.

Smaller openings are usually systems within a system—for example, a small creek spilling into a large canal inside an estuary. There are small creeks that spill into sheltered water, and some do flow into open water, but most have stone jetties or natural structures that protect the opening from rolling seas.

Every opening that finally enters the sea is the mouth of an estuary. Estuaries are the nurseries of the sea, places where many small sea creatures' lives begin. The foods that feed many of our inshore gamefish are the products of estuaries. These complex systems are networks of marsh areas, with water flows of varying size with bottoms of sand, mud, gravel, and some rock. There are two major types of systems: mixed fresh and salt water, and pure salt water. The pure saltwater systems are never 100 percent pure, because there are always small freshwater flows feeding them. But they have clear water, while the mixed systems have discolored water throughout the system or large sections of coffee-colored water. Both systems harbor tremendous amounts of bait. However, some foods thrive in mixed waters and need fresh water to spawn; other foods will not tolerate fresh water. Striped bass can survive in most levels of salinity; they spawn in fresh water and, after adapting, live there as well.

Fish hold in a creek mouth, waiting for the coming tide.

I will divide estuaries into these two categories: pure salt water and mixed fresh and salt. Although both systems have similar waters and you can fish them in a similar manner, I will split them up to avoid redundancy. In the clear-water system, I will emphasize visual fishing; in discolored waters, blind casting. Remember, fishing any water in low light requires blind casting even if the water is clear. The major difference is visibility. In a pure system, reading the water, finding bait, and spotting fish is easier. In a discolored system, you never have the luxury of **learning the water** by sight. Even such basic functions as wading and running a boat will be different because you cannot see. I will begin with saltwater systems. They are more fun to fish, particularly if you like sight-fishing.

Small Openings That Enter Open Water

A pure system offers excellent sight fishing, especially at low incoming tide. There are many small outlets and river mouths with good flowing water that resemble spring creeks with shallows, deep cuts, and gravel bars. Some places are cut off from the sea at low tide, filling quickly as the tide rushes in. I have seen fish landlocked at

Small, clear backwaters are ideal places to sight cast; this is similar to fishing a western spring creek.

low tide waiting for the flow to fill the backwater. Usually, the trapped fish are hard to take. It is best to wait for the inflowing sea before fishing, or you will just alarm them.

These locations are easy to find because they are small and the fish are visible, but the low, clear water makes fishing tough at times. Even at the mouth of a busy beach, the fish enter these small locations looking for food.

Look at the mouth, or the water just outside the mouth, for cruising fish. Sometimes sight casting can be effective as fish mill about, waiting for enough water to enter the estuary. If the mouth is small and shallow, fish might be spooky, so it is better to move back into larger water and let the fish settle into feeding.

Work carefully, walking without making noise and fishing with a floating or clear-tip line and a long leader. This is typical sight fishing in skinny water at low incoming tide, so use the techniques described in Chapter 6 (Flats and Shallow Water, Mud, and Sand). In big-tide locations, conditions will change once water fills the estuary. As the water covers the flats, look for the fish to feed in deeper sections along the marsh grass. Any point that forms a rip will hold fish. Fish the deeper sections and work the rip by letting the fly swing across current. This is a mixture of blind casting and working the water while watching for the movements of fish. Poppers and small flies can be effective when fished along the grass banks. You can usually cover the water quickly as the tide rises, because the water is small. For sight casting, try small crabs or shrimp patterns. Use small, lifelike baitfish flies when fishing the deeper areas.

There are many small marshes like this that run in from the sea for a mile or two, and the fish will move in with the tide. If there is a run of fish, it usually happens with the first good flow of water, and the fish will poke slowly up the marsh, feeding with the tide. If you see only a few fish once the flow has started, find another spot. I usually fish up inside these places only with overhead sun to spot fish. These locations can be very good on a falling tide as the bait flushes out into open water. At first light, you might find some good fish holding at the mouth. Most stripers that move up inside these small waters are schoolies to 10 pounds, with an occasional 15- to 20-pound fish that will make your heart stop. For low-light fishing, I will spend time in bigger areas, because if I'm losing sleep I want to fish deeper water with a better chance at bigger fish.

Small creeks and marshes are not usually places to catch large numbers of stripers; you will earn each fish. They are, however, unique areas because the fish will feed in overhead sun in 1 foot of water waving their tails in the air like bonefish. Some spots are good for only an hour daily for several weeks a year but are worth a look throughout the season. They are ideal places to park the car and hit for several hours. Not suitable for boats, they are a wader's delight, and a canoe or kayak will open up many possibilities.

Bigger Flows That Run into Open Water

A bigger outflow, one you need to cross to fish both sides, might be as wide as several football fields. Many such locations have jetties to keep the openings stable, to prevent them from filling with shifting sand. If the jetties are large, fish them as described in Chapter 8 (Jetties). For locations with smaller jetties or those with very strong rips, work the current along the rocks. Some openings have tremendous flows of current if the backwater is large. Some, such as the breachways in southern Rhode Island, continue to flow in for more than 2 hours after high tide. They have the same delay on falling tide. On big-moon tides, the water races through with a rush that you can hear.

On outgoing tide, the flow in front of the jetties will hold fish. Cast into the flow and work the feeding lane, the line that forms between the fast outflowing water and the slow water. This line shows up well in most strong outflows. The fish hold along this edge, as well as in the flow. You are fishing a rip: covering water, then working the fly back through the feeding lane or through the slower water in front of the jetty. A fast-sinking line works well here. Try casting at different angles to the rip, drifting the fly on the swing. Use an upcurrent mend on some casts to get the fly down. Also try mending a large loop of line downcurrent, then feeding more line before retrieving quickly. This will let the fly sink, then make it swing quickly to the surface like a fleeing baitfish.

The water at the mouths of outflows is excellent for boat fishing. Some locations have good water flow for several hundred yards. Give the surf anglers room, staying well out beyond their casting range. Work this moving water by drifting and casting into the current, using sinking lines if the water is deep. Cast across current, fishing baitfish-type patterns with a medium to fast retrieve. On some casts, let the line sink to work the fly deeper in the water column. When it is safe, anchor on one side of the rip and cast at different angles to the flow, as you would when fishing a rip from shore. An outlet that faces the open ocean will have breaking waves on outgoing tide if a sea is running. These are not places to trifle with. Unless you know a location well, do not run any outlet when big swells are rolling into the mouth. When outflowing water hits incoming waves, sea conditions are frightening. In a boat, avoid these locations in heavy seas.

Openings without Jetties

Some openings, such as Cape Poge Gut on Martha's Vineyard, are very stable, even though they have no structure at their mouths. You can fish these areas as you would an opening with a jetty. There can be good footing that allows wading close to the flow, providing ideal access for fishing. In protected water, the outer areas of the flow are ideal for boat fishing.

Open ocean outflows without structure or jetties to fend off the sea keep changing, however. Sand openings can move great distances; those on Cape Cod are constantly shifting. The shifting sand forms bars and cuts, creating large deltas at the mouths of these openings. When the sea is not big, the whole delta can offer ideal sight fishing for stripers. On a flowing tide, drift, pole, or use an electric motor to search for fish along the bars, where they will hold facing the flow on the downtide side. In the bigger shallow sections, look for fish to cruise on incoming tide. Try anchoring on an edge of a big shallow, working the deeper water in a cut while watching for fish up on the flat. This can be ideal flats fishing, using the shallow-water techniques discussed in Chapter 6. Depending on the bait type, there can be fish all season long, but May and June are excellent if you find fish when they first arrive.

On the falling tide, the delta is a good wading spot to sight fish, but watch the tide and the walking. In locations with shifting sand, stay back from the edge. Avoid the distant waters on incoming tide.

The deltas can be great during low light at the bottom of the tide. As the water funnels into a few strong flows, stripers feed in these main channels. Usually there is a delay of several hours before the rising water will chase you from the bars. If you plan to fish at night, research this water in the daytime to learn where the best cuts are, what tide is best, and if the wading is dangerous. This research should be current, because conditions will change frequently. The tides that expose the delta, making it accessible for better wading in the morning, are big full-moon tides; at night you want a big *new*-moon tide. Avoid these places in a boat at night if there is any sea.

Work the stronger outflows as you would a rip, casting at different angles to the current. You will be fishing a river-type flow, so keep walking along and blind casting to find where the fish are holding. Many times the fish will feed at the mouth where the flow meets the ocean. Wave action over the bars adds movement to the flow, making feeding easier. Work the white water around the bars, getting the fly to swing with the flow into the rolling water. Keep the casts short, alternating both dead drifts and retrieves to keep in contact with the fly. Don't get fancy here by trying to mend or make long drifts. This water is broken, and if you must make long casts, make them quartering downtide, not across, unless the water is slow. In low light, the fish should strike aggressively, especially when the water is rolling. If the water is flat, use some mends, but keep it simple. An intermediate line works well, but carry a fast sinker if the water flow is strong, if there is a hard roll, or if there are deeper pockets to fish. Often the fish are holding along the edges of bars or just below the bars, taking anything that moves. Dark, active flies, or patterns with green or blue backs over white with some flash, work well. In all but flat, calm conditions use larger flies, 4–6 inches long. Sand eels are a major food most of the season. In the fall, small, flat-sided baits, 2–4 inches long, are also important.

When there are several good cuts, keep working different water to find fish. Sometimes the rolling water between the flows holds fish. Stripers move along the bars, slipping into pockets of deeper water as the tide begins to rise. Most outflows have outrushing water even well after the tide begins filling the delta. The bait will hide in sheltered pockets, and as the holes begin to fill, look for stripers to move with the coming water, searching for the trapped baitfish. Be aware that rising water means it is time to seek higher ground, so begin fishing your way back to shore. Some places allow a full range of the prime waters for only several hours, and this time might be cut short if a sea is running. Most of the time the outer bars break the sea, but once the outer bars cover over, look for the waves to intensify.

On calm days, the outer edges of the delta are good sight-fishing locations to work from a boat. Pole or run an electric motor, working the outer bars to spot fish. As the water begins to rise, look for the fish to move over the outer bars and swim into the estuary. On a falling tide, look for the outer bar to collect fish if there is good holding water where they can wait out low tide.

This is an ideal situation for presenting a fly at close range to a big fish. With good supplies of bait, expect to find fish at any time, but nighttime is ideal to fish deltas.

Inside a Clear-Water System

If the system is large, there are countless types of water with ideal sight-fishing opportunities. The waters are complex with rips, bars, gullies, and cutbanks, and in some of the sandy locations, there will be sections of scallop-shaped holes. In places with heavy current, look for washboard sections of water, a long series of small, lumpy bars with pockets in between. Depending on the sand's texture, water speed, and length of flow, these washboard sections of water can be large and the holes between the bars quite deep. From a distance, the water will look wavy; at low tide, if the bars are exposed, they will look like sand waves. If the pockets are several feet deep, they offer excellent holding water for stripers.

In small sections of pocket water, work the closer downtide pockets first so you don't disturb other fish holding in pockets farther away. In places where there are series of pockets for several hundred feet, try to fish the pockets methodically. Cast a clear-tip or intermediate line above the pocket, and make the fly swing over the bar's edges and

When fishing small pockets, work the closest one first so you do not spook the fish from other pockets.

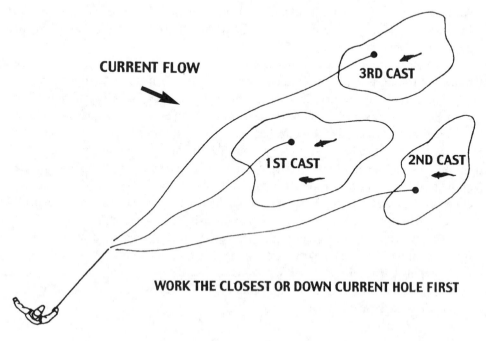

CURRENT FLOW

3RD CAST

1ST CAST

2ND CAST

WORK THE CLOSEST OR DOWN CURRENT HOLE FIRST

drop into the hole. Three- to 4-inch-long, light-colored attractor patterns work well. Use the basic technique of working a rip, casting above the bar and swinging the fly from the faster water into the drop-off. The difference is a smaller target to fish the fly through. Be sure to cast the fly above the bar, not right into the pocket. Give the fish a chance to see the fly coming so you're not just whacking the fish on the head. Usually you get only one chance with fish in a small pocket; if you draw the fish out with a poor cast, it will take a long look at the next presentation.

Many of these pockets are the size of a pool table, with the fish usually sitting near the middle. The fish must react quickly in fast current, because the fly is in range for only a brief time. When fishing a section of water with a series of holes, give each pocket just a few casts and then move on to the next. The fish might be scattered, sitting in the deeper holes, and most pockets will not hold fish. The better ones may hold several. In low light, move more slowly, working each pocket with a dozen casts to different locations above the hole. Even though the water is small, it is not easy to get the right drift when you cannot see. This is trial and error until you learn a location well enough to know precisely where to cast.

Pocket water can make for good sight fishing. You won't always see the fish before the take, but you will see the fish's reaction to the fly and see the strike. If fish are looking but not striking, try a smaller, more precise fly, or try to present the fly at a different angle.

Gullies with Sharp Banks

In some places, particularly in smaller systems where the main channel is cut deep, you will find gullies that look like a trench surrounded by shallow bars. Big systems might have feeder creeks, sections, or gullies along the main flow that resemble Bahamian bonefish creeks. There might be shallow, light-colored sand with a cut running through, or clear blue-green water. Stripers use these cuts as feeding areas, as traveling routes for moving around inside the estuary, and as holding areas to wait out a tide. Inside a big system, there are many small parcels of water that hold pockets of fish and are good fishing spots for a short time in the tide. The bigger cuts offer excellent opportunities throughout many phases of the tide.

The smaller locations are ideal for wading; in the bigger, deeper places you need a boat. Many of the smaller spots have hard, light-colored sand bottoms that you can cover by walking along one side of the cut. Fish cruise up on the edges of the flats, looking for food or feeding with their noses in the sand. If fish are working the banks, actively feeding in the shallows, use sight-casting techniques, casting to visible fish. When there is no fish activity on the banks, blind cast, letting the fly swing across current to fish the edges of the banks. Work any bar, point, or bend that forms a rip. Move slowly, getting the fly to swing into the pockets while watching the fly for fish activity. In small water, expect action on the first cast and try to make it count. A sloppy first cast might attract a fish, moving it from its lie, but because the fly was poorly placed the fish only follows it. Let this fish settle down; try coming back later when the fish is ready to feed. Sometimes it will take on the next cast, but waiting several minutes or changing to another fly will increase your chances.

I enjoy this fishing because it's visual and simple. You will see most stripers before they take, and even when they refuse, the fish usually show themselves, giving you another opportunity to try for them. This water is simple to cover; you need only a few casts to attract a fish. An intermediate line works well, but perhaps a clear or clear-tip line is the best choice for fishing any small clear water in the daytime.

Bigger Systems

In bigger locations, wading works well, but a boat opens up the entire system. Most estuaries have limited walking access because of the system's character. The network of canals, cuts, and creeks makes walking difficult. To reach a spot 50 yards away, you might need to walk a mile. Even if you plan to wade, a boat, canoe, or sea kayak will open up many fishing opportunities.

Using a Boat

When working from a boat, keep it on the edges, being as unobtrusive as possible. Avoid the smaller areas, as the boat's presence will just drive the fish out. Set up on one side of a shallow sand bank, anchoring so you can cast into shallow water and still work the deeper cut, much the same as if you were wading along the cut. You will fish in the same manner, but try a fast-sinking line to work the deeper sections of the cut. Fish as if you were working a deep rip, getting the fly down. Some of the bigger systems will have 20-foot holes.

On rising tide, work the bigger flats that border a section of deep water. Look for fish to move into the shallows when about 18 inches of water covers the flats. A boat provides a higher viewpoint, but also a taller profile for the fish to see. Keep well back from the deeper water, about 70 feet, which gives you time to spot the fish and make a cast.

On falling tide, look for fish to move to the deeper holes or to secluded spots with little boat traffic. In the smaller systems, most fish will move to the open water outside the estuary, and even in bigger systems, some fish will move out with each tide. The mouth is always a good place to look.

Some systems are a network of many creeks without large areas of open, deep water, or with small shallow flats that border the creeks. Without running room, low tide is not the time to fish unless you can enter from the open water and fish the rising water. If you are coming from inside the estuary, fish the high outgoing tide, then fish the low incoming tide back home. In places with big tides, plan on getting trapped until you know the tides well. In a new location, never fish when there is a big low tide at dusk; you might have a long, tough run back in the dark. If you anchor and wade, leaving the boat, use both a bow and stern anchor, or the boat may be high and dry with a falling tide. With a strong offshore wind, expect to have lower-than-normal water, and on big tides or with onshore winds, be aware that the entire area, including the marsh grass, might be covered. Without the grassy sod banks for reference, running in low light is difficult, and your boat might end up looking like Noah's Ark in the desert.

Pure, clear estuaries usually have good wading and little structure, and even if there are strong currents, 9-weight outfits with floating or intermediate lines and smaller flies are standard tackle. In some of the discolored estuaries, big tackle is a necessity. I have purposely not mentioned some water types found in both types of estuaries, because these waters make up the bulk of a mixed water system, which I will cover in the next chapter. Remember, both pure and mixed systems have the same water types. You can fish some locations using the same techniques; in low light, fish all locations in the same manner. The only difference is visibility, or lack of it, which can be significant at times and makes a mixed system quite fascinating.

The timing of runs during the year is also similar. In the mixed systems, I have emphasized the runs of herring in the spring, but they also occur in many pure systems, as do runs of spearing in early spring. The mixed systems just offer more and bigger runs of different baits, because they have more fresh water. Again, I must emphasize that you should treat both systems the same, because you will find that many of the fishing techniques are similar.

Estuaries 10

Water visibility was perhaps 6 inches; a big, bright fly would vanish after hitting the water. It made my home water on the Connecticut side of Long Island Sound look clear. In the summer, you sometimes can't see your feet in 3 feet of water—only in late season when the temperature chills will it clear up. But this muskiness is common in the big river systems of Maine and New Hampshire, and just as prevalent in the systems of Delaware and Chesapeake Bays. This water in the Piscataqua River, which separates Maine and New Hampshire, was not dirty, just rich with nutrients and heavily laden with fresh water. Probably, in some locations, the water down several feet was fairly clear because fresh water does not mix well with salt water.

It was the late 1960s, and my longtime fishing partner Pete Laszlo and I were anchored on a reef inside Great Bay. The rip had just started moving. We were working big herring patterns with sinking lines while waiting for the flow to increase. It was a new moon the first week in July—in the past, I had witnessed good hatches of cinder worms in this location. It looked like we would be disappointed; the flow was intensifying, but there were no worms appearing.

Sitting down for coffee, we were just discussing why the hatch had not materialized when the first splash broke the surface. It was like opening a floodgate. In a few minutes, the water was filled with worms and feeding stripers. Perhaps the worms were there and had not surfaced, but I believe we would have seen the fish feeding.

The rip was now alive with fish. Switching to small flies and floating lines, we both hooked up on the first cast. There are times when fishing in a worm hatch can be frustrating, with many feeding fish and few takes. But this was one of those times you dream about. The fish were not large, perhaps to 10 pounds, but the action was non-stop and lasted for several hours. We'd make a quartering cast downcurrent, let the fly drift, and a fish would take on the swing.

I don't remember really examining the worms, but I recall they were different from those in other worm hatches I had witnessed. I later discovered they were possibly palolo worms. The worms were brighter red and shorter, without the small black head or white section that the *Nereis* or cinder worms have. The last time we fished in a worm hatch, it was in this location, but the worms were of the *Nereis* type.

Estuaries are wonderful places, providing plentiful foods, shelter, feeding locations, and breeding grounds for stripers. There are many river systems in Chesapeake Bay and sections of the Hudson River in New York where most stripers, plus many other species, spawn. Mixed fresh- and saltwater estuaries are literally the basis for most of the life in the sea. They are the zones that connect fresh water to the ocean, allowing a flow of many creatures to pass back and forth throughout their lives. Without this connection, many species would perish. The striped bass as we know it today, and much of the food that provides its nourishment, would not exist. The rich inshore fishery that we enjoy on the East Coast does not exist in many areas on the West Coast, because these areas are devoid of estuaries.

Estuaries are the places where life begins in the sea. Whether large or small, they are excellent locations to find stripers.

Estuaries have a variety of water types, in addition to the important ones that I will mention later. There are open beaches, bars with rips, flats, and cuts. Bigger estuaries have reefs, huge sections of open water, and large jetties at their mouths, where the estuary meets open water. Big estuaries are complex. They take time to learn because there is so much water to cover.

The changing nature of the estuary also makes it a demanding fishery. Some years one bait will dominate a system; the next year there might be several foods, or a lack of foods, which will quell the fishing. The amount of rain and winter snowfall affects the water levels in big systems by changing the salinity levels in different locations throughout the system. Different levels of fresh water can drastically change the fishing from one year to the next in a mixed system. Keeping a log helps to forecast possible events like worm hatches and the arrival of different baits, but each season you must take a fresh look at the fishery, and assume nothing.

There are numerous large mixed systems scattered along our coast, such as the Kennebec in Maine, the Merrimack in Massachusetts, the Hudson in New York, and Delaware Bay between New Jersey and Delaware. The biggest, however, is Chesapeake Bay. All the bigger estuaries are systems within a system, and most will take a lifetime to learn. The Chesapeake Bay would take three lifetimes.

One dominant feature of all estuaries is the miles of grass-covered marsh banks glowing a yellow-green in the morning sun. In the estuaries from Pamlico Sound, North Carolina, to northern Massachusetts, there is limited structure, especially in the southern systems. The big systems of New Hampshire and Maine have tremendous structures of rock and ledge covered with weed and kelp. This structure makes the northern systems unique, providing holding water not found in estuaries with little structure.

On a map or nautical chart, a typical system looks like a giant tree. Its branches are the smaller rivers and creeks, and the trunk is the main river or main section of the bay. Unlike the water in pure, clear-water systems, the water in mixed systems is generally coffee colored or has a tannic tint with no subsurface visibility. A chart will offer information about water depth and structure in the main section of the system. Reading the water's surface and exploration are the only ways to learn the back areas in a system, which is the reason that it requires time to learn to read the water.

Learning a Location

To learn any system, you must take one section and spend time determining where the fish hold, when the best tides are, and how to move about without getting into trouble. Reading the water flows will help. Look for rip lines that tell you where the bars and sections of structure lie. If you are wading, locations with good flow should have decent footing, but some places can be muddy. Take small steps, use a wading

In small systems, canoes, sea kayaks, and float tubes are ideal for exploring and give access to fishing waters not reachable on foot.

staff, and feel with your rod tip for the drop-offs. In a boat, move slowly in uncharted water, watching for signs like rips or weeds that are stationary, indicating structure just below the surface. Explore at low incoming tide, and in structure-filled systems, expect to chip the prop. It is wise to use a softer aluminum or plastic prop when you are doing extensive exploring. I change props, using softer ones in different locations, to protect the expensive internal drive of the outboard motor. The softer props do not last as long, but they are cheap insurance when exploring new locations if you must bump around the rocks and hard bars.

Look for Early-Season Spearing

Popping bugs are very effective in locations with large spawning shiners. In the spring, 5- to 6-inch-long spearing sometimes appear along grassy banks in shallower areas of the estuary, in 2–6 feet of water. These are the leftover, surviving shiners of last year, and most will die after spawning. When you find these baitfish congregating in the grassy back areas of estuaries, fish poppers along the banks, at the edges of the drop-offs, and over the sunken grass beds. This is ideal fishing with a floating line and popping bugs or other surface flies.

Look for breaking fish in any of the back, slower-moving pockets. In wadable places with smaller tides, you can work these fish from shore if there is access. Small boats, canoes, and sea kayaks will open up many places unreachable to the wading angler. A boat with a push pole or an electric motor can prowl along, letting the angler take fish after fish when stripers lock onto this food source. You cast to the open water between the grassy patches, popping the bug along the banks, then letting it rest along a bank or over the sunken grass. Try popping several times and letting the bug sit, or fish it fast with loud, splashy pops. Also try a small, short, chunky popper using a slow, steady pop-pop-pop. In the early part of the season, this fishing might be hot all day long.

Working a Cutbank

Every marsh bank with current flowing along its edge is a potential fish-holding location. In big-tide locations, the holes against the bank might be 15 feet deep, and even in places with small tide fluctuations the marsh banks can have good holding water. Some banks offer good shore fishing, but working the banks requires careful planning. Otherwise, the bigger fish will depart before you can show them a fly. Sod or marsh banks transmit sound. If you step hard, leap over cuts, or walk briskly to a location, you will fill the surrounding water with noise. To prevent spooking fish, you must have a plan when fishing these places.

Let's say you are fishing a 100-yard bank with a good current along one bend and a quiet pocket at the bank's end. It is incoming to high tide, and the water along the bank ranges from 8–10 feet deep. Once you have researched the area and know the better lies, begin fishing some distance from the prime water, working up to that location slowly. Pip Winslow of the Orvis Company taught me a trick that works well when fishing from shore along a bank. Pip makes his first casts while standing well back from the water, landing 20–25 feet of fly line on the grass and another 30 feet in the water. He then fishes the fly back to the grass while remaining back from the water. With weedless flies, you can continue fishing back from the bank, working a section of water until you have cleared that section of bank. Then move carefully to the water's edge and begin fishing the fly along the bank. This technique lets you fish every piece of water without spoiling one area just to reach the water's edge.

Once you reach the bank, walk as if stepping on eggs and begin to work the water along the edge. In the spring, when there are big baits—such as herring—that frequent estuaries to spawn, stripers will trap them against banks. Fish a 6- to 8-inch-long, flat-sided fly, swimming it near the banks, making it look crippled. Use an

BANK

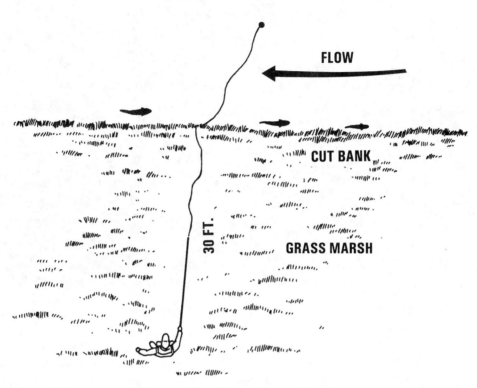

FLOW

30 FT.

CUT BANK

GRASS MARSH

Before walking up to a cutbank, cast while still some distance from the water.

intermediate or clear-tip line, stripping with a stop-and-go action, letting the fly hold and bolt as if it is stunned. Fish the fly right to the bank, then let it remain there for 10–15 seconds, as though the baitfish is hiding or seeking a resting place. Remove the fly too quickly and you might see a huge boil from a striper where the fly left the water. That fish will never come back.

Keep working the banks, casting into the current at different angles and letting the fly swing. Any small flow or gully that flows into the main stream is a feeding location. If there is little activity, try a smaller fly, working the water where the small flow meets the main stream. Smaller foods wash into the deeper water as this small flow flushes out.

Cutbanks hold fish at high water. Research them at low tide to find the deeper pockets.

Make the fly swing into the eddy behind the small flow, or try casting so the fly lands right in the middle of the flow like a bait that washed from the marsh gully into the main current. Be ready in case a fish takes when the fly hits the water.

Keep watching the calm water along the edges and the flat, slow-moving water in the quiet pockets. Stripers like to drive bigger baitfish into a pocket, like a pack of wolves herding their prey into a corner. When baitfish begin to swim in small circles, quiver on the surface, or rush about, they are being pushed by predators. If the baitfish act frightened, or you see bigger explosions and baitfish flying into the air, move quickly to get a cast into the action. This feeding may not last long, so begin moving at the first signs of activity.

In the spring, blueback herring and alewives spawn in many estuaries. There can be hot fishing for big stripers for several days to a few weeks when conditions are right. If you find big baitfish holding in one location or know that big baits frequent an estuary, keep watching and fishing that area. The trick is **learning the water,** to discover the right time and place to find this action, because once the big baits leave and the water warms, this opportunity is generally lost for the season.

Fishing Undercut Banks

Stripers hold like trout along the banks, particularly in places where the current undercuts the marsh bank. The difference between a cutbank and an undercut bank is that the cutbank drops straight down, while the undercut bank is eroded or hollowed out below the top of the bank. The bends along a marsh bank will erode over time from the flowing current. Places with grass right at the edge with no visible sod out from the grass are probably undercut.

You should begin fishing upcurrent of the hole using a sinking or clear-tip line so the line and fly settle or swing into the hole. In the spring, when big baitfish are active, stripers will take a herring pattern near the surface; at other times, getting the fly

From shore and upcurrent from the undercut bank, the current will usually sweep the fly naturally into the hole.

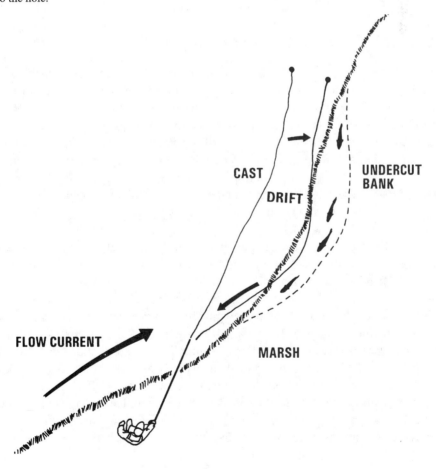

CAST

DRIFT

UNDERCUT
BANK

FLOW CURRENT

MARSH

down is the key. The natural flow of the current sweeps the fly under the bank when you fish from shore. Remember to use the same precautions as previously mentioned: Walk slowly and stay back from the banks. A quartering cast downtide lets the fly swing under the bank. Then you can retrieve back upcurrent, working the fly along the bank. On some casts, let the fly rest in the flow under the bank. The water right next to the bank on some bends has less flow, so allow the fly to swim in this water, retrieving it uptide with a stop-and-go movement.

From a boat anchored above the undercut bank, cast the fly close to the bank, throw a mend downcurrent, and let some additional line slip to make the fly sweep into the hole. Try different mends and drifts to swing the fly under the cutbank. Even if the boat is straight upstream from the hole, the current will sweep the fly away from the undercut bank as soon as the line tightens. When worked from a boat, the fly will be in the sweet spot for much less time than when fished from the shore. However, you can still fish effectively; just keep swinging the fly into the hole—and do not be afraid to get the fly down.

Covering Water from a Boat

Using a boat allows you to work many sections of water that are unreachable from shore. Working downcurrent with an electric motor, you can move without noise and fish one section after another. In bigger locations, boats offer you many different sections of water, whereas you are usually confined to a small piece while wading.

There are two ways to fish from a boat: drifting and anchoring. Drifting works well in locations that are more than 100 yards wide with a deep channel between the banks. In bigger water, you can fish a spot repeatedly by drifting, letting the boat get below the fishing area, then running a good distance around the spot and drifting over the location again. This allows you to work an area from different angles. After several drifts, you will know if fish are holding in a location. In a small location, where you can cast to either shoreline from the middle of the channel, anchoring is a better technique. If you drift through the spot and want to fish it again, running the motor so close to the fish just alarms them.

In a tight location, I like to anchor above the rip or cutbank. Start above the lie, casting so the fly flows downcurrent, swinging into the deeper water, then turning upcurrent as the line tightens. After working the water from one position, keep letting out more anchor line, about 10–15 feet at a time, to fish the location from different angles. When you are fishing from directly across or from below the spot, cast upcurrent, fishing the fly on a sideways drift into the deeper water. Fishing across from or below the spot is the most demanding, because the line will have a large bow in it and will be drifting downtide. When casting uptide at angles, you must begin retrieving when the fly lands. This is not to move the fly, but to keep pace with it by taking in the slack line, so when the fly flows into the hole, you have a tight line. This is trial and error, casting at different angles in the current to catch the right drift. Also remember to try adding different mends. If you detect any bump, tug, or tap on the line—or movement of the line during the drift—make several quick strips to set the hook.

Working Steep Drop-offs with a Boat

In the northern estuaries, particularly in Maine and New Hampshire, some locations have extensive ledge structure. Similar structure also exists in some of the backwaters of Rhode Island, which may be more sheltered bays than true estuaries, but you can fish the ledge in the same manner. This fishing is much like working offshore ledges without wave action. (See Chapter 7, Cliff Fishing.) I will discuss situations here that differ from cliff fishing. These techniques also apply when fishing bridge abutments, which are very similar waters—namely, sharp drop-offs with heavy current.

Along the face of a bridge or ledge, there are sharp drop-offs. Some places can plummet to more than 30 feet. When fishing quieter water, such as a back eddy flowing against a steep wall, cast several yards from the ledge and let the line flow toward the structure. In deeper water, use a fast-sinking line, letting it sink for a count of ten to start with; use a longer count if needed. Try to get the fly to swing along the ledge, retrieving with long pulls. Work the ledge by casting to different sections of water, covering the entire area. If the flow is strong, drift along the ledge, casting into it and letting the line sink before retrieving. Keep casting, swinging the fly so it fishes right alongside the structure. Watch your drift if the flow is pushing the boat into the ledge. This can be dangerous in a small boat with strong current. Make the first drift well away from the structure, and keep working closer until you are getting the fly to brush the ledge.

Many good holes exist in back areas with no flow. Work this water by letting the fly bump the bottom on some casts. In darkness or low light, stripers will be up in the water column, but once the sun hits the water, they will hold deeper. The best strategy is to fish deep with a fast, pulsating retrieve.

When fishing an estuary ledge from shore, you generally have one game: to work the small section of water that you can reach. Often the ledges are steep and tough to walk. As when fishing a cliff or jetty, be sure to fish the fly right to the edge, letting it hold there. Use the same swing and flow techniques to fish the fly from the flow into the structure. Be persistent. Keep working the water, and let the fish find you. Stripers will keep moving in some locations, and the angler who hangs tough will have good fishing. Still, a boat is the best way to fish most large estuaries with ledges.

In very large locations, there will be open water similar to a bay or sound or the open ocean. Look for surface-feeding fish, bait activity, or birds working over feeding fish. Cover this water as described for open-water fishing (see Chapter 11, Big Rips and Open Water). When you are looking for birds, watch the ones on shore as well. Pat Keliher, an excellent Maine guide, told me something interesting about birds watching fish from shore. He noticed that when seagulls were sitting on structure and kept looking into the water, they were not just sight-seeing. Pat watched a bird one day that kept pacing back and forth and peering into the water. He motored over to the spot, dropped a fly into the water, and was into a striper immediately. It seems that the birds find a holding striper and hope it will drive some food their way. Pat has used this trick to find fish on many occasions.

Small Funnels That Flow off a Bank

I have already mentioned briefly how to fish a small flow running off a bank. Although small, these flows demand attention, because they are feeding troughs and draw stripers to one location along a bank. Many years ago, small channels and gullies were cut into marshes for drainage. On a falling tide, they collect food and funnel it into the main flow. As the tide drops, water trapped on the banks flows into the channels and pours out into the main flow. On falling tides, look for places along the bank where water pours out as from a drainage pipe. (Incidentally, any spot that has a drainpipe flowing into it—a small backwater draining into open water—is a good location.) Along some banks, this flow spills into the main channel like a small waterfall. Work the water around and downstream from the flow. Fish will hold right under the spilling water, taking food as it tumbles into the flow, or will hold along the bank in the current below the outflow. Don't expect schools of fish in these locations, but the patient angler fishing from shore might have a steady flow of stripers as fish keep coming to these small spots. A good technique is to keep coming back to a flow like this after fishing different locations along the banks. These small channels flow best on bigger tides when there is more water left on the banks and the water level drops quickly.

A Flow into a Flow

Water flowing into another flow is a universal place to catch many types of gamefish in all waters throughout the world. It is a place you never pass up. Where two flows intersect, the water movement creates confusion; this disrupts the bait, making easy feeding for stripers. Inside an estuary, this water type is prevalent, but it exists in many locations and should be the focus of all anglers. Anytime I encounter a flow into a flow, I will work it carefully. It is one of the favorite ambush spots for stripers.

The variety of intersecting flows is endless, from a small creek flowing into a large river system to flows of equal size merging together. A small creek entering a big river is a good place to start, and it usually offers better fishing on higher tides. In places with bigger tides, the creek might dwindle to a trickle as the tide drops.

A small creek is an ideal shore-fishing location. Most of the fish will hold along the shore within several hundred feet of the creek, and they should be well within casting distance. If you can cross the creek, start working the water above the outlet, casting above the outflow and letting the fly swing into the merging water. An intermediate line is a good choice unless you are fishing a cutbank with deeper water. In that case, try a fast-sinking line as well. If you notice a bait type, match it. Otherwise, use an attractor pattern, such as a 4- to 5-inch-long chartreuse Deceiver.

Fishing from above the intersection, let the main current drag the line into the creek's flow so the fly looks like a baitfish trying to reach the safety of the backwater below the creek. Try several casts dead drifting and several casts retrieving, but always get the fly to swing through both flows. To get the fly deeper and to change the fly's swing, cast quartering downstream and make a mend across and upstream, forming a large bow around the merging water. Let the fly and line swing into both flows, then retrieve quickly, making the fly dart into the slack water below the creek. If the creek's size or water flow does not allow this, then cross the creek and try fishing on its lower side.

In this spot, you will notice that a good feeding lane forms right near the creek's mouth and runs for a short distance along the shoreline. (Although the term *feeding*

Cast and work both currents, letting the flow swing the fly into the feeding zone.

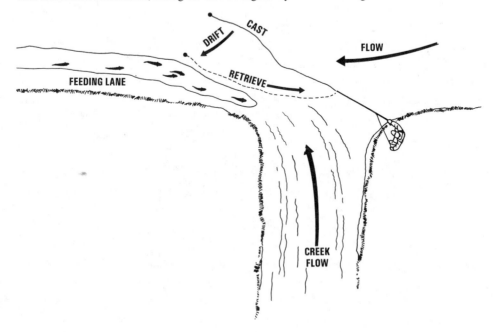

lane belongs in a trout-fishing book, stripers use feeding lanes constantly to pick off baitfish trapped in the mixed water.) If the outflow is larger, the feeding lane will be longer and wider. Use short casts, and keep swinging the fly from the faster water into the feeding lane and retrieving back along the shore. Try making some casts angling uptide, retrieving the fly so it enters the lane at right angles, not just from downstream. It is important to work this water from all angles. If the feeding lane is close to shore, do not wade; sneak to the edge along a cutbank and fish carefully.

After fishing a short line, begin working more water with a longer line, but continue to fish at different angles. Depending on the lane's size, move downcurrent and keep working the water in the same manner.

Anchor a boat above the outflow and cast so the fly lands near shore and the line lies inside the feeding lane. Executed correctly, this maneuver makes the current from the creek sweep the fly from the slow water through the feeding lane and out into the main current. Work this first with a straight cast, then try mending line. Just after the fly lands, throw a mend toward the shoreline, which will cause the fly to settle deeper and swim toward the creek, then turn quickly and dart through the feeding lane. Mending out over the feeding lane will cause the fly to swim angling downcurrent

From the creek's other side, work the feeding lane and the water down from the flow with short casts.

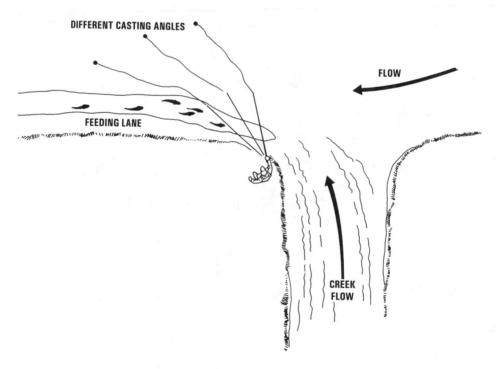

and make quick swings through the feeding lane. Keep letting out anchor line to change the casting angle until you can make the fly swim through the feeding lane effectively. Working the feeding lane carefully is essential for catching fish.

Fish bigger flows in a similar manner. The main difference will be a larger feeding lane that will extend farther out from the shoreline. From a small creek, you might pick up a few fish along the feeding lane; from a larger feeding lane, fishing can be steady for some time. A feeding lane the length of a football field with a strong back eddy can hold good numbers of fish. From shore you may not be able to reach all the water in the lane. Work the edges of the feeding lane and the back eddy that runs along the shoreline in the opposite direction of the main flow. In bigger areas, this is usually deeper water, and a fast-sinking line might be necessary if the fish are holding down in the water column.

Fish the downcurrent side of a large opening when fishing from shore; from the up-current side, you may not even reach the feeding lane. Let's say you are standing on a shoreline. The 100-foot-wide outflow is to your right, and the main flow is more than 100 yards wide. The water depth is 5–12 feet, and the backflow is strong, running left to right. When fishing any big back eddy, cast the fly just into the feeding lane at different angles to the flow to make the fly sweep along the edge of the lane. This flow moves back toward the mouth of the opening, forming either a quiet pool or a section of swirling water if the flow is very strong. Cast straight out, or cast quartering downcurrent, and keep swinging the fly from the feeding lane into the slower water. If you mend down, the flow will add speed to the fly as it drifts. Try mending, then feed some line and retrieve quickly to make the fly dart from the faster water into the slow water.

I like to begin fishing downstream from the opening and keep working toward the pool that forms just below the flow. In this case, fish from left to right, moving with the flow of the feeding lane but walking upcurrent of the main flow. While working toward the opening, keep swinging the fly from the outer flow through the feeding lane and into the pool, then retrieve it back along the shoreline. Once you get near the opening, carefully work the section of water at the top of the feeding lane. Try casting almost parallel to the shoreline, landing the fly in the faster water about 10 feet beyond the feeding lane. Begin retrieving as the fly lands, and work it right into the pool. This simulates a baitfish caught in the outflow trying to reach the slower water inside the feeding lane. In bigger water like this, spend some time fishing, changing fly patterns, or using a different line to work the water completely. This is good holding water: Hang tough.

From a boat anchored above the feeding lane, cast so the line swings from the faster water into the back eddy. This is the natural flow of a baitfish or crab seeking the shelter of the slower water. Once the fly enters the slower water, retrieve it quickly downcurrent, back through the feeding lane into the faster water. With the boat in the right position, the cast should be quartering downcurrent. If the boat is too

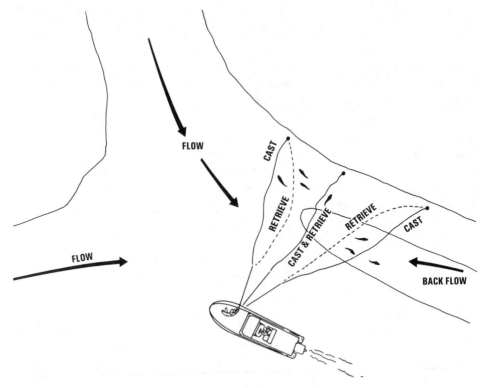

Cast to different locations to cover all the water around a creek mouth.

far away from the feeding lane, try mending line into the back eddy after landing the fly in the faster water outside the feeding lane. The fly should swing through the feeding lane into the back eddy, then back through the feeding lane into faster water. Getting the fly to crisscross the feeding lane is very effective.

If drifting or using an electric motor to maneuver the boat, work the water in the same manner. Be sure to keep the boat well away from the feeding lane. While drifting, cast at different angles and keep working the water with numerous drifts, keeping well back from the holding water when running the motor. If the current is fast, you will only get several good casts before flowing by the spot, so make each one count.

Drifting Large Middepth Areas

There are many sections of moving water from 3 to 10 feet deep that hold fish. Submerged areas along the edges of bigger flows or large flats are ideal to drift in a boat. In locations with soft bottoms, wading is out of the question.

Look for moving water and sections that form rips. This need not be a sharp rip line, only a subtle break in the current that could offer a holding spot for a striper. Fish will hold even in long flat sections of current. Drift these sections in a boat casting across or upcurrent using a fast-sinking line and a quick, pulsating retrieve. This is not fancy fishing, just covering as much water as possible while flowing downtide. Most of the time, you should retrieve when the fly hits the water, working water depths of 3–6 feet. In the spring, when big baits are around, use 6- to 8-inch-long, flat-sided patterns. At other times, try attractor patterns 3–5 inches long. On higher tides in low light, look for surface action and watch the birds. In big, flat locations, watch the water level on a falling tide; the flats along a river will flush out quickly, leaving you stranded. Avoid being swept onto a bar by the current. A strong wind blowing offshore with a falling tide will leave some areas that normally hold water looking like a desert.

Fishing with the Flow

The open waters of big estuaries allow fishing at any time and tide. However, small systems or the back sections of bigger waters require timing and planning. When possible, fish the system by moving with the flow. On an incoming tide, begin at the mouth and fish the rising water up into the back section. On a falling tide, begin up inside the system and work the falling water to the mouth. Moving with the flow requires less motoring and keeps you flowing with the fish. In some systems, the fish flow with the tide, spreading out on incoming tide and dropping back into the deeper channels as the water level drops. If you hear or see fish feeding in a location beyond your reach, hold tight, because they will come to you as the water drops. **Learning the water,** knowing a system well, will make fishing easier.

The Seasons

Time of year is important in many systems. The Chesapeake Bay and Hudson River systems are major spawning areas, but they lose their stripers early in the season when the fish migrate to their summer locations. The best time for the spawning systems is March and early April; for the Chesapeake, November and December. Actually, the Chesapeake can have good fishing all winter long, but check the legal seasons. Remember to avoid the spawning areas when the fish are breeding so you do not disrupt them. Most systems have early spawning runs of big baitfish such as herring from April to early May, and the stripers are not far behind. Look for big stripers to enter the estuaries early, from mid-May to mid-June, if there are good runs of big baits. In spring, stripers will travel into the back sections of the system searching for big foods. As the water warms and the big baits leave, the bigger fish seek cooler, open water and turn to night feeding. Locations that have runs of menhaden, which arrive later in the season, might get a second run of big fish. In the fall, look for activity at the mouths of estuaries or just up inside the large sections of the system. Unless the stripers have spent the season there, the back areas of the system will not have many migrating fish in the fall.

Expect to find many food sources throughout the season. On full and new moons in late May, June, and July, look for swarms of worms, as well as crab hatches. The same moon phases will have shedding blue crabs in the southern systems. In summer, smaller baits, such as shrimp, small crabs, and mummies—as well as schooling baitfish like spearing—will fill the striper's diet. In the dog days of summer, some estuaries become slow, but look around the mouth or just outside in open water. In the spring, the estuaries host big baitfish and these draw large stripers into fly-rod range.

Safety When Fishing from Shore

There are several reasons to walk carefully and stay back from the edge of a cutbank. In the previous chapter, I stressed walking and moving slowly to prevent spooking fish, but there is another reason—safety. The banks not only transmit sound, they are unstable. The edges can crumble, sending you plunging into deep water. The undercut sections are particularly dangerous. Stay back from the edge, venturing close only in places that taper out to the waterline with sod showing under the water. Bank sections with just a top edge that disappears might be undercut—not a place to walk near the edge.

Wading in soft mud is uncomfortable and tricky unless you know the place well. The next step might be over your head. Water draining off a flat or out of a creek will cut away the soft bottom, creating pits of soft mud. If you hit one of these pits wading waist deep, you are in trouble. Use a wading staff and shuffle along, using one foot to feel for hard ground while keeping the other foot on firm bottom. Watch out when crossing the small channels that crisscross the marsh; they can be deep and very soft.

Tackle

Big tackle—10- or 11-weight—is best for fishing the early run of big baitfish. Heavy rods handle the big patterns well and have more lifting power for fighting fish in tight quarters. They are a must when fishing the heavy rips in some of the bigger water systems, where a fish will head to the bottom looking for structure. Sixteen- and 20-pound-test tippets are a good choice if you must pull a fish away from a cutbank or a tangle of kelp. An 8- or 9-weight outfit is fine for open water and light rips or for fishing smaller flies, but in tough areas, the bigger rods will get the job done.

Estuaries are perhaps the best striper-fishing locations we have. If I needed to catch fish to live, these ecosystems would be my first choice.

Big Rips and Open Water

The big offshore rips that build wall-like waves and have current that wells up like the rush of a broken water main should be left to the pro guides. When the rips are flowing hard into a brisk wind or ocean swells are breaking over the reefs, fish quieter waters. However, with the right conditions, many places are safe to fish if the angler uses some common sense.

It was a snotty September morning, with wind from the east at 10–15 miles per hour and a good ocean swell walling up. The shallower sections of the reefs had breaking surf. I worked the deep edges of one rip, holding in the current, so we could cast into the edge of the white water. Both the wind and the tide favored this location; I could nose the boat up close to the breaking seas and the flow would just push me back into deeper water. I never put the boat where wind or tide could push us into danger.

Several other boats flirted with the sea. One was working the inner section of the reef, motoring broadside to the swells as the captain let the anglers cast downcurrent to the fish feeding around the submerged boulders on the reef. The boat's operator was so intent on the fishing that he never saw the large set of waves building up outside the reef. The first awareness, the first hint of trouble, was the boat dropping down and being dragged away from the reef as the sea sucked the water from under the boat. Turning, the boat's crew "saw God"—an enormous wall of gray-green water about to break over the boat. *Seeing God* is a surfing term, when you look up at a huge wave that will break on top of you. I have seen this from a surfboard. I never want to see it from a boat.

The boat's occupants were lucky. The wave broke outside, and a 4-foot wall of white water swept them across the reef into deeper water, rather than the wave pitchpoling them into the structure. Safely on the opposite side with the motor still running, they limped away slowly, trying to drain the boat filled with seawater. I have not seen that boat on the reefs since.

When conditions are bad, offshore rips are perhaps the most dangerous fishing water you will encounter. When ocean waves, fast current, and wind combine, the boater must use common sense, just as the angler fishing along the cliffs needs to move with caution.

Strong rips form, sometimes even several miles from land, in areas with drastic water-depth changes. A good example of sandy shoal water is the area extending from Monomoy on Cape Cod south to Nantucket, then east to Martha's Vineyard. An example of reefs and rocky rips is those that run from Watch Hill, Rhode Island, to Fishers Island, New York, then across the Race to Orient Point on Long Island.

Here is Ray Smith with a nice fish taken at first light from a hard-running rip.

Some of the shoal areas have sheer inclines, with water depths changing from 30–50 feet, down to just a few feet. The drop-off is like a retaining wall. On a chart, these depth changes are easy to see: the ones in sandy areas will constantly shift; the hard-bottom locations are stationary. When flowing water hits this wall, the surface boils up, creating stand-up seas even on a calm day and making ideal feeding conditions for stripers. This rolling water disrupts schools of baitfish, and the stripers holding behind the reefs and bars can pick bait off easily. When good concentrations of bait-fish or squid move into the rips, these locations come alive with feeding fish; it is almost a sure bet for excellent fishing.

Look for surface activity, feeding fish, or groups of diving birds. When fish are feeding actively in moving water, the approach is simple, and hookups should be easy. Use basic techniques: Fish a 4- to 6-inch-long white fly with a pulsating 6- to 12-inch-long retrieve, angling uptide and keeping a tight line. These fish will not be selective if there is ample bait in fast water, as long as you handle the boat properly.

Positioning the Boat Correctly

When you have an area to yourself, never run the motor over the fishing location. When drifting, calculate the current and wind so you pass through the fishing area casting at different angles to the flow. At the drift's end, run the boat in deeper water around the rip and drift the section again. Set up the drift so you pass through different sections of the rip on each flow. Even if you took fish from one alley, give it a rest for several drifts, then fish it again.

You should avoid entering some rips. If the water is standing up from big seas or there is not enough water depth to clear the structure, then you must use the motor to hold above the rip. Most fishing guides work a rip by running the motor, stemming the tide while one angler casts. It is very common to see several boats holding in a rip working a section of water. I prefer to drift quietly and fish while flowing with the current; I have never taken a really big fish with the motor running.

Anchoring works well in some areas, particularly in places with scattered structure near the surface. If you must keep running the motor to avoid hitting bottom, pick a good slot with a deeper section and anchor.

Anchoring

A rip flowing over a rocky reef will have pockets, areas where fish stack. The best way to learn locations is drifting to cover large areas quickly. However, once you know an area, anchoring can be effective. When fish lock onto one spot, anchoring allows continuous fly presentation to the holding area, rather than a passing shot. If the wind is strong, drifting is tough. Holding in one spot in the current makes fishing easier, because you can control the line and fly better from a stationary position. This will certainly help the novice to keep a tight line. If the fish are on top, it is as simple as casting, quartering downcurrent, and bumping the fly with short pulls until the fish hits. I have watched many fish take the fly as it hangs in the current.

The problem with anchoring is getting the fly down in a strong rip. Let's say you are sitting in a rip, and the boat's stern is holding right on the drop-off. The tide is strong, the water depth drops from 10 to 25 feet just below the boat, and you are fishing from the right side. If you must get the fly down, casting upcurrent and setting up the right swing and drift are essential. Cast well upcurrent, quartering at a 45-degree angle above the boat, using a fast-sinking line and short leader. If the bow is at 12 o'clock and the stern is at 6 o'clock, you are casting at about 1:30, angling to your left. After the cast lands, follow the line with the rod as it flows alongside the boat downcurrent. When the line flows below you in the current to about 4:30, begin retrieving, using

When anchored in heavy current, try casting well up the flow, letting the line sink and flow with the tide. When the line is straight out from the boat or just downcurrent, begin retrieving.

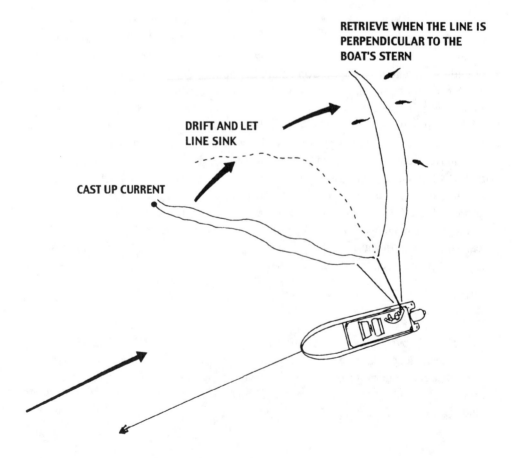

RETRIEVE WHEN THE LINE IS
PERPENDICULAR TO THE
BOAT'S STERN

DRIFT AND LET
LINE SINK

CAST UP CURRENT

long, hard, fast pulls. The key is to let the line settle into the flow. Most of the drift is used to set up the fly to fish a short section of water just below the drop-off. Try retrieving at different phases of the drift from 3 o'clock to 6 o'clock to find the best swing. Also change the boat's position up- or downcurrent to give a different presentation.

At times, holding below the drop-off, casting almost uptide and retrieving as soon as the cast lands is effective. The first half of the cast is for setup, but with the current flowing toward you, retrieving is necessary to keep in contact with the fly. Here is where a long cast helps; it gives more water penetration and a longer time in the sweet spot. I have had some great days working the fly downtide.

Release Anchor and Shock Line

A release anchor is a must when hooking big fish in a strong current. In some flows, two floats might be needed to retrieve the anchor line. If the rip pulls a lobster-pot float below the surface, it will do the same to your line and float. I also use a shock line system to make anchoring more comfortable. Between the anchor line and the

When anchoring in a rip, you need a release anchor to be able to follow a big fish quickly.

boat's cleat I have a heavy-duty, rubber shock section—called a snubber—with line spliced to both ends. If there is a surge from a big sea, the stretch removes most of the shock when the anchor tightens and prevents the bow from dipping below the surface. To prevent loss of the anchor, be sure to use a release float on the anchor line in case the snubber breaks.

Drifting

Floating with the tide while covering water allows many options. If fish are popping up, feeding for only a short time, you can move quickly to them. There is no lost time following a big fish that makes a long run. It is the easiest way to cover large amounts of water and let the line and fly sink. Using a countdown system, you can fish deeper water for longer time, not just a quick swing.

When fish are on top, the casting angle is not as critical; casting quartering into the wind will usually keep a tight line. The wind is the key to casting angle, and sometimes requires that you use casting techniques opposite to those used with a normal drift. A strong wind blowing with the tide speeds up the boat. Casting up-current into the wind helps keep a tighter line, but gives less penetration. Casting downwind requires excellent line handling, but it is the best angle to get deep. This is opposite to the technique used when drifting without wind, when the upcurrent cast requires good line management. When in doubt, cast across the wind and tide. This works the fly sideways to the flow, allows good line and fly control, and gives decent penetration.

Wind against the current slows the boat, and casting across current swings the fly so it settles down, then darts up to the surface. Casting upcurrent gets the fly down, but you must keep retrieving to maintain contact with the fly. Cast downcurrent only if fish are on the surface.

With a quartering wind, you must try different angles to see how the flow and wind affect the line. When drifting, keep experimenting until you find an angle and retrieve that work. In shallower areas, casting across the flow will give better line control with some penetration. In deeper locations and on the edges of the drop-offs, cast upcurrent and bring the fly downtide from the shallow water into the drop-off, but you must be sure to maintain line and fly control.

I have already covered much of this fishing in other sections, so I will not linger. The key is to keep a low rod and as tight a line as possible. Do not strike until you feel a positive connection between you and the fish. And keep working the water, never getting into a rut—unless, of course, you are taking fish on every cast.

When fishing in a rip or in wind, Dan Marini, an excellent Cape Cod guide, uses a rope with a section of chain that drags along the bottom. Dan uses this to slow the drift rate of the boat. He prefers drifting a section, then fishing it again rather than anchoring. If drifting with a wind, Dan likes to cast into the wind, even when the wind is blowing into the current, which moves the fly upstream into the current. Using the chain to slow the drift works well in places with smooth bottoms; in a fast current with a rough bottom, the chain can catch, sending someone into the water.

Stemming the Tide

Some of this could be called trolling, depending on how the captain runs the boat. Many years ago, I helped out at a trout school for kids in Massachusetts. On the last day of school, we took the kids out in canoes to let them try their skills. Some of them had trouble casting, so I worked out a system that helped them catch fish. I had the first kid make a roll cast, then feed out line as I eased the canoe back. With about 40 feet of line out, I told him to shake the rod tip as I kept backing the canoe away from shore. There was a pocket of stocked fish just off the shore, and the kid hooked up. This worked well with all my kids; they didn't know it was trolling, and they loved every minute of it. I did take some grief from the other instructors, but the kids enjoyed it. I figured they would learn soon enough about rules, so let them have some fun.

There are locations that require stemming the tide, places that would be too dangerous to fish without running the motor. On guided trips, running the motor allows the guide better control, and for many anglers, it helps catch more fish. Enjoy this style of

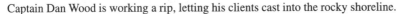

Captain Dan Wood is working a rip, letting his clients cast into the rocky shoreline.

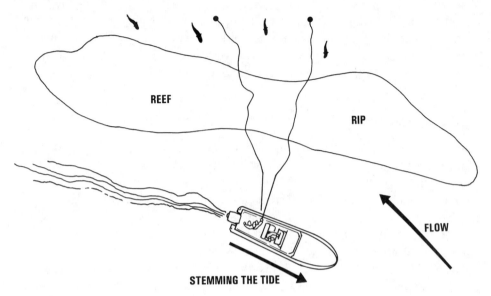

Many guides stem the tide, using the motor to hold in the current, letting the angler cast to holding water.

fishing because it is fun and productive, but realize that it is not accepted as fly fishing by the International Game Fish Association (IGFA). If you catch a world-record fish, it is not legal. Remember, for a world record, the motor must be out of gear when presenting the fly and hooking the fish.

Using the motor while working rips allows you to hold the boat straight into the flow or to slide it along the flow while the angler casts back into the moving water. One thing you need to watch out for is the spinning prop. Keep the line well away from the back of the boat; if the prop catches the line, it will suck in the rod tip like a 2-by-4 going into a wood chipper. In most locations, casting across tide works well and helps keep the line clear. If you need to fish deeper, cast and let the boat drift back into the flow before putting the motor into gear. If sliding along the rip, an angler casting in the same direction as the boat's drift will get better penetration. In some cases, this is just like anchoring, so fish different angles depending on where the fish are feeding in the water column. An angling-upcurrent cast will give the best penetration.

Slow and Slack Flows

There is very little finesse fishing when the water is flowing hard. Usually things happen fast, and the fish need to react quickly because the bait passes through, sometimes in seconds. Some anglers leave a rip when the flow slackens, but this is my favorite time to fish. If conditions are right—with light winds, small baits, and no dummies with outboard motors driving down the fish—slow water can offer hot but tricky fishing. A calm night can be a good time during slack water. The best time is first light, when stripers are cruising just below the surface searching for food or holding around the structure waiting for an easy meal. Fishing the surface is effective; a popping bug will pull fish up from their lies or draw them from a distance to eat the fly. If fish are surface feeding, approach them slowly, drifting with the wind or tide. An electric motor will allow a silent approach and let you move up quietly on the fish.

Without wind, the boat moves at the current's speed, and the fly needs to be retrieved to make it look alive. If the fish are on small bait in a slow flow, just a slight twitch is effective. Small baits are prisoners of the current, drifting with the tide. A floating or intermediate line works well to fish the fly several feet below the surface. In very clear water and bright sun, a transparent or clear-tip line works well. Stripers can be picky in slow, clear water when feeding on small baits. Use a slow retrieve, or drift and retrieve—moving the fly several feet and then letting it flow several feet with the current. Keep watching the line and the area around the fly for activity. A flash, a swirl, or a twitch of the line might be a strike. In slow water, stripers will sip the fly, making strikes difficult to feel. Use your eyes, and be aware of any slight sensation on the fly line. Several quick pulls—long retrieves—will not spoil the fly's action and might hook a fish that you would have otherwise missed.

As the tide slows, look for small pods of 1- to 2-inch-long baitfish. Sometimes they hold under big jellyfish or clumps of weed. With polarized sunglasses, kneel by the side of the boat to search for small, slow-moving baits; many anglers never see them. Watch the stripers. They will cruise slowly several feet below the surface or sometimes fin on top, leaving a wake. Frequently they will just nip the fly. Many times you will be hooking the fish only by the lips. This is unusual for stripers, which often take the fly well into the mouth.

First try fishing a faster retrieve with a small, 1½- to 2-inch-long white fly. Hooking fish is easier with a steady retrieve. If the fish are picky, then cast angling across or downcurrent, moving the fly slowly. On a clear, bright, calm day, keep watching the fly. Stripers will follow the fly, and their body language might indicate a strike. If the fish's mouth opens, or the fly disappears, or the fish turns quickly, try hooking with a short pull. Most of the time, these fish will not take a fly positively the way a striper usually does.

Following the Moving Tide

On a large area of shoal water with rips, the flow may be different in some locations around the change of the tide. Most rips have lag time; they are always behind the tide. A big rip might keep flowing in one direction for an hour or more after a tide change. As the current slows, many anglers leave, looking for better-flowing water. In an area with a series of rips, you can keep moving to stay with the flow. Rips that cover several miles might be flat at the north end and still have moving water at the south end, depending on the tide. Keep records of water movement to predict how and when different water flows work. This also works if you like to fish slower water—you can keep moving to stay with gentle flows. A good example of this is the Cape Cod Canal in Massachusetts, where anglers will follow the tide with bicycles to fish the flow they like. This is a place where an angler without a boat can fish an off-shore rip-type environment.

Because the Canal is similar to other waters we have discussed, I will add just a few brief thoughts on fishing techniques, even though we are talking about boat fishing. The Cape Cod Canal is a 7-mile-long, hard-running rip with excellent walking access, but most of the shoreline is tough to fish with a fly. Boat fishing is not allowed in the canal. Fish the flowing water as you would an offshore rip, concentrating on any small point or rock formation that breaks the flow. Fish close, and work the water in tight, focusing on the fish that feed along the edges. Follow the slower, lower tides, which give better access to some of the rock formations. This is big, fast water with structure; fish at least a 10-weight and 16-pound tippet. Use good nonslip wading chains over your boots and a wading staff. The Canal is a fishery in itself and requires time to learn. One word of caution: Never wade too deep, and head for shore if you are thigh deep and a big ship is passing through the Canal—the wake will bury you.

Fishing Open Water

Throughout the season, but mostly during the fall run, fish will feed in open water, not just on the reefs. If there are good concentrations of bait, fish will drive them to the surface, even in deep water. In the fall, keep watching for birds picking bait over feeding fish. A funnel cloud of birds over the water is a sure sign of hot action. These fish are feeding, and they usually eat any fly or popping bug that hits the water. The trick is getting a cast into the fish without putting them down. Never run over or into feeding fish with the motor; use the wind or tide to drift into the fish. Work the fly or popper fast, and use a popper that pushes lots of water. In the bedlam of feeding fish, a small, bubbling popper might get lost. If you are having trouble hooking up with a popper, use a sinking line and a large, 5- to 7-inch-long, bright fly. If you don't hook up quickly, check the bait size—they might be on small bait, so you will need to change to a smaller fly. Stripers will usually hold, feeding on the surface longer than other fish. If you seem to be chasing ghosts, never reaching the fish before they sound, they may be bluefish, bonito, or false albacore, which are not bad options!

Start out fishing on or near the surface using a fast action. If you do not hook up quickly, then go deeper, fishing under the feeding fish. At times, if there is too much competition on the surface, getting below the bait and using a slower retrieve will be effective. The fish will single out the fly if it looks like a crippled bait falling or swimming below the school.

The offshore rip needs food to hold the fish and make fishing hot. Spring and fall should produce good fishing in many locations. With the right bait, some areas will have excellent fishing all season, with good daytime action. Fast-sinking lines are the best tools, but carry an intermediate line in case you find picky fish on small baits. Even though you are fishing from a boat and can often follow the fish, use big-enough tackle. I like 10- and 11-weights in the big rips with structure, because a good striper will bury you in the rocks and kelp if it goes down. Even in the big sand rips from Monomoy to Martha's Vineyard, the heavier tackle helps, because in many of these rips you cannot follow the fish. If I could fish only one fly, it would be 5 inches long with a midsize body in white.

Large Points and Reefs 12

I slowly motored the boat up onto the reef off Watch Hill, Rhode Island. There were several submerged boulders that I wanted to anchor between. The swell was big enough that I wanted to maintain a safe distance. Being driven onto a rock the size of a bulldozer by a big wave is not healthy for the angler or equipment.

There were fish feeding in the current just behind and inside the inner rock, as well as good feeding activity right into the point. It surprised me that there were no shore anglers fishing the hot action right at the point; it is usually stacked in with anglers. Also, it was a shame that I could not get in closer, because most of the feeding activity was in the white water close to the point. But the tops of the waves were getting frosty just inside our holding location; any closer would have been suicide. We anchored so we could cast to both rocks, but all the action was between the boat and shore. The fish would move from the white water just around the rock to the flowing rip below the rock. As 2- to 3-inch-long herring flowed into the broken water, they were devoured by feeding stripers. Any small white fly cast into the feeding zone was immediately attacked. There are times when hooking fish is easy, and this was one of those days.

When fish stack into a large point of land, fishing can be exceptional. They might hold for extended periods. Places like Montauk Point on Long Island; Watch Hill, Rhode Island; Provincetown, Cape Cod; and Great Point, Nantucket, are just a few of

Points and reefs like this one at Watch Hill, Rhode Island, produce good runs of fish, particularly during the fall.

the many large points that have great fishing. Any size point can be a productive fishing spot, but some of the big points, particularly in the fall, have heavy concentrations of fish.

While I was fishing one day with Mike Laptew, the underwater cinematographer, he made a good point: If you fished only near the major lighthouses, you would find good fishing. Lighthouses mark many of the major points of land, warning ships to give a wide berth. Many of these locations mark not only the end of a point, but also a treacherous reef or shoal with heavy structure and strong rips. A large point that juts out usually creates good current flow. All these factors create ideal feeding habitat for stripers. Many lighthouses have excellent fishing right in their shadows.

One problem with some of the best-known big, open-water points is crowds. When large numbers of stripers lock in, shore fishing with a fly rod is difficult. And many locations are rugged without good backcasting room, or the fish are holding a good spin cast away, well beyond fly-tackle range. Fishing from shore, I usually avoid the ends of major points, fishing just away in less crowded conditions. If the point forms a reef and has breaking surf (most do), the better holding water will be a distance from shore at the point, but closer if there is deeper water back from the end.

Working most of this water is identical to fishing an ocean beach but with a hard bottom mixed with rocks (see Chapter 4, Ocean Beaches). The secret is to find a holding pocket—a section of deeper water with good movement—and hope the fish move into it. Avoid fast-sinking lines or you will lose too many flies to the bottom.

Avoid the Big Points

The melee at a big point will tempt you, but if there are shoulder-to-shoulder anglers, fly fishing is out of the question and not very appealing. Pick a section of deep water away from the crowds and hang tough. You will be surprised at the good fishing in this water; at times it can be as productive as the point's end.

Likewise, the water out from the point will get heavy boat pressure; sometimes there will be both surf and boat anglers competing for the same turf. I find these situations both unpleasant and unsafe, avoiding them when the runs are on. If there are no crowds, fish the outer reef as you would an offshore rip (see Chapter 11, Big Rips and Open Water).

Smaller points are better suited for fly fishing. Most form good rips, have structure or holding water, and the better ones have stripers throughout the season. Let's look at a typical point, one with a reef running out several hundred yards from shore. The reef's bed is sand and gravel with scattered rocks and a mixture of big stones, some the size of a refrigerator. There is a deep hole along the right side of the reef, and it slowly tapers into deeper water on the left side. The tide is high outgoing, running from right to left, angling away from shore out along the reef. Some reefs jut out from a straight shoreline, but many are the continuation of a point of land. (Reefs running perpendicular to a straight shoreline have crossing currents; those that protrude from a point have currents that run along the shoreline and angle out across the reef.)

Work the Uptide Pocket

From shore, fish the water both above and below the rip line formed by the reef. The deeper water to the right above the rip will hold fish, because it is deeper than the holding water below the rip. If the water were of equal depth on both sides of the reef, the better holding water would be below the rip. Start well above the rip line, casting at an angle to the flow, fishing the water so the fly swings into the pocket just above the reef. If you start too close to the reef, casting to the end of the deeper water, you might draw a fish up but not give it time to take the fly before it swings into the shallow water of the reef. Work this section carefully as a separate piece of water. Make a dozen casts, move several steps, and repeat the process.

Standing on the crown of the reef, fish both above and below the flow, swinging the fly over the reef and into the drop-off below the rip. Again, keep moving a short distance at a time to work all of the water. Concentrate on the hole below the rip and the water right on the reef. A clear sink-tip or intermediate line works best, and a floating line is effective on very shallow reefs or when fishing poppers.

Some points have rocks that provide good platforms from which to fish. The height of a rock offers easier casting and better line control. In many fishing locations, not just points, learn the rocks that allow the best access to the water at different tides. Use these perches to make fishing more comfortable.

Work the Big Rocks

Rocks that are out in the water are good holding locations for stripers. They break the current and provide an ideal ambush position. Cast just above the rock, swinging the fly so it sweeps past the structure. A rock in a flow will form a small slick, or a round-shaped calm spot on the water's surface. The slick will help to mark rocks in any rip you fish. Depending on the water's depth and current speed, this spot will be several feet to a few yards in the current below the rock. If the rock is well below the surface, 8–10 feet, cast right over the structure so the fly swims over the rock. Stripers will hold behind and all around the rock; work this structure carefully.

Because wading can be difficult, the higher tides are better for many locations. For the adventurous wader, some locations are good on low incoming tide, as long as the reef is not too long. On big reefs, when wading some distance from shore, do not linger on a rising tide. On bigger reefs, carry a compass in case fog sets in; a wading staff will make walking easier.

Shallow Reefs

Shallow reefs are good places to wade on a falling tide; in small-tide locations, you might be able to fish much of the coming tide as well. Depending on the reef's size, begin to move out as the tide drops, giving you access to more water. Do not ignore the base of the reef as you head for the end. Start fishing the first section of water and keep working out, fishing both sides and the shallow water over the reef. Concentrate mostly on the rip line and the drop-off below the rip. If the flow is fast, try dead drifting and mending to alter the swing. For most of this fishing, you do not need to get the fly down very deep—several feet at most—unless the water is cold. Expect to see some of the takes and to have action right on the surface. Here you need to cover water, using different casting angles and letting the fly swing to fish each piece of water.

Once you learn a spot, you will know the proper pace and speed to fish, where to hang tough, and where to move quickly. I have not gone into any special detail about fishing because shallow reefs are similar to other waters I have discussed. You are simply fan casting, covering the moving water.

Boat Fishing

Working this water from a boat is another matter, not because the fishing is different, but because boat handling demands a special approach. Any reef or rocky structure open to the sea will have dangerous water conditions. Anglers who attempt to venture too close to shore will put their boats in a bad position. Most anglers on shore are trying to reach the rich water out from the point. Just do what the shore anglers are hoping to do: Fish the deeper structure off the point. If you do attempt to fish the water just outside the breaking waves, back in with the motor running, and be ready to run if a rogue wave walls up.

I like to anchor in some places if it's safe and inoffensive. In popular locations, this is unacceptable. Anchor in the rip, or drift, working the water as you would an offshore rip. For most of this fishing, use a fast-sinking line. Look for bait to bring the fish up, and keep watching the surface for feeding fish. In the spring, squid and big, flat-sided baits are abundant, and in the fall, large schools of small baitfish will at times cover some points. In the fall, big points become striper magnets if the bait stacks in. The water off the points will always have some fish, but are not always in large numbers unless there is abundant food.

Find the Alley

On certain tidal flows, there might be one section of the rip off the point that will have a flow of food. The tide or wind funnels baitfish into a slot, as it does on an offshore rip. If you see one section of the rip that keeps showing fish, work that area. With a good flow of food, fishing technique is not rocket science; you swing a white fly through the moving water and a fish will take. A constant flow of food keeps fish up and feeding even at midday in the summertime. In low light and in the fall, the fish are up in the water column feeding more aggressively. Otherwise, only good flows of bait will keep the fish moving once it gets too bright.

In the fall, onshore wind packs bait into the bigger points, and the shore fishing can be exceptional. Several days of northeast winds will turn the hard-bottomed locations like Montauk Point into fish factories, but the sandy areas might become too riled up to hold fish. If the sea becomes too big, fly fishing is difficult, and you may need to search to find a quiet pocket away from the point. At times the backside of the point will pack in bait and fish, but not anglers. Always check these quieter waters for activity; they will be more suitable for fly fishing and less crowded.

The popular areas will have heavy fishing pressure on weekends and will become hectic late in the season. Expect tough fishing conditions, heaving water, and structure. Use 10- and 11-weight outfits. Three- to 8-inch-long white flies work well when schools of herring or menhaden move in, but try a 7- to 8-inch-long dark fly at night when there are no concentrations of baitfish. Points usually hold fish all season, but they are best in the fall when large schools of bait create a feeding binge of stripers.

Night and Low-Light Fishing 13

N ight fishing is something that everyone should experience. There are fishing events that occur only at night. It is a time when you can have fish so close that they will hit your waders. If you are looking for a big bass, the late-night and early-morning hours are the prime times to find them. There are more types of food available, and the baitfish are spread out and confused, making them easier targets for gamefish. Stripers are nocturnal. Night is the time when they feed more aggressively and are less wary. The wee hours of the morning, from 1 AM to first light, is both a good time to avoid the crowds and a very active feeding time for stripers.

Some years ago, when stripers were scarce, we needed to fish the wee hours just to find a little action. A group of us would haunt different locations, sometimes all night, looking for fish, and usually we could take a few. It was rewarding to stop at the local tackle shop on a Sunday morning and boast of taking fish while others went fishless. How I went to school or work with so little sleep amazes me now. But it was fun and exciting, and those dark, buggy, long nights taught me to hang tough and to learn the techniques of low-light fishing. When I took my first striper on a fly at night, some local anglers believed that a fish would not take a fly after dark. How times have changed.

I remember one night more than 30 years ago when we found fish in a rip just outside the mouth of a creek. It was a flat, calm, warm night at about 2 o'clock in the morning. We needed to cross several bars to reach the fish. That night we must have resembled squirrels trying to cross a busy highway. We marched up and down through the trough seeking a path to reach the outer bar, but it was too deep. The feeding fish sounded like cinder blocks dropping into the water from a tall building. There were not many fish, but they were big. It was so calm and the fish sounded so big that we thought the ripples on the water were from the feeding fish. I don't know whether that was true or not, but at the time, we believed it. We were like three starving men listening to steaks frying. The fish were between 50 and 100 yards away, and all we could do was pace back and forth, listening to the explosions. When we finally reachcd the bar, the fish had left. That night we did not take a fish, yet I remember it like it was last week. And when the three of us get together, we will always say, "Do you remember the night we heard those big fish feeding at Greens Farms Creek?"

Night fishing adds to the fascination of fly fishing because our best sense—eyesight—is drastically limited or sometimes eliminated. The ears and sense of touch take over, putting the body on high alert—at least when the action is hot. There are some nights when lack of sleep turns the angler into a walking zombie. And just when you drop your guard, a big fish explodes 10 feet from the rod tip, leaving you shaking

Cooper Gilkes, the veteran fly rodder from Martha's Vineyard, with a nice nighttime striper. Coop has caught fish that would make your eyes bug out; here he is just surprised by the flash.

with eyes like saucers. That first rod-tip strike from a big fish on a calm night will make another lasting memory.

Fishing in darkness presents some problems, but offers some advantages as well. Remember, when fishing at night you will apply many of the techniques you use during the day. However, the first time an angler fishes in total darkness can be a humbling experience. Casting, handling the line, trying to feel the fly, and even walking will be challenging. Remember, you are trying to do something that requires skill totally by touch. The better angler catches on quickly; the newcomer needs some patience. Move slowly, particularly if walking and wading where you might get hurt. Lights are poison; they spook fish, but use one rather than get into trouble. Remember that your night vision takes some time to recover after you use a bright light. For changing flies I use a dull light, shining it down away from my eyes. When wading, shine the light into your waders. In a boat, keep the light low, shining into the bottom.

A Good Time to Start

Begin your outing in the daylight so you can learn the surroundings and get your tackle in order. Try casting with your eyes closed to feel what it is like to cast in the dark. If you are comfortable with the fishing conditions and casting before it gets dark, it makes the transition into darkness easier. Once you begin to night fish seriously, continue the practice of arriving early. The evening change of light might make for hot fishing, but the main reason is to check out the location. Look for food types and where bait is concentrated, check the water conditions, and see how the tide is flowing. You might get to a location and find it unfishable. This prevents wasting precious time by goofing around in the dark. Once you know an area well, you can predict its fishability most of the time just from experience.

Casting

Casting is the number-one problem when fishing at night. To begin with, many anglers have trouble feeling the line in the air. Some rods are too stiff, requiring a longer line to make the rod bend. If you cannot feel the rod load with 30 feet of line out, it might be better to use a heavier line to make the rod load quicker. Some anglers overload the rod by two sizes so they can feel the line with a short cast. Be sure that you can feel the line with a short cast, or you will suffer in the darkness. Keep the casts short, using just enough fly line so you can fish easily. Use small, easy-to-cast flies and a short leader, about 7 feet long. Even good casters shorten up at night. Generally, the fish are close, at times taking the fly right off the rod tip; along some beaches they might be feeding a rod's length from shore. Long casts are difficult to make, and a long line is difficult to control at night. When casting a long line across a strong current, you might not feel fish taking the fly. On many occasions, I have caught fish only after considerably reducing my casting length. At night it is a good practice to vary casting length, sometimes making only 30-foot casts.

Casting into the wind will pose problems. The wind stacks up the leader and the end of the fly line. This causes wind knots, tangles, and loss of fly control. Shorten the cast, shorten the leader, and try to stop the cast so it turns over more crisply. This might shorten the distance of the cast, but it should keep the line straight. Casting a straight line is very important at night. Unless you purposely want to mend the line, make sure that the cast is straight.

The Orvis clear-tip intermediate is a good line for night fishing. You can fish just a short tippet, 3 feet long, because the first 10 feet of the line is clear. The line turns over well, and the heavier tip section gives extra punch at the end of the cast. You know when the fly is close because you will feel the splice hit the rod tip. There is 10 feet of fly line outside the tip.

Mark the Line

There are different ways to determine how far the fly is from the tip. The clear-tip line with a splice is perhaps the best indicator. You know precisely how much line is beyond the tip when you feel the splice touch the tip. I advise my students to mark the line by putting several nail knots of 12- to 16-pound monofilament at a given location in the line. If you mark the line 40 feet from the end, this gives a reference for both casting and retrieving. When your hand feels the mark, there is 30 feet beyond the tip. For many rods, this is a good length for loading the rod. When retrieving, begin to count retrieves once you feel the mark. If you are making 1-foot strips, twenty will leave 10 feet of fly line beyond the tip. Feeling for the fatter, weight-forward section of the fly line then starting a count also works, but is not as precise as a mark. By adding a mark to the line at a given distance, you can tailor a personal system that helps make night fishing easier.

Controlling the Line and Fly

Controlling the line and fly is extremely important at night. Fishing at night is similar to working a fast-sinking line in a current in daylight—it's all a matter of feel.

Locations with slow currents are easier to fish. It is possible to feel the fly even casting uptide if you use a fast retrieve. In strong currents, the casting angle is critical; the best angle for feeling a strike is quartering downcurrent. Cast, then either let the fly swing to a position below you before retrieving upcurrent, or begin retrieving until the line straightens. At this angle, most takes are positive. As you cast farther uptide and allow the fly to drift, feel becomes more difficult. Even in a slow flow, casting across tide and letting the fly drift for just a short distance will make it difficult to feel strikes.

When casting above a drop-off, dead drifting is a good way to let the fly settle so it dips into the drop-off, then comes to life when you tighten up on the line. Here most of the strikes will come after you begin retrieving, so there is a positive connection with the fly. Mending line upcurrent after the cast demands even more skill, because you are adding slack. When you mend upcurrent, you lose control of the fly until the current tightens the line. I mend line at night only to set the fly up above a rip line, so by the time the fly reaches the drop-off, the line should be straight. If fishing a section of water with a level bottom, the fish might be anywhere, and without constant fly control, you will miss many fish. In locations where the fish are spread out, use a quartering downcurrent cast and move very slowly to cover each section of water.

Slower retrieves work best at night. Usually you just want to keep in contact with the fly, particularly when working faster water. As in any fishing situation, alter the retrieve until you find the right one. In slow or flat water, try a faster retrieve. When working a fly down the flow in faster water, use a fast retrieve. To learn downcurrent retrieves, practice during the day to see how the fly works and what speed of retrieve keeps the line and fly in control. Try this with different types of flies, because each fly has a different feel as you pull it through the water. A fly with a spun deer-hair head, such as a Snake Fly, is easier to feel than a slim fly. Small, slim flies offer little resistance in the water. In tough-to-fish flows, select a fly that you can feel easily.

A slow upcurrent retrieve can be deadly at night. In a faster flow, try moving the fly, then dropping it back on every third strip. Also try shaking the rod tip to make the fly dance like a baitfish trying to fight the current.

Night fishing helps develop "touch"—the sense of feel that makes good anglers pros. The only way to develop touch is to practice. Start in smooth water, and keep working tougher conditions until you know what the fly is doing most of the time. In some water, you will never be able to feel the fly all the time, but in most conditions you will be able to sense a strike.

In calm, still water, fishing right on the surface with a small fly or using a fly that leaves a wake works well. In very clear water, small, sparse 1- to 2-inch-long flies are effective. In these conditions, you will usually see or hear the fish take. Always wait until you feel the strike to set the hook. Fish might follow the fly, swirling without taking on the first pass.

Try to position yourself so you are not too close to the fish. Along a shoreline, when fish are feeding in shallow water, do not wade. Actually, it is best to stand back from the shoreline so the fish are not taking at the rod tip. You might literally be retrieving the fly onto the beach. Hooking the fish is easier if they take the fly with at least 15 feet of fly line outside the tip. You will also spook few fish if you keep away from the immediate feeding area.

In a boat, it's even more important to give the fish room. Keep the boat well above a rip or drop-off, although no matter how you position the boat, there will always be rod-tip strikes. I prefer anchoring to drifting at night, particularly in areas with moderate to fast current. On a big flat with a slow flow, or with a soft wind, drifting will work, but with faster flow you cannot cover the water well enough. A drifting boat will spook too many fish.

When the Water Glows

At certain times of the year, the water, when disturbed, will glow with a pale blue light called "fire in the water," or phosphorus. Tiny sea animals ranging in size from a pea to a baseball glow when touched. A 6-inch Deceiver looks like a dead chicken, and the fly line resembles transatlantic cable. Watching fish feed is fascinating. You see bathtub-size flashes emerge in the darkness, jet streams of light from swimming fish, and areas of shimmering light as baitfish dart about in fright. At first, this scene will be a novelty, but it soon becomes irritating. I have had some success night fishing in phosphorus. If the fish are concentrated and competitive, the fishing can be hot. But these are rare occasions; most of the time, fish are tough to take when the phosphorus is heavy.

A bright moon or backlighting will diminish the effects of phosphorus. Flies with thin profiles and slick materials work best. Flies with spun deer-hair heads look like torpedoes. Use a long, thin leader and fish the fly slowly. Some locations will have less phosphorus—keep moving until you find a clear location.

One angler told me about a remedy that he claimed works well. On a back beach in Nantucket, there were a number of fish feeding in heavy phosphorus, and he could not take them. So he faced his truck into the water and turned on the lights. The fish stopped for about 20 minutes, then began feeding again. Walking out in the bright lights, he took fish after fish. I do not recommend doing this unless you are alone or discuss your intentions with everyone on the beach. On a crowded beach, you might draw gunfire.

Keep Checking the Fly and Leader

Casting at night is tough on leaders and flies; wind knots and bad tangles are common. Flies will break, bend, or dull a hook point on the backcast. Keep checking the fly, leader, and the knot to the fly. Also be sure that the fly line is not wrapped around the reel. In locations with floating grass or weed, check the fly before each cast. Most of the time, a whistling sound when casting signals a tangled fly or grass on the fly.

Best Moon Phase

On the first few outings, a bright moon makes fishing easier; once your eyes adjust, you can see fairly well. On black nights, locations with some illumination—street light, dock light, and harbor entrances—will comfort the freshman. These fixed lights do not bother stripers and might attract baitfish.

I prefer the darker nights, particularly in very clear water. However, I have had some great fishing on a full moon. One night on Nantucket, we had nonstop fishing from shore. There were times when you could see the fish. It was like watching a movie with frames that keep stopping. With the rolling water, the fish would show up in the waves only when viewed at a certain angle. You would spot the fish moving toward you; they looked frozen in place because you saw only a glimpse of them. I did not believe I was seeing fish until I cast to one and hooked it. It was one of those nights with great action for several hours, and the fish were a nice size. On brighter nights, the fish see better; they are more alert and do not feed with the aggression they normally exhibit on dark nights. In spring and fall, the brightness may not matter, but

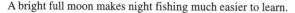

A bright full moon makes night fishing much easier to learn.

during the summer months, choose the darker nights or the darker periods of the night. Some anglers check the times that the moon rises and sets, fishing before or after the moon appears. I have enough trouble keeping track of the sun's actions; I just go fishing and work around the brightness.

Carry two lights, one for walking and one dull light for changing flies. Some anglers use a red light to change flies because it does not affect night vision. In a boat, carry a good spotlight, but don't use it to find fishing spots—it spooks fish and drives other anglers nuts. It will come in handy for finding the ramp, signaling other boats, or spotting buoys. Use a light only when necessary. If wading along a shoreline, back away from the water to change flies. I once fished with an angler who would threaten death if you shined a light; he wanted no one to know we were fishing a certain location. Lights tell other anglers your position, and many lights along a beach mean fish action. If you see the flash of a camera, head toward the spot, because someone is into fish.

Active Baits

Sand eels burrow into the sand at night to hide. Other schooling baitfish, such as spearing, break ranks, which makes them easy targets for stripers. Many bottom-dwelling baits, such as eels, sandworms, crabs, and lobsters, become active at night. Squid move into beaches to feed on small baitfish at night. I use a 4- to 6-inch-long, light-colored fly if there are squid around, even when small baits are prevalent. Check for squid under the lights at night in a harbor close to your fishing location. If you see squid there, they are also feeding along the beaches nearby. Even when small baits are thick, a big fly will draw the attention of stripers when squid are present.

Perhaps the most exciting event that occurs at night is the worm hatch, or swarm. For details, check the bait section (Chapter 17, Fly Design, Food Types, and Fly Patterns). On a calm, hot, buggy night in June or July, this can be a time to remember. Being in the middle of a full-blown worm hatch for the first time might cause a mental breakdown in beginning anglers. Fish act like wild piranha—sometimes twenty to thirty fish feed at the same time in a space the size of a two-car garage. In still water when the best swarms occur, it might resemble feeding time at a fish hatchery. There will be stripers feeding everywhere, but you might never hook a fish.

The worm hatch is usually a time for floating lines and surface flies. I like an active fly, 2–3 inches long. A black Snake Fly or an orange one with a black head works well. Any fly that leaves a surface wake can be effective, because the worms will swim along the surface. With background light on a calm night, the water will look like a mass of ripples with fish boiling everywhere. Fish the fly along the surface with a slow retrieve, or fish it in the current slowly on a swing. When the worms are very thick and the fish are not cooperating, try fishing a weighted fly like a Clouser, letting it tumble toward the bottom, feeling for a slight strike. The worms swim on the surface, and at times during the swarm, they spiral downward to the bottom and swim back up. Fishing below the worms sometimes works. However, there are times when catching is impossible. You might take a fish or two, but for the number of stripers present, fishing success will be low.

When the hatch is not thick, fishing can be fabulous. At these times, the fish will single out your fly. Usually, a thin swarm the night after a heavy one produces great fishing. The fish are waiting for the big feast, and there is not enough food to go around, so they take anything that moves. The hatch can occur anytime, but the best swarms usually develop in the evening or at night.

Even on a night when fishing is tough, just being in the middle of so many feeding fish is an event. If fishing is tough, be patient. Sometimes after a heavy hatch has died, there are still enough feeding fish that some will single out your fly. I have had some hot fishing just after the swarm has stopped.

If you like to be alone and don't mind walking, many beaches offer solitude and some exciting action in the wee hours. Beaches with no vehicle access are ideal for the walking angler. From midnight to 4 AM can be a tranquil time on the water. In the dog days of summer, it is perhaps the best time to fish. Certainly it will be quiet. These are the times when the die-hard bass hounds will roam, looking for that pot of gold. There are some anglers who fish only at night. It is certainly a good time to find a trophy striper.

Choosing an Outfit 14

I s there one all-around outfit that will fish every striper situation? No. If I had to choose one outfit, it would be a 10-weight. Remember, although this is a striper book, when choosing tackle you must consider other species. At all the saltwater fly-fishing schools I teach, the favorite outfit is a 9-weight.

An angler who owns two outfits has the luxury of covering more bases. With a 9- and an 11-weight, you can fly fish the Northeast, as well as much of the world's salt waters. These are my choices for the anglers selecting two outfits. Those who fish more sheltered waters might choose an 8- and a 10-weight. But for bigger waters, a 10-weight is the lower limit. Yes, you can fish in many locations with an 8-weight, but limitations will become apparent as conditions get tougher.

Stripers do not have the fighting power or speed of offshore species, nor do they have the strength of bluefish. However, stripers use the environment better than any other species; they can swim and feed in water that would destroy some fish. If trapped in the surf, even the mighty tuna will become confused and succumb to the rolling white water. The striper uses the surf's power or a rip's force to feed and to help it fight when hooked. It is not the striper's strength that requires heavier tackle; you need that tackle to outmuscle not only the fish, but also the heavy water it fights in.

The other considerations when selecting tackle are fly size and wind. Casting big, bulky flies and popping bugs is difficult enough with a 10-weight. It is foolish to attempt casting a large fly into the wind with an 8-weight. Even very good casters suffer when they combine big flies with light fly tackle. If you add wind, some locations are impossible to fish.

Rods for Different Locations

For sight fishing, the best rod is a 9-weight. This would also work well for sheltered waters, bays, small estuaries, or beaches without surf. A 9-weight is certainly a workhorse in salt water. For heavy rips, ocean jetties, rolling surf, fighting wind, and casting big flies or poppers, a 10- or 11-weight is my choice. From a boat you can cheat and go lighter, and you can also carry several outfits. When wading, if you venture any distance from the car, you must fish with the outfit you brought.

I would never fish a big striper flat on foot with anything less than a 9-weight. That holds true for bonefish as well, even with the small flies. When I need a delicate presentation, I lengthen the leader. When fishing stripers, a flat might become a big rip at the flat's end, with fish feeding on big baits. If the wind comes up and you must cast a big fly into its teeth to reach the fish, an 8-weight won't do it. I prefer a 10-weight for most wading and an 11-weight when fishing open locations with surf. In more than 3½ decades of saltwater fly fishing, I have seldom used an 8-weight, because every time I do, either the wind blows or I hook a good fish that outmuscles the tackle. If nothing else, you owe it to the fish to have ample tackle to land it before it is totally exhausted.

Overloading the Rod

If you lack the strength to handle a large outfit, try overloading your rod by one line size. Some rods are too stiff for casting large lines. There is not enough bend in the rod, which puts all the strain on your casting arm. A stiff rod requires more force when casting because the weight is a greater distance from your hand. Try lifting a given weight, then lift that same weight at the end of a 3-foot stick. Overloading the rod with a larger line size puts more bend in the rod, making it cast from the midsection rather than the tip. Overloading a rod also makes night fishing easier. The rod will load with less line outside the tip and give the angler more time to make the cast. I know serious night anglers who overload rods by several line sizes because they make numerous short casts.

Rod Length

The most popular rod length is 9 feet. Nine-foot rods are the best for casting and handling ease. Nine-and-a-half foot rods work well in the surf, giving extra height for a backcast and extra reach for jetties and cliffs. For special types of fishing, when the

Some of My Favorite Striper Flies

A Snake Fly variation with saddle hackle instead of ostrich herl.

SAND EEL PATTERNS
(Top to bottom): epoxy sand eel with eyes; Glen Mikkleson's Sand Eel; my old, basic sand eel; Eric's Sand Eel.

SQUID PATTERNS

(Top): Benjamin's Squid; (middle): Glow Squid; (bottom): Deceiver.

PRECISE EPOXY PATTERNS

(Top two flies): small herring-bunker patterns; (middle): epoxy sand eel; (bottom left): Surf Candy; (bottom right): Glass Minnow.

SMALL SPECIAL PATTERNS
(Top right): Worm, Snake Fly; (bottom right): floating shrimp; (bottom left): Merkin Crab Fly, all-tan. (Top left): small shrimp pattern;

FLAT-SIDED PATTERNS
(Top): Enrico's Bunker; (bottom right): Deceiver tied with a wide profile; (bottom left): Slab Fly; (left middle): Mark's Baby Bunker.

These patterns are very popular—they are all "workhorse" flies for stripers. (Top right, clockwise to top left): thin Snake Fly; thin Deceiver; Clouser; Bill Peabody's Rhody Flat-wing, tied Deceiver style; full-tied Snake Fly; full-tied Deceiver.

SURFACE POPPERS

(Top): foam-body Edgewater Popper; (middle): Pop-Hair Bug; (bottom): cork-body Popper.

angler needs to manipulate the line, a 10-foot rod would give more reach, but it would also require more strength when casting into the wind. For boat fishing, some anglers like 8½-foot rods. In some locations, a Spey rod might be an advantage. With a Spey rod you can pick up a long line and make a backcast or a long roll cast and cover great distances. But a Spey rod is a specialty rod, not built for fishing short distances. Spey rods are designed for fishing waters between 50 and 100 feet away—places where you fish a section of water that requires a long cast but where water closest to you is undesirable. If you are fishing the fly right to your feet, the Spey rod's length would be a disadvantage. Most striper fishing requires fly and line control with a short to midrange cast, 30–70 feet long; a 9- to 9½-foot rod covers that water well.

Rod Action

Try before you buy. Don't choose a rod because it casts a narrow loop to 90 feet at rocket speed. In the protected environment of a consumer fishing show, experts can make rods look great. A great casting rod might not be the best fishing rod. If you can, try a rod outdoors with a hookless fly. Ten to 15 minutes of steady casting should give you a hint of how the rod will feel after a day's fishing. A stiff rod will begin to tire or hurt the caster in a short time. Remember, much of our fishing is blind casting. Midflex or medium-action rods with less speed are easier and less tiring to cast. A midflex rod roll casts better, handles sinking lines better, casts big flies easier, and fights fish with fewer break-offs than a tip-action rod. It is more forgiving to cast than a fast-action rod. A fast-action—or tip-flex—rod is better for speed casting to sighted fish and throwing tighter loops. My choice is a midflex action rod.

If you travel frequently, the multipiece rods are great. Besides the convenience of packing into a small container, I think they cast better. The one drawback is you must be sure that all the sections are tight. If a ferrule is not firmly tightened, the rod will break under pressure. Check each section before fishing. To assemble a rod, push the ferrules together with the guides at a 90-degree angle and twist until the guides are straight. Tighten firmly, but not with a death grip.

Rod Materials and Hardware

Graphite is the favorite material for most fly anglers. Its lightness, slim diameter, and strength—and now its affordability—make graphite the overwhelming choice in the sea. Modern fly rods spoil the angler. Very few casters are skilled enough to appreciate how well they throw a line. Rods of 4–6 ounces that can easily cast heavy fly lines can still dead lift well over 20 pounds if used properly. In 30 years, the evolution of fly rods has gone from the stone age to the space age. And we keep improving them at a rapid pace. My only concern is that some new rods are too light—that the maker is sacrificing strength to shave an ounce off the selling weight. I want strength, lifting power, and durability. If shaving weight from the rod blank weakens it, it's an unwise decision by the manufacturer. Fly rods for the sea should withstand abuse, even improper handling. They will certainly take a beating not just from fishing, but also from rough handling, such as getting banged around in a boat or bouncing off the rocks when wading.

The guides need to be firmly attached and durable. Two stripping guides are better than one, and snake guides are more durable than single-footed guides. Look for big, thick snake guides and a big tip-top. Where the rod tip's ring meets the sleeve, the connection should *not* form a narrow groove that will pinch the fly line. When the tip pinches the fly line, it prevents it from shooting on the backcast.

The reel seat should have two threaded locking rings, and the reel should lock in place with no movement. A fighting butt at the reel seat's end is important. Rounded soft rubber or cork butts work well; they should extend back 2½–3 inches. I prefer fixed fighting butts; I keep losing the removable ones.

Rod handles come in many shapes, but a full-wells grip is the choice of most striper anglers. Fighting butts are important. A round cork or rubber butt about 3 inches long works well.

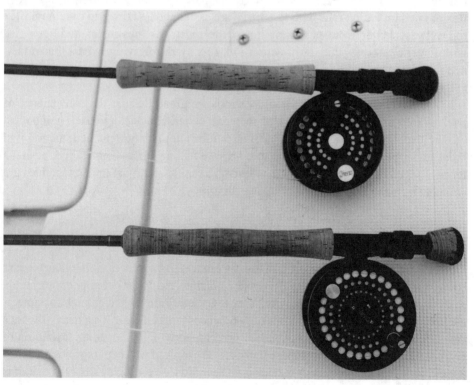

Reels

Most modern fly reels have sound-enough drags, particularly for stripers. Many of the better reels are overkill, with drags built for offshore species. Today reels in the $100–300 price range are of high quality compared with many of the early reels that were used in the salt. Any of the basic reels, even those with simple drags, will work for stripers. However, think about other species, especially when choosing your reel. The Orvis Battenkill or DXR, the Cortland 140D, and the Scientific Anglers System 2 are just a few of the many quality reels in this price range. If you wish to spend more, some reels are incredibly well built.

The first choice you need to make is between a direct-drive and an antireverse reel. Direct drives are less expensive, simpler, and the choice of most anglers. When a fish takes line off a direct-drive reel, the handle spins and can whack your fingers if they

There are many different reel designs. From top right, clockwise: antireverse DXR, Orvis multiplier Battenkill, Orvis direct-drive Battenkill, large direct-drive Fin-Nor #4, large-arbor Tibor Riptide.

are in the way. Most experienced anglers choose this reel because with each turn of the handle, the reel takes line. Even in the dark, you know when you are reeling line back on the spool. If you are surgeon, play a musical instrument, or would lose substantial income without the use of your hands, the antireverse might be the better choice. When a fish takes line with an antireverse reel, the handle remains stationary so you can hold the handle. Both types work well, and this is a matter of personal preference.

Multipliers and large-arbor reels retrieve line faster than conventional fly reels. Large-arbor reels are becoming very popular. They are bigger in diameter and take in line faster than a standard fly reel. The bigger arbor allows for a large drag surface. Besides a faster retrieve, the fly line coming off the reel is less likely to tangle because it is wound in larger coils.

Multiplier reels use a gear system to spin the spool faster than the handle. Also the handle does not spin as fast as a direct-drive reel handle when the fish runs. But with a fast-running fish, you will still have tears in your eyes if the handle finds your knuckles.

Reel Drag

A reel's drag is a braking system, slowing down the progress of a fish as it runs. A big striper can make a powerful run, but not like a little tunny. A high-tech drag is not as important for stripers as it is for offshore species. A run from a striper will not overheat a reel.

What I want in a drag system is smoothness and dependability. Drags that gum up from sand or need constant cleaning are not ideal, especially if they are used in the surf. For the last 5 years, I have used reels with disk drags and found them very dependable. Check the drag's smoothness by rigging up an outfit and running line off the reel. Tie the leader to a fixed object and run yourself, or have someone run off the line while you hold a bend in the rod. If the rod holds a steady bend, the drag is smooth, but if the rod bobs like a woodpecker's head driving a hole into a tree, the drag is poor. Some drags work better once they are "burned-in." Use the speed of a car or boat to run several hundreds yards of line off the reel. Be sure to use a very light tippet in case the driver becomes vindictive or misjudges the distance, so you can easily break off before you run out of line.

I prefer a light drag, applying most of the pressure with my fingers. (I will explain this technique in Chapter 20—Hooking, Fighting, and Landing Techniques.) Most modern reels have an exposed spool rim. The rim on the handle side of the reel is not covered by the frame, allowing the angler to touch the spool's rim as it spins. With a light drag setting, you can apply the pressure necessary to slow the fish's run and keep applying the proper drag to land the fish. Your hand is really the best drag, and most skilled anglers prefer using their hands for applying heavy drag, even for fast-running fish. I use a light drag, about 2–3 pounds—just enough to prevent the reel from overrunning—and do the rest with my hand.

All new reels should have noncorrosive parts, particularly in the drag system. Some of the older models might work fine, but keep checking the working parts for corrosion. Any weak parts show up quickly; salt water is destructive even on noncorrosive parts. With any reel, you should check the drag system to be sure it is clean, because salt builds up and begins to clog the working parts. A freshwater bath and some lubricant will keep the drag and the entire reel running smoothly. Before adding anything to the drag system, check to see what the manufacturer recommends for drag care.

How to Set the Drag

Most anglers should set the drag with a good tension scale. If the drag is set to 4 pounds, it will double with a full bend in the rod and the heavy part of a floating line in the guides. As the fish takes line, the drag increases, because the line on the spool arbor decreases. A 5-pound drag straight from the reel will become 10–12 pounds if a fish runs off several hundred yards of backing. Three to 4 pounds is a good drag setting for a 16-pound tippet. Test the drag to see if it takes more pressure to start the drag. After sitting, some reels might require twice the pull to move the drag; this is called drag "start-up." Some reels require a lower setting, because the drag needs more pull to get it moving. It pays to test a reel's drag after you fish a while to see if it has tightened. When surf fishing, keep testing the drag with little pulls to be sure the reel is free. Waves can wash sand into a reel, locking up the drag. Once you become familiar with a reel, pull with your hand to check the drag's tension.

I prefer reels with a quick-change spool. These have either a lever or button on the reel that releases the spool without using tools or removing any parts. The obvious reason is to change spools quickly. But more importantly, you can open the reel quickly to clean or check the working parts with less chance of losing pieces. Taking apart a reel with many loose parts on a sandy beach or in a rolling boat is asking for trouble.

Line Types

Weight-forward fly lines have a larger-diameter front section, tapering smoothly to a thinner-diameter running line. Weight-forward lines vary in their front dimensions. The weight-forward section, or thicker head section of the line, can range from about 30 to nearly 50 feet long. A line with a shorter front section—called a saltwater, quick-load, or bass taper—is better for quick casting, because the rod loads with less line outside the tip. The shorter-headed, quicker-loading lines also make casting easier at night, because you can make shorter casts and still feel the rod loading. Longer heads are better for distance casting and for roll casting. To make a good roll cast, the thicker section, the head of the line, must be inside the rod tip. With a longer head, you can leave more line outside the tip and make a longer roll cast. For most anglers, heads of 32–38 feet work best. A better caster can handle the long head.

Fly lines come in lengths from 70 to more than 100 feet. Very few casters can throw 100 feet of fly line, especially under fishing conditions. Determine the amount of line you can cast under ideal conditions, leave some for improvement, and remove the rest. Most anglers will find that a fly line between 80 and 90 feet long is ideal. Removing the rest leaves more room for backing. Remember, if you cast 85 feet of fly line, the fly is landing more than 90 feet away; that's a great fishing cast.

The intermediate-density (very-slow-sinking) line is the most popular fly line for stripers. It casts better than a floating line, it fishes a larger variety of waters than any line, and it evades the wind's effects without sinking too aggressively. It certainly should be the first choice of the shore angler. Even for sight casting, the intermediate line works well. I prefer it for all but the shallowest areas. For shallow locations with current and varying depths, the new clear intermediate lines are ideal. You can present the fly with less chance of spooking the fish and still get the fly down along a drop-off in a deep pocket. An intermediate is not an ideal popper line, but if dressed with a flotant, it can fish poppers. If you use a big popper, the slowly settling line will pull the bug down, giving a louder pop. The intermediate fly line is my workhorse for perhaps 60 percent of my fishing. The clear intermediate is becoming my favorite line.

My second line is a very fast sinker. If fishing deeper, faster water from a boat, this might be the primary line for some anglers. Even for the shore angler, when fishing surf along cliffs or on a steep beach, this line will track better in heavy water. Fast-sinking line is the only way to get the fly down in locations with deep cuts and steep drop-offs that have fast water flows. In any of the big rips, unless the fish are surface feeding, getting down is the key to taking fish. The Teeny and Depth Charge–type lines are very popular. Built like a standard weight-forward line, they have a 25- to 30-foot head of very-fast-sinking line with an intermediate or floating running line. They cast and handle like a standard weight-forward line and fish like a shooting head. The new Airflo sinking line is a full-sinking line that is thinner in diameter with little stretch. These lines sink faster; with less stretch, they have more feel and better hooking power than other lines. I must caution that they are still new and might not be for everyone, but my first impression has been very favorable.

Floating lines work well when fish are feeding on the surface or sipping on small baits. The time to work the surface is when small baitfish, shrimp, worms, or crabs are hatching or swarming in and around estuaries and along sheltered beaches. Here you must present a fly that will hold on or near the surface and move slowly or dead drift with the current. Remember, this is specialized fishing that is done mostly in sheltered waters with lighter tackle. It is the type of fishing made for an 8-weight outfit or lighter. This is one of the few cases where I will suggest light tackle. For fishing poppers, for working very shallow areas with structure or grass bottoms, and for fishing flies that leave a wake, a floating line is the only choice. Of course, floating line also works well for sight fishing; it is the choice of most anglers when fishing the flats.

I do not fish standard sink-tip lines. The only sink-tip line I use is Orvis's clear sink tip. It has a clear, 10-foot intermediate tip spliced to a floating line. It fishes like a floater but gets the fly down a little better. For anglers who like floating lines, it is a good compromise between a floater and an intermediate. This is a good line for sight fishing, because the clear tip allows closer casts to the fish with a shorter leader. In the wind, long leaders are hard to control. It is also an excellent line for fishing poppers. I have made up some lines with a similar design, but lengthened the heads and added more weight. Cutting back the floating line, I added more clear to make the intermediate section 20–30 feet long. And I splice a 10-weight clear section to a 9-weight floater. The splices work better because they are both the same size, and the added weight makes them cast like a miniature shooting head. The standard 10-foot clear tip will do everything a floating line can, but better. It is expensive but well worth the money in some environments.

Shooting Heads

Shooting-head systems consist of two separate sections: the fly-line head and the running line. The head is heavier and larger in diameter and is the section that carries the fly to the target. The running line connects to the head and is the line that you handle and that shoots through the guides. Shooting-head systems allow the angler to fish several density lines on one reel spool. A shooting head is a 25- to 40-foot-long fly line with a loop connection on one end. Twenty-six to 30-foot heads are ideal for casting; longer heads take more skill to fish. The head attaches to the running line that is on your reel. (See Chapter 16, Rigging Up Your Line System, for connection information; see below for running line information.) By carrying several shooting heads, you can change from a floating line to a sinking line without changing spools. Shooting heads are very popular on the West Coast but are used much less in the Atlantic. Economically, this is the least-expensive way to have many different lines, and you need only one reel spool.

When I started saltwater fly fishing, I used shooting heads because I could not get the fly lines I wanted. The running line on most big fly lines was too thick and tangled easily. So I would splice the head of a big fly line to the running line of a lighter fly line with a permanent connection, making a fly line with the dimensions of a shooting head. Today manufacturers build full-length fly lines resembling shooting heads. With the number of fly-line styles, types, and densities, any angler can find a line for his or her casting style and fishing conditions. For this reason, I seldom use shooting heads. I do still have some lines with a permanent splice. One line design I like is made by splicing a 5- or 6-weight fast-sinking fly line to a 10- or 11-weight extra-fast-sinking head. The line handles well, gets deeper, and tangles less than other sinking lines. A sinking fly line by Airflo has just come on the market. It handles well, has a light running line, and sinks like a stone.

Shooting heads cast well, giving extra distance when using a heavy, fast-sinking head with light running lines. For fishing deep, a lead-core shooting-head system will penetrate the depths better than most fast-sinking lines.

The negative side of shooting heads is the constant thump of the connection going through the guides. Also, they do not roll cast well, and with a light-density head (floating or intermediate), they do not cast into the wind or cast big flies very well. Shooting heads do not backcast well if you must use a backcast rather than a forward cast to reach a fishing location. Shooting heads might work well for some special conditions, but they are less versatile for most anglers in a number of conditions.

Running Lines

Level fly line, .025–.035 inch in diameter, is manufactured in floating, intermediate, and full-sinking for running line. The larger sizes are better, but they all tangle in the cold. Monofilament line of .018–.022 inch is the best running line for distance, but it tangles and is tough to fish from a basket. Braided monofilament lies flat in a basket, and the bigger-diameter 50-pound test is easy to grip. Either tape your hands or use a two-handed retrieve, because it grooves wet fingers quickly. Orvis makes a flat running line that shoots and knots well but is difficult to fish from a basket and hard to grip. With each running line, there are advantages and disadvantages. My choice is the braided monofilament in 50-pound test.

One of the reasons I seldom use shooting heads is that there is not a running line I really like. Each one is a compromise. Perhaps I am spoiled by the development of all the excellent fly lines in recent years, or I'm just lazy.

Other Equipment 15

fter choosing the basic tackle, you must now select other gear. Although
the rod, reel, and line are the important pieces of equipment, take care to
choose the other gear properly. Waders need to fit properly and be well suited to all
types of fishing. And some of the small items—like gloves, sunglasses, pliers, and
lights—will make fishing easier and more enjoyable. Having the right gear will add
to your fishing pleasure.

The Stripping Basket

Other than the rod, reel, fly line, and flies, the stripping basket is the single most important piece of equipment the saltwater fly rodder can own. There are locations that
are difficult to fish without a basket, and jetties, rolling surf, and cliffs would be impossible. Fishing with a sinking line while wading would be a chore. I use one even
from a boat. Today's market offers many well-built baskets at a wide range of prices.
Orvis makes the best hard basket, but you can make one from a plastic dishpan that
works well. I prefer the hard baskets. The line tangles less, you can move from one
location to another and leave the line in the basket, and they do not blow around in
the wind. The soft baskets are convenient to store, however.

The stripping basket makes fishing easier. Here my wife, Barb, is using one even in a boat.

I use one with a solid bottom without drain holes. If you do any deep wading, a basket with holes will keep submerging. To remove the buildup of water, just dump it after a cast. An elastic wading belt or just a shock cord with hooks makes a good belt.

Other Gear

Waders are far superior to hip boots. With any wave action, you will get wet in hip boots, and deep wading is out of the question. Waders and a rain jacket will keep most water out—even the pounding spray from a wave. Fishing in the cold or at night is not the time to take a soaking.

Today's waders are light and comfortable to walk in, and some are nonsweat. Wearing the new breathable waders is like fishing in jeans; they make long walks and climbing around rocks a pleasure. I prefer bootfoot waders because they are lighter and easier to change. If you can afford the luxury of two pairs, the neoprenes are great in cold water. My wife uses light neoprenes all season. I sweat too much to use them in the summer, but in the cold weather they keep you comfortable. Neoprenes also act like a wet suit—if you take a spill, they retain body heat and are buoyant.

There are several hand tools that are important. Some pliers include enough devices to perform open-heart surgery. Pick a pair that will cut through a hook or wire, crush a barb, and remove a hook. A small pair of snippers will do a much better job trimming the leader. Pliers will not cut as close. A hook hone is important. The ceramic ones do not rust and work well to maintain sharpness. They are the only sharpeners to carry; steel ones will rust. For sharpening bigger hooks at home, a fine mill file works well. I know of a fast sharpener called the Diafold Hook and Knife Sharpener, by Diamond Machining Technology; it has a diamond grit surface that cuts quickly and does not rust.

A good pair of polarized sunglasses is important for general daytime use to protect your eyes from the damaging rays of the sun. They are essential when fishing the flats. For shallow-water fishing, glasses with wraparound frames or with side shields

Other important items are (clockwise from top) hook sharpener, forceps, neck light, pliers, small gooseneck light, and (center) compass.

cut the side glare and improve vision. Both amber- and copper-colored lenses are good; amber-brown is the preferred shade for flats fishing. On the darker sand flats, black mud, and grass flats, I feel that copper gives more contrast.

To be an all-weather angler, you need two types of gloves. Some people are affected by the cold. For those anglers, neoprene gloves with full fingers are the best choice. The fingerless fleece gloves are much better for fishing because they allow free use of the fingers. For most marginally cold conditions, the fleece gloves will work. In very cold weather or frigid wind chills, full neoprenes are a must. The new thin neoprenes allow decent dexterity while keeping your hands warm.

There are several different types of fly boxes. For small to midsize flies, I prefer a box with soft foam, using the hook point to secure the fly to the box. For wading and for using bigger flies, a box with several large partitioned sections will keep the flies fresh without taking up too much space. In the boat I use a bigger, thicker box with soft foam, which does not crush the flies.

In slippery locations, use either wading cleats or chains. If you use soft-footed waders, studded boots will work, but they do not hold as well as chains. Felt is acceptable on some surfaces, but not on black, slime-covered rocks.

I prefer a neck light with a cord long enough to hang down inside my waders. With the light inside the waders, there is no chance of spooking fish when tying on a fly. Headlights are handy because you don't need hands to shine the light. The problem with headlights is the constant shining of light with every movement of your head. If someone says something while you are tying on a fly, you look up, flooding the whole beach with light. Red lenses or bulbs do not affect night vision and are less offensive to fish. But they do not illuminate very well, and some anglers will have a problem trying to walk using a red light. A red light is great for a boat, but be sure to have a good spotlight as well.

Carry a compass when wading. You can get lost in the fog on a large flat or when walking a reef on incoming tide. Without a compass, this can be a terrifying experience. Even walking 100 yards from shore, in a dense fog with an uneven bottom, it will be difficult to determine the right direction to dry ground.

I prefer a spray-on insect repellent to keep my hands from being coated. Insect repellent adds an offensive smell and makes the fly line slippery and hard to hold. And some repellents can damage the fly line's coating.

The items mentioned are just some of the extra gear you can own. I have listed what I feel is important. Some anglers fish with a fly-rod outfit, one box of flies, and sneakers; others resemble pack mules wallowing down the beach or need ten trips to load a boat to the gunwales. I like to carry spare tackle and gear when fishing from a boat and when traveling. When wading, I carry only the essentials. After a season or two, you will know what items are important.

Rigging Up Your ⬤**16** Line System

T he key to catching fish, especially strong fish, is having a sound knotting system. One poor knot in the system and the whole system fails. One day I watched an angler fight a big striper from the beach. His technique was poor, but I believe with a good knotting system he would have beaten the fish.

The fish hit just outside the wash. First a big boil appeared, followed by several washtub-size explosions as it ran line from the reel like a racehorse out of the starting gate. The first part of the battle went well. The angler cleared the line—actually, the fish performed on cue, taking line quickly while the angler stood with rod in hand, mouth gaping open. Running along the beach, the fish quickly took more than a football field of line. The angler, still recovering from shock, just stood still. So I offered advice, yelling, "Follow the fish down the beach, and do it quickly." After much walking and some cranking, the angler gained ground on the fish. But now the tough part began. The fish was about 70 yards out behind a bar, holding in the ripping water just outside the hole.

Big stripers use their environment better than most species; this fish was holding all the cards. Walking down the beach, the angler tried to change the angle and possibly move the fish. But each time the fish kept moving out, putting more pressure on the frail tippet. The wave action was strong, giving the fish a good flow to keep taking line. Leaning back, the angler put good pressure on the fish, not too heavy, yet enough to stop the slow run. As the angler lifted the rod to start taking line, it straightened. It looked like the fish had given ground but then there was no resistance; the line had parted.

There is a sick feeling when you lose a good fish, and I walked over to console the angler. It was a tough environment to land a big fish. Ocean beaches have such heavy water movement that it is tough to stop a fish. The tackle must be in top shape, because heavy pressure is the only way you will win that fight. I told the angler that when he stopped the fish, I thought he might land it. He just held up the remains of his leader and walked away in disgust. The tapered leader had parted in the middle, where the material was heavier; one of the knots had been poorly tied or was worn. It's a tough way to lose a big fish. I know the feeling all too well.

Unfortunately, poor or worn knots fail only under the strain of a big fish. The story is usually the same: "I never had problems with my knots before," the angler will say. This is because smaller and even midsize fish in mild conditions will not push tackle to the limit. A poorly tied or worn knot on a 16-pound tippet still might break at 8 pounds. Under normal fishing conditions, many anglers have never needed to pull that hard on a fish. When you're pulling on a big fish is not the time to find out if your knotting system is sound or to discover that you should have changed the leader or retied a worn knot.

I have lost very few big fish in my life. I feel the major reason for my success is using good knots, tying them properly, and taking the time to replace worn materials. It is also important to use good, fresh materials when building the system.

The First Section

I will start by discussing how to build the system, listing some of the knots without knot-tying instructions. A complete list of all knots and tying instructions appears later in this chapter.

The first part of the fly-fishing line system starts with a knot to the reel arbor and runs to the loop at the end of the fly line. It includes the backing, the fly line or running line and shooting head, and the first connection of the fly line. In most cases, this section will remain intact; the only exception would be changing the head if you are using a shooting-head system. This first section might not be touched for years other than changing a knot that becomes abraded or replacing a worn fly line. I have backing that is many years old and is still sound.

The Backing

Years ago we had Dacron; now there are many choices, but Dacron is still the mainstay. Micron is thinner, but is less durable and does not knot as well. The new gel-spun poly backing in 35-pound test allows more yardage, giving a small reel larger line capacity. It is strong, but beware: The small-diameter line can cut like a knife. If you touch the backing while a fish is running, it can groove your fingers or cause a nasty laceration. The 50-pound poly backing is a better choice for most anglers. If you do choose the lighter poly backing for extra capacity, use 100 yards of 35-pound backing at the bottom of the spool for insurance, connecting to it a large-diameter backing. This gives extra backing for those few long-running fish, while offering safe handling for 95 percent of your fishing. The poly backing is tough to knot, because it is very slippery. It is better to use a loop-to-loop system to attach the fly line. Put a whip-finish loop in the fly line and a loop in the backing large enough to allow the reel to pass through. (See the knot section later in this chapter for the proper knots.) Some anglers prefer this loop in the fly line to loops in the backing for a quick-change system. If you prefer to knot the poly to the fly line, use non-water-soluble glue on the knot, and be sure to strip the fly line and put an overhand knot in the core of the fly line to prevent slipping.

If you choose Dacron or Micron, use 30-pound test. The heavier line is more durable, and the knot strength is better than with lighter, 20-pound material.

I add roughly a 100- to 150-foot section of 20- to 25-pound monofilament between the backing and the fly line. This gives better durability and allows for a stronger knotting system. The first 100 feet of backing will endure most of the punishment, and monofilament is much more durable than Dacron. Any braided line loses strength quickly once one fiber is broken. The monofilament also adds a little stretch if a fish wraps the line around a rock or tangles in weed. Monofilament knots much better to

The loop-to-loop system allows you to change a tippet quickly. Interlock the loops carefully; top is correct, bottom is incorrect.

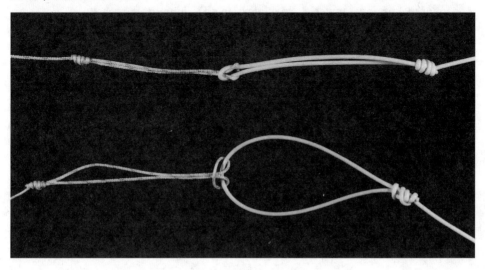

fly line than braided line will. *Do not use all-monofilament backing—it could ruin your reel spool.*

A Loop-to-Loop System

Many fly-line makers supply a loop fixed to the fly line's end. Some are braided monofilament; others use a section of standard monofilament. If you use the manufacturer's loop on the fly line, test it to be sure it is sound. You might get a "coffee break" loop that pulls off with just minimal pressure. I prefer to attach my own loop setup with a nail knot using 30- to 40-pound monofilament. For a simple leader system, use a short section of line about 4 inches long with a loop at the end. This loop system attaches to many leader systems. Whenever you make a loop-to-loop connection, regardless of the types of material used, put it together this way.

The Simple Leader

Using a loop-to-loop system allows you to quickly change the leader system. The simplest leader setup is a knotless tapered leader either 7½ or 9 feet long. Interlock the loop on the fly line to the loop on the tapered leader, tie the fly to the end of the leader, and go fishing. This is the best system for the freshman angler. It's simple, easy to use, and very effective with the new materials.

Some experienced anglers still use a "store-bought" tapered leader. Using a tapered leader, the angler needs only one knot, for tying the leader to the fly. However, you should also learn the Surgeon's Knot. As the tapered leader shortens with use, you can apply the Surgeon's Knot to lengthen the leader. With several tapered leaders and a spool or two of tippet material, an angler can go fishing for the season.

Some anglers prefer knotted leaders, feeling that they turn over better. You can buy knotted leaders, or make your own tapered leader using several line sizes from .024-inch diameter to the tippet. A simple system that works well is to use a Surgeon's Knot to connect 3-foot sections of .024 and .020 monofilament, and add a 3-foot section of 12- or 16-pound monofilament for the tippet.

Fluorocarbon leaders and tippet material have improved my success rate and made fly fishing easier. It is less visible to fish, ultraviolet-ray resistant, and very abrasion resistant. In many cases, I do not use a shock tippet because fluorocarbon is so tough. (It will not replace wire for toothy species, however.) And I can use a heavier tippet because it is less visible.

The downside of fluorocarbon is lower knot strength. With some knots I have experienced very poor knot strength when connecting it to some types of monofilament, particularly Maxima. It also has less stretch, so the impact strength is not as good as monofilament's, and it is expensive. With all that said, I still like it. For tough-to-take fish in clear shallow water, fluorocarbon is a must, and when fishing structure, you will land fish that would have sawed through monofilament in a heartbeat. If you buy your flies, fluorocarbon will probably save you money.

The Advanced System

The system I use requires several knots—one of them takes some time to learn. It is the strongest knotting system you can use—in some cases, it has a full 100 percent break strength. And you can change tippets quickly without using knots.

The key to this leader system is the Bimini Twist. To some, it is the "dreaded" Bimini Twist, for it is a knot that has tried the souls of anglers. Once it's mastered, you will find it to be the only knot that breaks at 100 percent every time. I have never had one fail. Equally important is the twisted part of the line that is formed by the Bimini, which adds a miniature shock absorber to the tippet. This slight elongation of the twisted section can prevent the sudden snap or shock that will stress a knot, or break a tippet, below its actual break strength. You can substitute a Spider Hitch for the Bimini, but it is not as consistent and does not have a twisted section unless you pretwist the line before forming the knot.

My advanced system has a butt section of heavy monofilament nail-knotted to the end of the fly line. For floating and intermediate lines, I make the butt section 3½–4 feet long with a Surgeon's Loop at the end. For sinking line, my butt section is about 8 inches long. Some anglers use a very short section of monofilament, 3–5 inches long, for all their fly lines. They then loop the butt section to the fly-line loop, and loop the tippet section to the loop on the butt. This way you can vary and modify the butt section, but I do not like the extra loops in the heavy line. My choice is to have a permanent butt and just add the tippet.

The tippet section for most of my striper fishing is a combination of a Bimini Twist and a Surgeon's Loop. (See the knot section later in this chapter.) You first form a Bimini with a section of tippet material, then fold over the double lines and form a Surgeon's Loop. After trimming the tag ends of the knots, attach the tippet's loop to the butt section's loop by interlocking the two. This completes the leader. Then you are ready to tie on the fly. To change tippets, you need only remove the spent one and replace it with a fresh one using the loop-to-loop system. This system allows you to quickly change tippets without tying a knot in the field other than tying on the fly. I pretie all the tippets at home, store them in labeled plastic Ziploc bags, and keep them in my fly bag. This is a quick and easy leader to use, and the skilled knot tyer can have a 100 percent knotting system. And you can quickly change to a tippet with a shock or to a bite guard that also has 100 percent knot strength.

When making a tippet with a shock leader, tie a Bimini at both ends of a section of tippet material, tying the shock section to one Bimini and a Surgeon's Loop to the other. Knotting the double lines of the Bimini to the shock material makes a stronger knot. If using more than 30-pound-test shock material, the only way to get good knot strength is by knotting it to a Bimini. If tying 16- to 25-pound or 12- to 30-pound test, a Surgeon's Knot works well, but it will not give you the excellent break strength of the double line to the shock material.

I have become smart, or perhaps lazy, in my leader system. For rough conditions in structure, I use a straight tippet of Mirage fluorocarbon with no shock leader. Even fishing the cliffs, where the tippet is constantly being abraded, this material holds up. On a few occasions, I have fished one tippet for several hours, catching numerous fish, and the leader was still sound. One tippet was abraded along its entire length, and it still had excellent strength. When fishing structure, I use a 20-pound tippet of straight Mirage with no shock leader. Even if the tippet is reduced to 10 pounds because of damage, that is still enough strength to land a striper. I use a Four-Turn Clinch Knot to tie on the fly. That knot with 20-pound-test Mirage breaks at about 15 pounds. If you use a better knot—one that might break near 20 pounds—and must break the tippet to free a snag, the nail knot to the fly line could break instead. For stripers, I use 20-pound test only for abrasion resistance and tough conditions; otherwise, a 16-pound class tippet is more than sufficient.

Fluorocarbon is much tougher than monofilament because most of the strength of monofilament is in the skin. Removing 15 percent of the skin from 20-pound monofilament might reduce the strength by half; it will only reduce fluorocarbon to about 16 pounds. Remember, fluorocarbon will not solve all problems. Although manufacturers claim that the overhand knot strength is very good, and fluorocarbon is very tough, change your leader if it is nicked or has wind knots. When I talk about testing knots and leaders, I will cover this in more detail. My findings might be surprising to some anglers.

Why a System Fails

There are many reasons why your leader breaks. If a system is new and it breaks, the fault is usually a poorly tied knot. On rare occasions, it can be defective material. Monofilament will go bad if stored improperly. Exposure to sunlight and heat is poison to monofilament. A good test is tying an overhand knot, then slowly pulling to break the line. Damaged line will part easily.

I am not familiar enough with fluorocarbon to know its limits. Most of my exposure has been positive, but I'm still dubious about the way it knots. When I am tying a simple knot to attach a fly, I have never been able to make a 100 percent knot with fluorocarbon; some very good knots with monofilament are poor with fluorocarbon. With monofilament I can tie 95 percent to 100 percent knots fairly consistently. When connecting two different materials, be sure to test each knot with a hard pull.

Knowing a system and knowing the materials that make up that system is important. And once you have a good working system, stay with it. The saying: "If it's not broke, don't fix it" is good advice. Right now I'm using fluorocarbon for much of my fishing, but until I learn more, I will not abandon monofilament.

Test Every Knot

Usually, a poorly tied knot breaks well below the line's strength. A good knot might not break, or it will at least break very near the line's break strength. When tying a knot, be sure to tighten it firmly. If it's a poor knot, I want it to fail in my hands, not on a fish. It is also wise to periodically hand-test other knots in the system and to check these knots for wear. A knot that looks tattered should be changed even if it feels strong. When fishing is hot and heavy, change the knot to the fly if it looks worn. Even when the fish are small, you never know when the next fish will be big. If you hit the fly on the backcast, check the knot as well as the hook point. A slight chip in the knot can cause it to fail.

How to Tie a Knot

One trick to making a good knot is consistency. Once you have had success tying a knot, keep tying it the same way. Always feed the line from the same direction and follow the same steps each time. Also, wet the knot with saliva. This lubricates the knot, preventing heat buildup, and allows the knot to tighten. If a knot is not tightened properly, it can slip or lock together too quickly. Either way, the knot will be a poor one.

Pull up the knot with one smooth motion, and do not be afraid to use some force, especially when tying heavier lines. Some knots might require two pulls, but this must be performed uniformly with no sharp pulls. Hard, quick pulls will burn and weaken the line, drastically reducing knot strength. Use enough line to tie the knot so you can form it easily and have ample material to grab on to.

For tying butt sections or heavy shock tippets, you might need gloves and pliers to lock up the knot. Even with a 16- or 20-pound tippet to the fly, use pliers and wrap the line around your hand several times. Wet hands are soft, so be careful, because the line will cut into your fingers, and these cuts take forever to heal.

After tying the knot, take a look at it. If the knot is not smooth, or if there is a loose loop or a loop that is crossed over, retie the knot. It might feel strong, but if it slips, it will fail.

Be sure your hands are clean and, if possible, dry. Substances like sunscreen, reel or outboard oil, and grease from foods will make knot tying difficult and might affect the knot's strength. It's smart to have a small towel to wipe your hands, and if necessary, some soap to remove grease. I carry both when fishing from a boat. Oil, gasoline, and other oil-based products will soak into monofilament, weakening it and adding scent to the line.

To the permanent knots in the system's first section, I add non-water-soluble superglue. This bonds the knot and makes it more durable. Some materials do not knot well and loosen with time. The glue will add insurance to the system, but don't rely on the glue to hold the knot together.

KNOTS TO BUILD THE SYSTEM

Backing to the Reel
Three-Turn Uni-Knot

Backing to Monofilament
Double Nail Knot
Double Uni-Knot

Backing or Monofilament to Fly Line
Nail Knot
Offset Nail Knot
Loop-to-Loop, backing to fly line

Make a loop in the fly line by doubling over the line and putting a whip finish over the fly line. Put a loop in the backing using a Bimini Twist, then a Surgeon's Loop, and interlock the loops.

Butt Section or Loop to Fly Line
Speed Nail Knot
Nail Knot

Making a Loop
Surgeon's Loop

Knots for the Leader
Surgeon's Knot
Improved Blood Knot
Bimini Twist
Spider Hitch
Surgeon's Loop
Orvis Knot

Knots to Tie on the Fly
Twice-through-the-Eye Clinch
Improved Clinch
Rapala Knot, Free-Swing Loop
Surgeon's Loop
Homer Rhode Loop Knot

Important Facts about Knots

The knots that I use are proven and tested. I do offer some alternatives, and there are other knots that work well. I have just not had enough experience with them to make suggestions. If you use knots that work well, do not change. There are perhaps a dozen good knots for tying on the fly. The problem is that some knots work better with certain materials. The Berkley Company did some extensive knot testing some years ago. They feel that the Twice-through-the-Eye Clinch is the best knot for all types of monofilaments when tying on a fly or lure. Berkley calls it the Trilene Knot. It is very similar to the once-popular Clinch Knot, except that you feed the line through the eye twice before tying the knot. Berkley feels it would be an easy knot for most anglers to tie. With some lines, I consistently get excellent knot strength with this knot. However, it is important that you choose a knot that you can tie easily and quickly. A 95 percent knot will be useless if you cannot tie it, particularly when fishing in the dark.

Some information about knots, especially their break strength, is incorrect. The type of material, the diameter of the line, and the person tying the knot can all alter knot strength significantly. How the test is performed can also make a big difference. Under laboratory conditions, some knots and lines can appear to be much better than they really are. Many knot testers slowly draw up the line, giving the knot time to form while creating little heat. Knots that tested well with a slow pull did not fare as well with a faster take-up, which is what we experience from a running fish under normal angling conditions. An overhand knot in a leader of monofilament or fluorocarbon reduces its strength by nearly 50 percent. Yes, sometimes higher breaks might occur, but don't count on it. If the overhand knot is tightened slowly before the test, it fares better; with a loose knot and fast take-up, the break strength is poor.

While writing *Inshore Fly Fishing,* I tested knots with a slow take-up tester, and some of the findings favored the lines and knots. I found that testing with a faster take-up made many knots less consistent. You would still get some high-break tests, but some knots are inconsistent or have a much lower break strength. The claim that Surgeon's Knots have a consistent 95 percent break strength is wrong. In 6- and 8-pound test it was better, but in 16- and 20-pound test it broke at 70–85 percent. The Spider Hitch, also called a Five-Turn Surgeon's Knot, ranged from 75 to 90 percent, depending on the line type. The Surgeon's Knot seemed to work better with stiff lines. I'm not going into detail on every knot with every line type—that would take another book. My intent is to warn anglers that knot-strength claims might only be for some brands of line under ideal testing conditions, not fishing conditions. Find a brand of line that you like and stay with it. I use Berkley Trilene, both XT and Big Game, for all monofilament. The Big Game works well for butt sections and for the monofilament section between the backing and fly line. The Berkley XT and Big Game are both good tippet materials. For fluorocarbon, I use Orvis Mirage.

Tippet material with more stretch might be an advantage for certain types of fishing. When hooking fish with a short line, there is no give. The line comes tight, sometimes with a quick shock. Here is when low-stretch tippet material is at a disadvantage. The sudden impact catches the angler off guard, parting the tippet in a heartbeat. Monofilament absorbs water, which decreases its strength by about 10 percent but gives it more stretch. This is called a zone of toughness, and it is like trying to break a rubber band. In some cases, this extra stretch will prevent break-offs. If you are having problems with break-offs at short distances, use a monofilament with more stretch. The new low-stretch fly line combined with fluorocarbon might cause some anglers problems.

I have mentioned following a routine when tying a knot. Form the knot carefully, wet it with saliva, and pull it up firmly. Do not rush a knot, even when fish are breaking all around you. I feel that most anglers do not take knot tying seriously. Most of the time you will not need to put tackle to the limit when landing a striper, but you still want the best knot strength possible.

Anglers interested in pursuing world records should join the International Game Fish Association (IGFA). You will receive a book containing a list of angling rules, tackle requirements, and leader specifications. Learn all the rules, take the right measurements, and get the right pictures or you will be disappointed if you lose a record on technicalities.

BACKING TO THE REEL

Three-Turn Uni-Knot

Use this knot to attach the backing to the reel spool.

Double Nail Knot

To connect one backing to another, or Dacron to monofilament. This is the knot that I use in my system.

Double Uni-Knot

To connect one backing to another or Dacron to monofilament.

BACKING OR MONOFILAMENT TO FLY LINE

Nail Knot

To connect Micron, Dacron, or monofilament to fly line. I have never had a Nail Knot fail, even fishing 20-pound test for tuna. If you tie it carefully and glue the knot, it will break at better than 20 pounds.

Offset Nail Knot

To connect backing to monocore fly line or when using gel-spun poly backing. Same as a Nail Knot but with an overhand knot in the core of the fly line to prevent slippage. *Loop in fly line*—whip finished or with monofilament Nail Knot over line to form a loop. If you plan to use loop-to-loop connection between fly line and backing.

BUTT SECTION OR LOOP TO FLY LINE

Speed Nail Knot

The easiest and best knot to put a butt section of solid monofilament loop onto a fly line. Like a standard Nail Knot, I have never had one fail.

Nail Knot

MAKING A LOOP

Surgeon's Loop

Used to make a loop at the end of the butt section or in a double line. Also used to make loop knot to put on a fly.

KNOTS FOR THE LEADER

Surgeon's Knot

The quickest and best way to add tippet to a tapered leader without tying a Bimini. A good knot to connect lines of different diameters. If the diameters are vastly different, the knot strength will suffer.

Improved Blood Knot

For knotting different-size lines to make tapered leaders. It is a straighter knot than the Surgeon's but not as strong with some materials.

Bimini Twist

The best knot to form a double line, it is the key to making very strong tippets.

Spider Hitch

A fair substitute for the Bimini but less consistent and not as strong.

Surgeon's Loop

I use this knot for all my loop connections.

Orvis Knot

The strongest knot for knotting fluorocarbon together.

KNOTS TO PUT ON THE FLY

Twice-through-the-Eye Clinch

It is the best knot for tying monofilament to the fly.

Standard Clinch

An old standby, still good for tying heavier tippet to the fly.

Improved Clinch

A very good knot, perhaps the best knot for tying the fly to fluorocarbon.

Rapala Knot—Free-Swing Loop

For tying on a fly with straight tippet when you want a loop to allow the fly more movement. It is the strongest loop knot for tying on the fly.

Surgeon's Loop

A fair loop knot to tie on the fly.

Homer Rhode Loop Knot

To form a loop in heavy shock tippet to give the fly more action.

Knot-Tying Directions

KNOTS TO TIE THE FLY TO THE TIPPET

Uni-Knot

This is a good knot and has many uses. Other than attaching the fly, the Uni-Knot works well to link lines of unlike material and size.

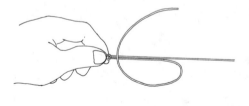

STEP 1 Run the line several inches through the hook eye and fold back, making two parallel lines. Bring the tag end back toward the hook eye and forward again to form a loop.

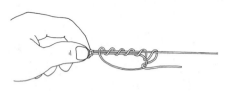

STEP 2 From the hook eye, make six turns around the double line and inside the loop with the tag end. You are forming a Clinch Knot over the double line, wrapping away from the fly.

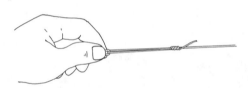

STEP 3 Hold the double line near the hook eye and pull the tag end just enough to tighten the turns. Do not lock too firmly, or heat will build up if a tight knot is drawn down over the monofilament, weakening the line.

STEP 4 Draw the standing line to slide the knot down and lock it against the hook. Tighten smoothly in one motion to snug the knot. Trim the tag end. For a loop connection that will give the fly a free-swinging action, do not draw the knot to the hook eye. Stop ½ inch short and pull the tag end to set the knot. The knot will snug up after a fish is hooked.

Twice-through-the-Eye Clinch (Trilene Knot)

For most types of monofilament, this is the strongest knot to use for attaching the fly to the tippet. It is an easy knot to make.

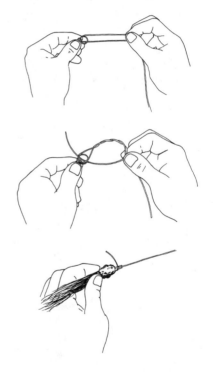

STEP 1 Thread the line through the hook eye, leaving a 6- to 8-inch tag end.

STEP 2 Run the tag end through the hook eye again from the same direction as the first loop, and form a dime-size loop at the eye. Pinch the hook eye and loop with your thumb and index finger to hold the loop steady.

STEP 3 Wrap the tag end around the standing line four to six times, and bring the end up through both loops. Essentially, you are making a Clinch Knot, but are going through two loops. (Use six turns for lighter tippet of 2 to 6 pounds—less with heavier line. I use four turns with 16 pounds.) Pull the end tight, and when snugging the knot, be sure that the two loops lie next to each other evenly and do not cross.

Improved Clinch Knot

This is an excellent knot for connecting the fly with fluorocarbon and a very good knot for monofilament as well.

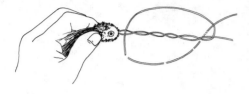

STEP 1 Thread the line through the hook eye, leaving a 6- to 8-inch tag end. Wrap the tag end around the standing line four to six times, and bring the tag end back through the loop. Essentially, you are making a Clinch Knot. (Use six turns for lighter tippet like 6-pound test; with heavier line, 12 and 16 pounds, use four turns.) Before tightening the knot, run the tag end back through the loop you first formed to make a Clinch Knot. This added step improves the Clinch Knot, making it stronger.

STEP 2 Pull the end tight, and when snugging the knot, be sure that the loops lie next to each other evenly and do not cross, and that the tag end pulls up tightly against the hook eye.

Loop Knot

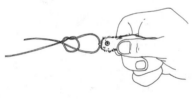

STEP 1 Tie an overhand knot in the tippet 8 inches from the end, and thread the line through the hook eye, leaving the loop several inches from the hook's eye.

STEP 2 Run the tag end through the overhand knot so the line exits the knot in the same manner as the first line. Do not cross the lines in the overhand knot.

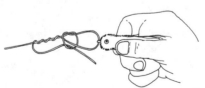

STEP 3 Make five to seven wraps over the standing line, and pass the tag end back through the overhand knot. Again feed the tag end back in the same flow without crossing the lines. For the best strength, feed the tag end through the outer edge of the loop, not through the inside loop.

STEP 4 Pull slowly on the tag end to tighten the wraps. To set the knot, pull on the standing line and the fly. For certain patterns, a free-swinging knot gives better fly action. This knot also has very good knot strength.

TYING SHOCK LEADER TO FLY USING 30- TO 50-POUND MONOFILAMENT

Three-and-a-Half-Turn Clinch Knot

To tie on shooting heads or to tie a fly to shocker (more than 30-pound test). This is a low-break-strength knot. Do not use it with straight tippet.

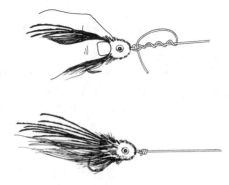

STEP 1 Run the line through the hook eye, and bring a tag end of 6–8 inches back along the standing line. Wrap the tag end over the standing line, from the hook eye back, three and a half turns. Bring the tag end forward, and thread it through the loop formed at the hook's eye.

STEP 2 Pull tight and hard, using pliers to hold the hook.

Homer Rhode Loop Knot

This knot is for shock leader only—monofilament or coated wire—to give a free-swinging action to the fly.

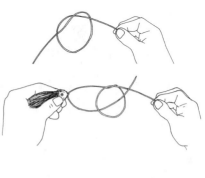

STEP 1 Tie a loose overhand knot in the leader, leaving a 5-inch tag end.

STEP 2 Run the tag end through the hook eye and back through the overhand knot. The tag end must pass through the overhand knot running parallel to—not crossing—the standing line.

STEP 3 Snug the overhand knot down onto the standing line—not hard, but firmly. Pull the tag end to bring the overhand knot against the hook.

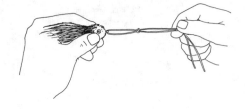

STEP 4 Take the tag end and make a single overhand knot with wire or heavy monofilament with the tag end over the standing line. Tighten the knot onto the standing line. (With light shocker—25 to 40 pounds—use a double overhand knot for higher break strength.) Pull both the standing line and tag end to bring the overhand knots together. Tighten the knot by pulling both lines at the same time, putting more pressure on the tag end. For heavier lines, pliers are necessary to set the knot hard. Trim the tag end.

KNOTS THAT FORM DOUBLE LINES

Spider Hitch

A double line knots better and has more strength when connecting unlike or different-size materials. The Spider Hitch forms a double line easier than a Bimini Twist does, but it is not as consistent and does not hold up as well under impact.

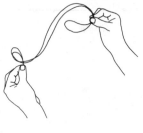

STEP 1 Form a 2-foot-long loop of tippet material. About 20 inches from the loop's end, grab the line between your thumb and first finger. Form a small reverse loop, crossing the double line under the standing line, and pinch the small loop with your thumb.

STEP 2 Hold the small loop between your thumb and forefinger, and extend your thumb beyond the forefinger. The loop must extend beyond the end of your thumb.

STEP 3 Wrap the double line from the large loop around your thumb and the small loop five to seven times. Thread the remaining line down through the smaller loop and pull. The loops will peel off your thumb and onto the standing line.

STEP 4 Finish the knot by pulling on the end of the large loop and the standing line. Bring the knot up tight and trim the tag end. This knot is actually a multiple-turn Surgeon's Knot.

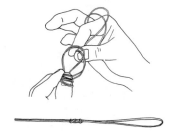

Finished Knot.

Bimini Twist

This is definitely a multihand knot. Remember to use your thumb, first finger, pinkie, and palm for holding points. Although it's tricky to tie, learning this knot is well worth your effort.

STEP 1 Form a loop of line large enough to fit loosely over your knee. Hold the tag and standing ends in one hand, and twist the end of the loop twenty times with the other hand.

STEP 2 Spread the twisted loop over your knee, holding the doubled line with one hand. Hold the standing line with one hand and the tag end with the other. Pull your hands apart to tighten the twists against your knee.

STEP 3 Run the hand holding the standing line down close to the V where the loop splits. Place the left index finger in the V, and hold the standing line with your thumb and middle finger. The standing line and tag end also form a V, and the twisted section lies between both Vs. The V formed by the tag end and standing line makes the knot, and the V next to your left index finger is the locking point.

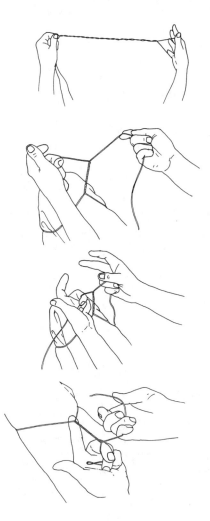

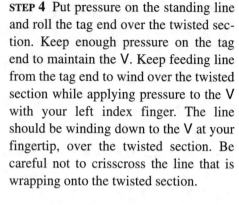

STEP 4 Put pressure on the standing line and roll the tag end over the twisted section. Keep enough pressure on the tag end to maintain the V. Keep feeding line from the tag end to wind over the twisted section while applying pressure to the V with your left index finger. The line should be winding down to the V at your fingertip, over the twisted section. Be careful not to crisscross the line that is wrapping onto the twisted section.

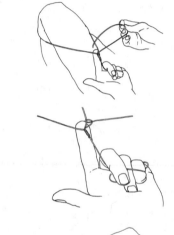

STEP 5 When the two Vs meet, pinch the junction with the thumb and index finger of your left hand. Take the tag end and make a half hitch over the nearest line of the loop. The half hitch should tighten into the V; this locks the knot and completes the Bimini, but a Clinch is necessary to prevent slippage.

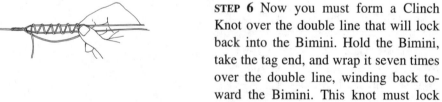

STEP 6 Now you must form a Clinch Knot over the double line that will lock back into the Bimini. Hold the Bimini, take the tag end, and wrap it seven times over the double line, winding back toward the Bimini. This knot must lock back into the Bimini.

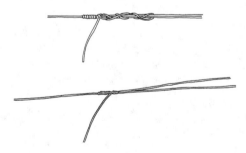

STEP 7 Pull the tag end and standing line while holding the double line to tighten the knot. Use the thumb and first finger of your other hand to smooth the knot. While tightening the knot, keep stroking the wraps back toward the loop, pulling away from the knot to prevent tangling. Pull tight and trim the tag end.

Knots to Add Tippet or Shock Material onto the Leader

Here are three popular knots used to connect lines. The Surgeon's Knot works well with all combinations of monofilaments, but is not a 100 percent knot and does not hold as well with fluorocarbon. The Improved Blood Knot works best to attach a heavier line (25 or 30 pounds) to a lighter 10- to 12-pound tippet. When tied properly, it is a 90 percent knot that works fairly well with fluorocarbon. But the best knot for adding leader material to the tippet with fluorocarbon, when the two lines are similar in size, is the Orvis Knot.

Surgeon's Knot

The fastest and easiest way to connect two sections of line. Works well with any size line, but knot strength is better with lines of similar diameter.

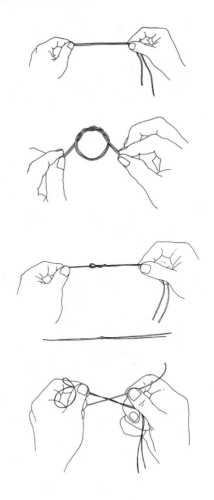

STEP 1 Hold the shock leader and tippet parallel for 6–8 inches. Either a single or double strand of tippet will work—double gives better knot strength.

STEP 2 Form a golf-ball-size loop and tie an overhand knot with both lines, pulling the entire leader through the loop, but do not pull it tight. Tie one or two more overhand knots; three would be strongest but might be difficult to tie with some materials.

STEP 3 Pull from both sides with all lines, snugging the knot together evenly. Cut the tag ends close to prevent snagging seaweed.

Improved Blood Knot

For adding a tippet section to a tapered leader when one line is heavier than the other—for example, 10 pound to 20 pound.

STEP 1 With thumb and first finger, hold a section of double line and a section of shock leader, crossing and pinching them together as they cross.

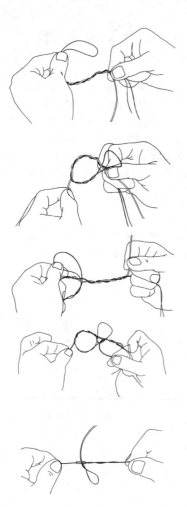

STEP 2 Wrap the double line over the shock leader five times.

STEP 3 Bring the double line back and place it into the V or cross formed by both lines. You have formed a Clinch Knot with both lines.

STEP 4 Pinch this section together and wrap the shock leader over the double line in the opposite direction. Make three and a half turns.

STEP 5 Thread the line back through the same opening as the double line. Be sure the shock leader and double line are heading in opposite directions. This will give better knot strength.

STEP 6 Pull both lines hard to tighten the knot. Trim the tag ends.

For a standard Blood Knot, tie the knot the same way without a double line.

Orvis Knot

To add onto the tippet when lines are close in size—very good with fluorocarbon.

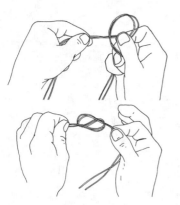

STEP 1 Lay both leader and tippet together with an 8-inch overlap and form a loop.

STEP 2 Wrap both lines together around the standing lines and through the loop—this will form a Figure-Eight Knot in both lines.

STEP 3 Bring both tag ends back through the same loop again.

STEP 4 Tighten by pulling your hands apart with the knot in the middle, holding all four lines. Trim the tag ends.

MAKING A LOOP IN LINE

Surgeon's Loop

Use this knot to form a loop in the line's butt section and in the double line of a leader. The loops interlock to make the loop-to-loop connection.

STEP 1 Form a loop in the butt section's end at the desired length, and tie an over-hand knot with the loop.

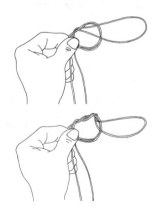

STEP 2 Leave the first knot loose and tie another overhand knot, pulling it up, but not tight.

STEP 3 Place a strong object in the loop and pull the standing line to tighten the knots. Make the loop several inches long, and pinch the loop ends together to make it tight. A narrow, tight loop is best for interlocking to a tippet. Trim the tag end.

CONNECTING LEADER OR BACKING TO FLY LINE

Nail Knot

Mainly used to connect backing to fly line, this knot also works well with Dacron or Micron to monofilament, or monofilament to monofilament, for a Double Nail Knot.

Although it's called a Nail Knot, a hollow tube is easier to work with when tying it. The best tool to use is a fly-tying bobbin. Tie this knot the same way, whether you're attaching backing or a butt section or are connecting two lines. When connecting two lines, lay both lines parallel, and tie a Nail Knot with each line over the other line. Tighten the knots, then draw them together so they butt up against each other.

STEP 1 Hold the hollow tube, fly line, and leader butt section between your thumb and first finger, and allow the main body of the fly line to trail out over your hand.

STEP 2 With fly line and leader pinched to the tube, wrap the leader's tag end back over the tube, fly line, and leader. Make six to nine tight wraps, running from your thumb toward the bobbin tip. Be sure the wraps are neat and not crossed.

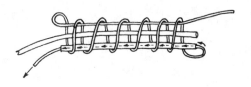

STEP 3 Slide your index finger up to pinch the knot to the tube. Pull the standing line to tighten the back section of the knot. Keeping the wraps tight is essential. Thread the tag end through the tube's tip and snug up. This will feed the tag end through the core of the knot so it can lock onto itself.

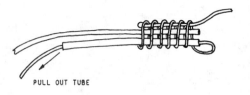

PULL OUT TUBE

STEP 4 Pinch the knot hard, and slide it off the tube. Keep pressure on the knot and snug up the standing line and monofilament tag end. Before locking tight, check the coils to be sure they are together.

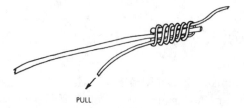

PULL

STEP 5 Pull hard on the standing line and tag end to lock the knot.

STEP 6 Trim both tag ends close, then pull the fly line and leader to test the knot. (A drop of superglue before the final locking is extra insurance, but I have never had a Nail Knot fail.) Illustrations: Kevin Sedlack.

Speed Nail Knot

A faster and easier Nail Knot, this should be used only for attaching leaders to fly lines. It's also called the Needle Nail Knot because a needle is used to form it. I prefer a straightened paper clip.

STEP 1 Pinch the paper clip and end of the fly line together, leaving about 1 inch of fly line beyond the clip. Place a length of butt-section material against the clip and fly line, with the butt section's tip facing in the same direction as the end of the fly line. Place the other end of the butt section in the opposite direction over your hand, and hold firmly. This forms a large loop of monofilament hanging below your thumb.

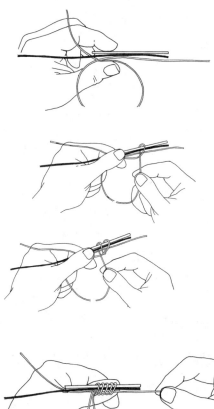

STEP 2 Take the section of leader that formed the large loop, closest to the tip of the fly line, and begin wrapping it toward your thumb, making six to nine turns. Keep the wraps tight and close.

STEP 3 Slide your index finger up to pinch the knot (as shown here, the knot is under the thumb). Pull the tag end of the butt section out slowly. You will feel it slipping between your fingers. The large loop will begin to disappear and may start to twist. Keep it untangled, because a knot in the loop will ruin the connection.

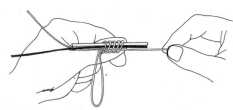

STEP 4 After the loop disappears, pull both the butt section and the tag end of the leader tight. Pinch the knot again, slide the clip out, and tighten. If the coils are neat and tight, lock the knot by pulling hard on both ends of the leader. Trim the tag ends close and pull hard to test the knot.

JOINING BACKING TO MONOFILAMENT

Use either a Double Nail Knot or Double Uni-Knot.

Double Nail Knot

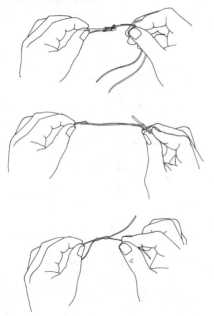

STEP 1 Hold the two lines to be joined together; they should face in opposite directions. Make a Nail Knot with one line over the other. Snug the knot. It should slide freely over the line.

STEP 2 Tie a second Nail Knot with the other line. Snug firmly, but do not lock tight.

STEP 3 Pull each standing line, drawing the two Nail Knots together. Once the knots touch, hold the line firmly and pull tight. Trim the tag ends. Follow this same procedure for a Double Uni-Knot.

Offset Nail Knot

Use to connect fly line to backing. Tie the same way as you would a Double Nail Knot, but make an overhand knot for the fly line's Nail Knot.

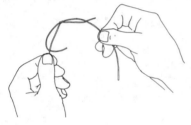

STEP 1 Strip off several inches of coating from the running line's end. Lay the two lines together, make a single or double overhand knot with the stripped fly line over the backing, and snug down.

STEP 2 Form a Nail Knot with the backing over the stripped fly line; then snug down.

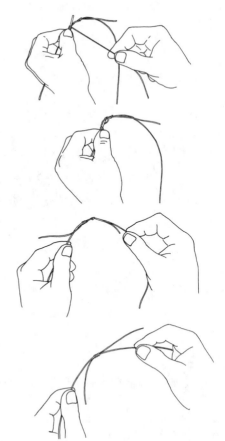

STEP 3 Pull the two knots together and tighten. If using a braided backing, superglue will make the knot stronger.

Backing to Reel

To tie backing to a reel arbor, wrap the backing around the spool several times. Then tie a Uni-Knot, draw tight, and clip the tag end.

Fly Design, Food Types, and Fly Patterns

What I have always liked about saltwater fly fishing is the simplicity of the flies. Anglers who choose to fish with several patterns in a few colors can still go out and catch fish, at times as effectively as the angler with hundreds of fancy flies. For a portion of one season, I fished two patterns tied in different sizes, either all black or all white. My catch rate was excellent, at times better than that of anglers using complex patterns.

Stripers are opportunistic and feed on many foods. If a fly looks and acts like some food source, and if it has good movement, it does not need gills, fins, and scales. Perhaps 80 percent of the time, the fly's *action* triggers the strike. Certainly this is true in locations with wave action or fast current, or in low light and discolored water, where the fish sees movement and must react before the opportunity passes.

At times, stripers lock onto a food type, feeding heavily on that bait while passing up other foods. A good example of this is when stripers are feeding on sand eels and become so focused on these small baitfish that they will not take any other offering, even ignoring fresh bait. Like trout, stripers can become very selective when they zero in on one source of food.

Length and shape are at times critical in fly selection. Stripers are particularly aware of a fly's length. In some cases, removing an inch from a 5-inch-long fly will increase strikes dramatically. When in doubt, use a smaller fly. The shape and profile are less significant when matching smaller baitfish. A 3-inch-long spearing, herring, or anchovy all have similar body shapes. As the big baits grow, they develop a wider, deeper body. When matching adult herring-type baits, a wide, flat profile is important.

In bright sunlight, or when the water is clear or shallow, or when the fish has ample time to examine the fly, you need a more precise pattern. There are times when you need a lifelike fly—or a fly of the same size and shape as the food—to take fish.

Color can be important, especially when fish are picky. Remember, baitfish are like gamefish. They change color to fit their surroundings, and different light conditions will affect how bait looks. After watching Mike Laptew's striper video, I could see why yellow is so effective in certain lights. He showed a school of herring that glowed gold-yellow in the early-morning light. In clear water, subtle colors or lighter shades work better. A baitfish that looks bright over a dark bottom might look pale over light sand. Over dark bottoms, on dark nights, and in discolored or rolling white waters, use a darker fly. Black shows up the best in conditions where visibility is difficult. Use a lighter fly in clear water, over light bottoms, and on bright nights. These are good general rules to follow, but keep an open mind.

Stripers are the garbage cans of salt water; they will eat anything. There are few fish in the ocean that consume such an assortment of foods. Perhaps there is not another fish in the sea that feeds in such a variety of waters. In times of abundant food, bigger fish prefer large baits, and all fish will take advantage of the easiest food

One of our major and most abundant baitfish is the sand eel. Precise identification of foods is unnecessary; just match the bait with a fly.

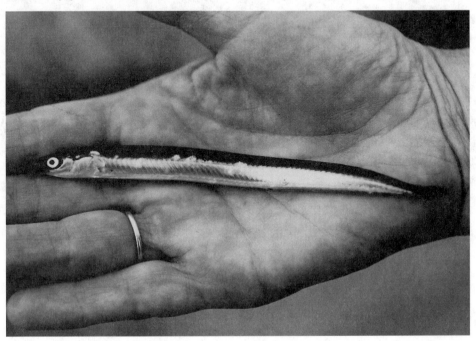

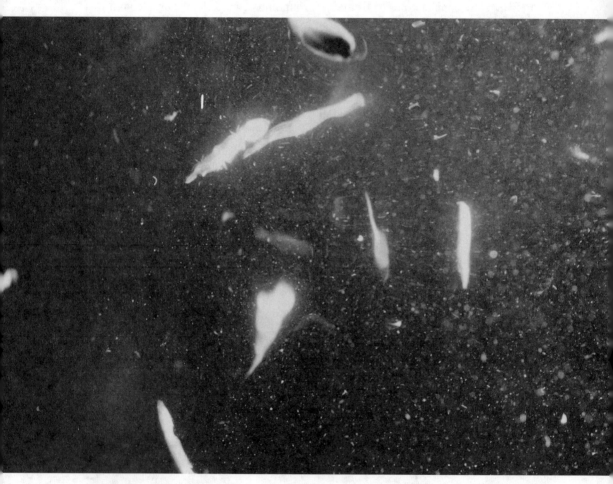

A worm hatch like this is an exciting event, but it is not a dependable food source throughout the season.

source. The food supplies in some locations have dwindled in the last 10 years; many of the bigger baitfish, such as herring, menhaden, and squid, are in short supply. With these major food sources gone, stripers are seeking other foods. They are looking for smaller foods and spending more time in very shallow water than stripers did 30 years ago. Even larger fish that seldom pursued smaller foods now feed regularly on tiny baits. The new breed of stripers feeds on small foods that were seldom considered important baits years ago. Now, don't dump all your big flies and start fishing with bonefish patterns. Instead, add some small flies to your arsenal.

As we discuss food types, I will cover the important foods, namely the baitfish, first. These are the meat-and-potatoes foods that stripers live on. There would be few stripers left if there were only amphipods to sip on.

Two important foods are sand eels and spearing. Sand eels range from southern Maine to New Jersey. Spearing are found throughout the entire range of the striper. The big baits, such as menhaden and herring, are most important when the juveniles reach eating size. This is particularly true in and around estuaries. The adults are less important because of their size; some are too big to match with a fly. And some of the adults are not available as a food source for very long. In the spring, blueback herring and alewives move into freshwater tributaries to spawn. This is the ideal time to concentrate inside the estuaries or at the mouths using big flies. It is a time when big fish move into sheltered waters and are on the feed.

The Important Baitfish

SAND LANCE—*AMMODYTES AMERICANUS*

Commonly called sand eels, these are actually small, thin fish, not eels, ranging in size from 1 to nearly 8 inches long. They are olive to bluish-green with a light underside. Most sand eel patterns are 2–5 inches long, light green, yellow, or black. They are a very important food source and the ideal baitfish for the fly rodder. Sand eel patterns are easy to make and are light and easy to cast.

Sand eels have a unique way of hiding: They burrow into the sand. Sometimes they hide at night, coming out at first light. The angler who finds sand eels along a beach should plan to fish that location before first light. If you suspect that there are sand eels in the bottom, stamp your feet. This will drive them up, making them jump above the surface.

Sand eels form tightly packed schools during the daytime. Fish feeding on them can be tough to take when they are feeding in the middle of the thick baits. If there is heavy surface action but no interest in a fly thrown into the breaking fish, try fishing under the school of bait. This is true with many types of baitfish that hold in thickly packed schools. You must fish under them, working the fly so it looks like a crippled bait falling below the school.

Sand eels hold in and around estuaries, along both ocean and sheltered sandy beaches, and in open water. They are found in great numbers on sandy shoal waters with good current flow. They are a food source throughout the entire season.

Slim flies with breathing action work well, but also try a stiff-bodied fly with an active tail. Yellow is the best sand eel color, along with all white and all black. Tie up some flies with a yellow, brown, or olive back over white for a more precise-looking pattern. Sand eels swim quickly, darting in different directions, and have very active tails. Bigger sand eels swim, then glide, but they can have a wiggle action as well.

Midbodied Baitfish

SILVERSIDES—*MENIDIA MENIDIA*

Also called shiners, or spearing, these baitfish are a mainstay for stripers, holding in estuaries, along sheltered beaches, in bays, and around rocky areas. Spearing are mid-bodied baitfish, 2–5 inches long, with a light green back, white underside, and a silvery stripe along each side. Spearing and smelt look alike, and in locations where they mix, you might not be able to tell them apart.

Silversides hold in schools but usually not in tight packs. In most locations, particularly at night, they spread out, allowing easy feeding for stripers. Along a calm shoreline, they will hold in several feet of water, swimming around in large circles. They are perhaps the most widely distributed baitfish in the striper's range.

Flies with a green, gray, or yellow back over a white body with some flash work well. All-chartreuse, all-black, and all-white flies also work well. The Deceiver and the Snake Fly are excellent spearing patterns. Tie the fly so it has about a half-inch profile when it is wet.

At night, a slow to medium gliding action, or a stop-and-go retrieve that lets the fly pause for several seconds, is effective. On calm nights, try a surface fly that leaves a wake. During the day, use a quicker retrieve, adding short pauses, pulsating the fly. Poppers are very effective in locations that hold spearing.

BAY ANCHOVY—*ANCHOA MITCHILLI*

This is a small baitfish that holds in tightly packed schools in and around estuaries. In late summer and early fall, anchovies congregate at the mouths of estuaries. The schools resemble flowing balloons filled with water, appearing dark or bright green in the right sunlight. The schools of tiny baitfish flow through the water like a single object. Late in the fall, they move into open water. At times stripers drive them onto a beach or up against a shoreline, feeding on mouthfuls of the small baits. Anchovies offer a food supply for stripers from early September through October. They are not a major food source north of Cape Cod.

Most anchovies are small, 1½–2 inches long, with a green to brown back and silvery sides. They look like small spearing, so any small silversides pattern will also match an anchovy. At times small, precise patterns or small epoxy flies work well when anchovies are around. Work the fly around and below the schools of baitfish. Make the fly look crippled, as if it is drifting from the school. In thick concentrations of anchovies, fish can be picky and hard to take.

Large Flat-sided Baitfish

BLUEBACK HERRING—*ALOSA AESTIVALIS*, ATLANTIC HERRING—*CLUPEA HARENGUS HARENGUS*, ATLANTIC MENHADEN—*BREVOORTIA TYRANNUS*, AND ALEWIFE— *ALOSA PSEUDOHARENGUS*

There is a constant flow of flat-sided baitfish from early spring to late fall throughout the striper's range. Above I have mentioned the major flat-sided baits, but there are other members of the herring and shad family that provide a significant food source for stripers. Although they are important in some locations, they are too numerous to mention. All the baits have a similar appearance: wide, silvery-white sides; darker-shaded blue-green or gray back; and light underbody. Juveniles will have less color. Anglers need to research their fishing areas to learn when these baits spawn and when the juveniles become active. The entire Chesapeake Bay and the estuaries to the south have countless varieties of flat-sided baitfish.

Blueback herring and alewives move into freshwater spawning grounds in the spring. Big bass follow these runs, looking to trap or ambush the baitfish up inside estuaries. Large schools of menhaden, also called bunker or pogies, begin to show in late spring to early summer. Both bunker and Atlantic herring spawn in deeper water, then move inshore to grow, developing into eating-size food for stripers by early fall. If spawning is late, some locations have juvenile baitfish that hold over and might become active baits in the spring as well.

These baitfish spawn earlier in southern locations, moving north as the water warms. The growth and development of young flat-sided baitfish varies from year to year. Expect to see very small flat-sided baits beginning to show from late spring right through the summer and into the fall.

Estuaries are the major nurseries for all these baits. In early spring, look for concentrations of adults around freshwater outflows. In some estuaries, different amounts of rainfall might change the holding locations of some baits. As the water warms, keep watching for tightly packed schools of juvenile baitfish up inside estuaries or around the mouths. By early fall, expect to find schools of juvenile flat-sided baits along beaches and roaming in open water.

Last summer, tiny butterfish *(Peprilus triacanthus)*, looking like flat peanuts, appeared on the offshore reefs between Watch Hill, Rhode Island, and Fishers Island, New York. The stripers devoured them like candy. The tiny baits would at times congregate under jellyfish or clumps of weed. If you lay them next to baby bunker or herring, they look alike. Small, chunky white flies with some flash worked well, as did small epoxy flies.

For any of the small flat-sided baitfish, make the flies with a wide silhouette. A round pattern is not as effective as one with a flat side and thin profile on top. For small flies, 1–3 inches long, a slightly rounded shape is fine, but when tying flies 5 inches and longer, they should be wide sided and thin. This makes the fly look right from any angle and makes it easier to cast.

Fly design is important for big flies. You must build the fly so it looks big and casts well. A heavily dressed fly with bulky materials is too difficult to cast. I use light materials, tied sparsely onto both the top and the bottom of the hook shank. (See the fly-tying section of this chapter for details.)

Work the bigger flies with long pulls, stopping briefly between strips. Try making the fly roll or wobble with quick, short, pulsating pulls. When the baits are small, use a slow retrieve, letting the fly hold for several seconds. Make the flies white with some flash and a gray, green, blue, or black back, and make some flies all yellow as well.

The runs of baitfish in early spring can be a bonanza for big stripers. Certain locations have predictable runs of herring. Keep searching the known spots while looking for other spawning areas to learn when and how the baits move. Log this information each year, and learn to predict the time the baits and fish arrive. Although the young of the year are less predictable, it is possible to get a rough idea of their movement.

Stripers become aggressive predators and take flies well when feeding on 4- to 10-inch-long, flat-sided baits. Smaller flat-sided baits create ideal fishing conditions for fly anglers.

BABY BLUEFISH—*POMATOMUS SALTATRIX*

Another flat-sided food for stripers worth mentioning is juvenile bluefish. They begin to show around mid-July, when they are 2 inches long. Called snappers, they grow about an inch a week, disappearing in early to mid-September. Use a wide-bodied herring pattern. Because stripers are constantly splashing on the surface while feeding on smaller baitfish, popping bugs are effective. Work them fast with loud pops.

Round-Bodied Baitfish

MULLET—MUGILIDAE

These round-bodied baitfish are an important food source from Rhode Island to the southern limit of the striper's range. They are a major food source in southern areas, as are flat-sided baitfish. From Rhode Island to Cape Cod, you will find schools of 3- to 5-inch baitfish in the fall. In the southern range, they grow to several feet in length.

The two major types of mullet—there are more than 100 species—are white and striped. Striped mullet spawn in the fall, white mullet in the spring. Like menhaden, they spawn in deeper water, and the larvae move into estuaries to grow. In locations with both species, there is a constant flow of young mullet.

The smaller baitfish, called finger mullet, move from the estuaries, forming larger schools in open water. In the northern range, the schools are usually small, while from Long Island southward they tend to be larger. The small mullet are silvery white, moving very quickly when chased. Fall is when the major runs of mullet begin to move along the outer beaches.

Three- to 5-inch white spearing patterns with flash are good mullet imitations. Build the fly with a rounder body than a spearing pattern. The smaller mullet are close in size and shape to a spearing.

ATLANTIC MACKEREL—*SCOMBER SCOMBRUS*

Mackerel are fast-swimming baitfish with stiff, cigar-shaped bodies. They have a green to blue back with black squiggly lines and a silvery-white underside.

Adult mackerel gather in deep water to spawn in the spring. There was a time when these concentrations drew large schools of big stripers. Sadly, those days are gone. The stocks of mackerel have diminished, but they are still a good food source in the northern part of the striper's range, Cape Cod and north. The coast of Maine still has a good spring run of mackerel.

Mackerel hold in large schools on the surface during their spawning period. When there are large concentrations of any big baits, fly fishing is tough. Fish a big mackerel fly around the schools, as well as working open water. Mackerel will hold in deeper water along rocky cliffs. In late summer and early fall, the young "tinker" mackerel appear. This is a good time to use 3- to 5-inch-long Deceiver-type flies. Make the flies either bright green or with a barred green hackle, and tie in a white bottom with some flash. Move the fly quickly with long, sharp pulls. Look for these small baits in open water and in and around estuaries.

SQUID—*LOLIGO PEALEI, ILLEX ILLECEBROSUS*

Squid have ten arms and tentacles and a roundish shape with fins on their tail. They are basically pearly gray to white in color but can change to red, brown, pink, yellow, and blue in rapid succession.

They swim in a rolling glide like paper airplanes. Squid are fast swimmers when frightened and can quickly stop, go backward, or hover with their fins fluttering.

They spawn in the spring, gathering in harbors or holding along beaches and over areas with structure and good current flow. They are a very important food source for stripers from Cape Cod to New Jersey.

When abundant numbers of squid show up in rips and along beaches, the fishing can be excellent. Squid feed on small baitfish, and locations that have large concentrations of tiny baits attract squid. At night, squid move into very shallow water to feed, and stripers follow them. Even when there is small bait along a beach, I fish a larger fly if I think there are squid in the area. A bigger fly stands out among the smaller bait, and stripers will single out that fly because they believe it's a squid. In open, flowing water, heavy concentrations of squid create a feeding binge; the action can run all day long.

Use a squid pattern, a Deceiver, or a Snake Fly tied in all white, light blue, or a blend of yellow and gray. In clear water on a sunny day, big eyes on the fly are important.

Work the fly slowly at night, with a stop-and-go motion. Let the fly glide, then hold to make the materials breathe. During the day, move the fly faster with long pulls, at times letting it hold for several seconds before moving it again.

MUMMICHOGS—*FUNDULUS HETEROCLITUS*, *FUNDULUS MAJALIS*

These small 2- to 4-inch-long baitfish are called "mummies" or "killifish" up north and "bull minnows" in Chesapeake Bay. They are found mostly in shallow water along shorelines in harbors and estuaries and have round, cigar-shaped bodies with flat heads. Mummies have olive to brown backs, silvery-yellow sides, and yellow to off-white undersides. Some have dark horizontal bars along their sides. Not a major food source in New England, they are of some importance inside estuaries, particularly in the tidewater areas of the Chesapeake Bay.

Mummichogs are robust and durable, most of the time holding in only several inches of water or up inside marsh grass. In marshy areas, a falling tide will drive them from the grass into open water. Locations like a drainage trough that spills into the main flow of a marsh will deposit mummies into the main stream. With the decline of other foods, stripers have turned to these tiny baits. Mummies, like shrimp, crabs, and many different small baitfish, now make up a portion of the striper's diet.

Small, dark, bushy flies—a Snake Fly is a good pattern—3 to 4 inches long, will match mummies. Make the flies all-yellow with a dark back, with just subtle flash. Cast along the shore, move the flies slowly with a short darting action, or work the spill-offs that flow into the deeper water along a marsh.

Sandworms and the Worm Hatch—Nereis

The worm hatch is one of the marvels of fishing in salt water. It was certainly my first introduction to fish feeding on small swarming foods. John Posh, a great friend and veteran saltwater fly rodder, and I have witnessed some hot worm hatches over the years. I remember the first worm hatch when John called saying, "Lou, I was into feeding fish for 3 hours and never had a bump."

The next night we sat in his boat waiting for the action to begin. He had described the activity to me, and I brought some different flies to see what might work. When the feeding started, it was totally foreign to me. Fish were breaking everywhere, yet not one take. We tried different flies, fishing them in various ways. One fly that finally worked was a small black Muddler fished right on the surface. Casting this fly across the slow current and letting it swing, leaving a wake, produced some action. But for the number of fish feeding, the success rate was only fair.

It is a fishing event that does not seem to fit in salt water: big fish feeding on small foods, like trout sipping tiny flies. We were gung ho then, thinking, big flies—big fish. Of course, that is true some of the time; but times have changed, and anglers are doing well using smaller flies. Stripers have always fed on smaller baits such as baby sand eels, but given the choice, a 40-inch fish is not going to chase 1-inch-long baits if it can grab several 1-pound herring. Unless the small foods are easy to catch, the fish use too much energy chasing the food. However, when there are no bigger baits, the fish must depend on what is available.

The worm hatch is a time of "easy" food for stripers; worms swim blindly in circles, not trying to avoid capture. The hatch is actually a spawning swarm that might last for several nights. During a normal cycle, the first night has moderate activity, the next night is the heaviest, and the last night there is scattered action. Wind, cold fronts, and active weather disrupt the swarms. Hot, calm, sticky nights have the best activity.

Full and new moons in May, June, and July offer the best opportunities for a swarm. Some locations have only nighttime activity, but other areas might have a swarm at any time. Falling tide starts the swarm, which can last for several hours. Swarms mostly occur in estuaries or along beaches near marshy locations. With stable weather, you can predict the hatches from year to year—however, it may be a full moon one year and a new moon the next. Keeping accurate records of weather, wind, water temperature, and moon phase will help predict activity in a given area.

The worms are actually sandworms, which bait anglers use for flounder fishing. They transform, swarm, spawn, and die. In the swarm, they are 1–4 inches long, red to orange with dark heads. Some have light-colored sections. The worms move through the water, rippling and spiraling as they swim. On calm nights, the worms' wakes and dimples cover the surface.

At night, a black Snake Fly works well. There are numerous "worm hatch" patterns, and the right pattern and the proper technique to employ depend on the thickness of the hatch and the time it occurs. If the worms are spread out, I like to fish the surface so the fly leaves a wake. In thick swarms on dark nights, getting the fly below the thick bait might be the only way to take fish.

Eric Peterson developed a fishing technique that works well in a thick worm swarm when there is enough moonlight or background light. He observed that fish take up feeding stations in flowing water when there are thick concentrations of slow-moving bait. When food sources are easily available, stripers have a small feeding window, and they will move only short distances to take a fly. The key to success is presenting the fly right to the fish's nose. However, judging the fly's position in low light is difficult, and to get the fly in the proper slot you must know the fly's location. Eric uses a floating fly line with a worm fly tied to the leader and a floating fly tied 2–3 feet behind the worm fly. When the flies are presented, the floating fly must leave a visible wake on the water's surface. By watching the floating fly, Eric can set up the drift and manipulate the line to direct the fly precisely to the fish's feeding zone. This technique will work when you encounter tough-to-take fish that are feeding on small baits, and there is enough light to see the floating fly.

During a daytime hatch, I fish below the surface. Patterns with active materials such as marabou, ostrich herl, and rabbit work well along with black, orange, or red flies with dark heads. A Clouser Minnow will work if you need to fish below the worms. Move the fly, then let it sink to simulate a spent worm swimming to the bottom. In thick hatches, some of the worms die early; the sinking fly looks like a worm falling to the bottom. Watch how the worms swim, and work the fly to match that action. A steady retrieve adding short pauses can be effective. Sometimes catching is difficult to impossible when the worms are thick. Be patient. As the swarm diminishes, some fish will continue feeding; these fish might single out a fly, and you can have decent action.

Eels—Anguilla rostrata

Eels are perhaps the best fishing bait for big stripers. Eels live throughout the striper's range and are active mostly at night. Estuaries, areas with structure, and locations with soft bottoms all hold eels. Smaller eels, 4–10 inches long, move inshore early in the season. Adult-size eels, 15–20 inches long, are difficult to match with a fly. In the spring, try fishing 4- to 6-inch-long, thin, dark fly patterns. Large flies, longer than 8 inches, are hard to cast; most anglers will suffer casting a full-size eel fly. Long black, olive, or purple flies tied with saddle hackle, rabbit strips, or long hair work well. The fly should have lots of movement and a good wiggling action. One problem that occurs with all long, thin flies is material fouling the hook. In the fly-tying section below, there are several techniques to use when building a fly that prevent some of the problems. However, with any long fly, be aware of tangling and check the fly constantly.

Fish eel patterns after dark using a stop-and-go retrieve. Try different speeds, making the fly's tail swing. Eels are nighttime hunters; they prowl looking for food. Even though eels seldom venture into open water, try eel patterns anywhere; stripers will take live eels everywhere.

Bottom-Crawling Foods

Shrimp, crabs, lobsters, sandworms, sand fleas, sand bugs, and the larvae of many sea creatures are part of the striper's food chain. Although most of these foods are bottom-dwelling creatures, you will find them at all levels in the water. When spawning or traveling, or if forced by water movement, they can end up away from their hiding areas.

SHRIMP: COMMON SHORE SHRIMP—*PALAEMONTES VULGARIS,* AND SAND SHRIMP—*CRANGON SEPTEMSPINOSA*

Shrimp inhabit the small creeks, estuaries, and shallow bays and flats. Shore shrimp spawn in the spring. Look for them flowing out of creeks with the tide or drifting over shallow flats, suspended near the surface. At other times of the year, look for shrimp along the bottom in sand or mixed sand and mud areas, or clinging to structure in bays and harbors. The shrimp are light tan to light brown and 1–2 inches long.

Small bonefish patterns, which mostly simulate shrimp, also work well for stripers. The fly's color should match the bottom's color. Use patterns about 1–1½ inches long. Add weight to most shrimp flies, but tie some that are unweighted and a few that float to simulate the spawning shrimp in the spring. When shrimp are spawning, fish the fly on or near the surface using a dead drift, or let the fly swing across the current. Retrieve the fly with short, 2- to 3-inch-long strips. For sight fishing, cast the fly in front of the fish and let the fish take it on the drop or off the bottom.

LOBSTER—*HOMARUS AMERICANUS*

This bait likes rocky bottoms and ledges but will move into open areas at times. Lobsters grow slowly. Undersize lobsters, 3–6 inches long, provide food for stripers. When working rocky areas, try fishing chunky flies in all black, black and red, or all red. Get the fly down, bouncing the bottom. Along ledges and cliffs, wave action will pull small lobsters from their lies. A dark 4- to 6-inch-long fly tied with thick, active materials looks like a free-swimming lobster. Move the fly with short hard strips to simulate their tail kick when swimming. Patterns with big spun deer-hair heads and bushy, active materials work well.

CRABS: LADY CRAB—*OVALIPES OCELLATUS,* BLUE CLAW—*CALLINECTES SAPIDUS,* AND GREEN CRAB—*CARCINUS MAENAS*

These are the major species of crabs that stripers feed on. All three inhabit estuaries, marsh banks, soft-bottomed areas, and structures like jetties. The blue crab has an olive to bluish shell, bright blue claws, and a white underside; it is king in the

Chesapeake Bay area. It is a good food source for stripers in and around estuaries from Nantucket Sound south of Cape Cod to the Carolinas. Blue crabs are very mobile, both along the bottom and in the water. They can hide in a heartbeat, even on sand bottoms.

The lady crab, also called calico or spotted crab, is equally mobile. These crabs are found on open sand beaches and sandy flats, where they are devoured by stripers. This 1- to 3-inch-long, reddish-yellow crab is common in many striper feeding areas.

The green crab is dark olive on top with a yellowish underside. It is a poor swimmer and is mainly found on gravelly bottoms, under rocks, or in the crevices of seawalls and jetties. Fish this crab pattern slowly, at times letting it just drift in the water. If you work the fly over a soft bottom, move it at a slow crawl.

The mole crab *(Emerita analoga)* is a small, tan, egg-shaped crab that lives along sandy beaches. This crab burrows into the sand or gravel along the water's edge. Wave activity dislodges the crabs, allowing stripers to sip them as they roll in the wash. Use a small tan Clouser, bumping the bottom right at the surf line.

If sight casting in shallow water, use a weighted crab fly, such as the Merkin, casting it in front of the fish so it settles to the bottom. Like shrimp, crabs seek the bottom to hide. Do not move the fly; let the fish take it off the bottom. Try a neutral-density crab fly with active materials, working it along marsh banks and in flows around estuaries. Work the fly slowly, with a pulsating action, letting it swing in the flow. A swimming crab expresses action. The back fins, legs, and claws all move as it glides through the water. A fly that simulates a swimming crab must have constant motion, even when just holding in the water. Sinking crabs should drop to the bottom at an angle with legs scrambling like an eggbeater.

Swarms of small dime- to nickel-size crabs occur all along the Atlantic coast. I have experienced this hatch a few times, and as in a thick worm hatch, catching stripers is tough. Surprisingly, I have had some success with a small, white baitfish pattern. In locations with heavy blue claw populations, small crabs are constantly appearing. In the Chesapeake Bay, there is a steady flow of small crabs. On full moons, crabs shed their hard shells, turning into soft-shell crabs. This is a time when blue crabs are easy picking for stripers.

The Midges of Salt Water

There are things floating and swimming in the sea that baffle me. I have run into hatches of inch-long, shrimpy-looking creatures that fish eat. I took a striper off the Maine coast several years ago that had what looked like ¾-inch-long "Letort scuds" falling out its mouth. Ed Mitchell, the author of *Fly Rodding the Coast,* had the same experience in Long Island Sound, and he thought they were amphipods.

I've looked in several reference books and it seems there are many tiny creatures, among them isopods, amphipods, scuds, and skeleton shrimp, that provide a food source for stripers. At times, these tiny food sources are important to the fish, but are they important to the angler? In a heavy bloom of very small baits, your fly becomes one of a thousand targets to the fish; your odds for a hookup are poor. As previously discussed, fishing in thick concentrations of any bait is difficult, let alone dime-size bait. It may be better to try fishing a larger fly, because baitfish such as spearing will feed on these small foods. The times when you really need to use dime-size flies to catch stripers are rare. An angler stalking the coast armed with only a box full of tiny, scud-type flies might need to search hard for an opportunity to fish them. Carry several tiny, "buggy"-looking flies so you are prepared for these rare cases, and hope you never need to use them.

Fly Types

Some advice on flies: Keep it simple. Choose a few good patterns in the beginning— all white, all black, all chartreuse, and all yellow—then add in some fancy flies. Keep adding patterns to your fly box to match the foods in your local waters. Fish flies that you can cast. Flies with active materials catch more fish. Length is very important at times.

Many fly rodders believe they must use elaborate flies and have an extensive variety of many patterns. I use a few basic patterns that catch fish in many situations and add special flies only for certain conditions and locations. A few patterns in different sizes and colors are better than a mishmash of flies. Anglers still use the old standbys for a good reason: They work!

Most saltwater flies are easy to tie; if you can eat with a knife and fork, you can tie many saltwater patterns. Begin by tying simple patterns such as Deceivers, and learn the basics of tying before trying more difficult flies like epoxies.

When using active materials, tie them near the bend of the hook, or add a loop of monofilament at the bend of the hook to prevent the materials from tangling around the hook. The monofilament loop should extend beyond the bend, resting under the material that forms the tail.

Use active materials like marabou, rabbit strips, and saddle hackle, and add some flash to suggest movement. I like flies that breathe, suggesting life and movement even when the fly is just holding in the water. Epoxy-bodied flies are lifelike and work well in clear water for fussy fish but don't breathe well in the water; they do not appear as alive as active patterns do.

To make flies more durable, apply epoxy or superglue (the non-water-soluble kind) to the head and sometimes the body. Superglue soaks into the materials and helps keep stacks of heavy, bulky materials from slipping off the hook shank. Use Goop to glue on plastic eyes. Many of the glues we have today not only make our flies easier to tie, but also make them more durable, to add to their useful fishing life.

There are so many new and different types of materials, it is impossible to mention them all. Success Flies offers some unique materials that are worth a look. The Fluorofibre actually changes shades when it rolls or turns, like a frightened baitfish. As of this writing, I am just beginning to see the potential of their other materials as well. They have certainly changed my convictions on fly tying and fly design. Using them has improved my fly arsenal.

Eyes are important to many patterns, making them look real, particularly in clear water on bright days. The Orvis Company offers a realistic plastic eye in several colors with a black pupil. To eye a fly without adding weight, paint the eye directly on the pattern's side with nail polish or waterproof paint, using a toothpick as a paintbrush.

For sinking flies, use weighted eyes of the appropriate size. Avoid heavy eyes on small flies. Small, heavily weighted flies do not track well and kick around during the cast. Some, such as the Clouser Minnow, are actually bucktail jigs; you can cast them with a spinning outfit. These flies are dangerous to cast and can break a fly rod or possibly hit the angler. They are fine for short casts but can lead to serious injuries; I know of several anglers who have lost an eye. My advice is to use only lightweight eyes on your flies, less than 1/16 ounce, unless the fly is big and heavily dressed.

What follows is a selection of popular fly patterns that will match the foods stripers eat. Some are for general use, others for special needs. Remember, one fly pattern can match many baits. Most of these flies are all-purpose patterns and will work in many locations. There are thousands of saltwater fly patterns. The ones mentioned are those I prefer. To learn how to tie flies and to see other patterns, consult the following: *Salt Water Flies,* by Deke Meyer; *Salt Water Fly Patterns,* by Lefty Kreh; *The Book of Fly Patterns,* by Eric Leiser; and *Saltwater Fly Tying,* by Frank Wentink. Lefty Kreh also has a tying videotape, "Salt Water Fly Tying," available through Dark Horse Video; or look for Bob Popovics's video, "Popfleyes Saltwater Patterns."

NOSE-DOWN SAND EEL—Lou Tabory

Hook:	Mustad 34007, #4 to #1.
Tail:	Marabou tied in just behind the hook eye to form a thin tail.
Body:	Slip E-Z Body Braid over the marabou and hook shank. The color will bleed through after epoxying the body.
Head and eye:	Tie on weighted eyes close to the hook's eye over the E-Z Body, then coat the body with epoxy.

This fly will dip down on each pull of the retrieve. It works well for sight casting because it drops to the bottom like a sand eel trying to hide in the sand.

CLOUSER MINNOW—Bob Clouser

Hook:	Mustad 34007, #4 to #2/0.

Eyes: Tie on weighted dumbbell eyes to the top of the shank to make the fly ride with the hook point up. Locate the lead eyes along the hook shank a quarter to a third of the way back from the hook eye.

First wing: Tie a wing on top of the hook shank, layering the materials over the hump made by the eyes. Secure the wing to both sides of the lead eyes so it extends along the shaft.

Second wing: Tie in materials to the bottom of the shank, stopping at the eyes with the wing lying over the eyes and flaring along the bend. Make the fly 2–3 inches long. Bucktail is often used for the wing, but marabou works well and gives more action.

Note: Add flash to some flies between the wings.

LEFTY'S DECEIVER—Lefty Kreh

Hook: Mustad 34007 or 34011, #4 to #3/0.

Tail: Six to eight saddle hackles or other long materials tied at hook bend; Flashabou or Crystal Hair can be added (tie in before the hackles).

Body: Optional on shorter-shanked hooks; longer-shanked hooks need the body. Mylar wrapped over shank or tubed Mylar slipped over hook shank. Try using a hot pink or orange body to simulate the insides of a frightened baitfish.

Wing top and bottom: Both top and bottom wings are the same: bucktail, or any hair-type fiber, tied behind the hook's eye so it extends just beyond the hook bend. Some versions leave the top wing longer.

Eyes: Optional. Glue to head.

This fly can be tied in a variety of ways to give different looks. Make a very thin Deceiver for a sand eel, or a little more heavily dressed fly for a spearing. The Deceiver is the best pattern for making big herring-type flies 6–9 inches long. Many fly tyers have tailored their flies after the Deceiver to match big baitfish patterns. Blend long hair or synthetic fibers with some flash into the saddle hackles in the tail, and add longer fibers to both wings to make a fuller-bodied fly.

ERIC'S SAND EEL—Eric Peterson

Hook: Mustad 34007 or 34011, #4 to #1/0.

Tail: Tie in a section of clear 20-pound monofilament at the bend of the hook.

Wing: Tie at the hook's eye bucktail, Polarfiber, Fluorofibre, thin saddle hackles, Flashabou, Crystal Hair, or a combination of several different materials. Eric's original used craft fur wrapped with monofilament, but other materials work well.

Body: Wrap monofilament over the wing materials, securing it to the hook shank. Coat with epoxy or clear nail polish. The color will show through after coating.

Eyes: Painted on, or stuck on before coating body.

Note: Fly should be thin but have tail action; softer materials will give better action.

TABORY'S EPOXY SAND EEL—Lou Tabory

Hook: Mustad 34007, #6 to #1.

Body: Bright fluorescent pink or orange Fluorofibre wrapped on body.

Wing: Split in three sections: white, pink, and chartreuse Fluorofibre layered light to dark. Add some flash, tied just behind the hook eye. Keep this sparse.

Head and body: Coat with epoxy, covering the body and wing over the body. Make the wing blend into the body, keeping it slim.

Note: This fly is also good with just a black-over-white wing. Make it 2–4 inches long.

SHRIMP FLY, FLOATING—Lou Tabory

Hook: Mustad 34007, #6 or #4.

Tail: Bucktail or calftail, ½ inch long.

Body: Spin light gray deer body hair on hook shank. Trim to a shrimp shape. Leave short side wings for better buoyancy, but leave the fly's shape straight.

TABORY'S SLAB SIDE—Lou Tabory

Hook: Mustad 34007, #1/0 to #4/0.

Tail: Layered long bucktail, marabou, or ostrich herl with some flash mixed between layers, 3–6 inches long. Make the tail wide sided to suggest a large, flat-sided baitfish.

Eyes: Either plastic or weighted, but keep the eyes near the hook shank, about one-third of the shank length from the hook's eye.

Head and shoulder: Spin deer body hair to form a large, flat-sided head. Trim hair flush to the eye on both sides, leaving the top and bottom tapered longer to the tail. Cut the underside closer to the hook for a better hook gap. Apply superglue or epoxy to the underside near the eye if you want the fly balanced. If using a sinking line, leave the fly unbalanced; it will roll slightly, giving it good action, and the fly will straighten on each pull of the retrieve.

TABORY'S SNAKE FLY—Lou Tabory

Hook: Mustad 34007 or 34011, #4 to #2/0.

Tail: Ostrich herl or saddle hackle tied near bend, 2–4½ inches long.

Wing: One or two sections of marabou tied about halfway between bend and eye. Leave room for head. Add flash between the marabou and the tail, or mix with tail.

Head: Spin deer body hair to produce a good flared head. Use fat hairs for best results. Trim head flat on bottom, rounding the top, and leave some hair long for a collar. Head shape and size will vary depending on the size and bulk of the fly. The action and density of this fly depend on its head size.

Note: A small hook makes this fly very buoyant. In small sizes, I use this fly to simulate a worm, "worm hatch," or tiny baitfish. In smaller sizes, just use marabou for a combination wing and tail.

ENRICO'S BUNKER—Enrico Puglisi

Hook: Tiemco 800S or Billy Pate Tarpon Hook or Eagle Claw #D67, #1/0 to #3/0.

Thread: Larva Lace, clear extra fine.

Body: Tie six to eight strands of fluorescent pink Krystal Flash at the hook bend, and take lengths of Enrico's Sea Fibers and tie over Krystal Flash. Then high-tie sections of Sea Fibers to both top and bottom of the hook shank, blending in the desired colors to copy a bait type. Glue the sections as you tie. You can make flies of differing bulk and thickness by varying the amount of material used. Add in some flash as you tie in the hair.

Tail: Tie in red Krystal Flash for gills and high-tie short sections of Sea Fibers to finish the head, again adding glue. Then glue in eyes—Enrico burns in eye sockets with a soldering iron before gluing.

Like most fine fly tyers, Enrico is an artist; I cannot duplicate the quality of his fly, but mine still looks pretty good in the water. This fly is an excellent lifelike pattern to match big baits. Make flies 4–10 inches long. Beauty is in the eye of the beholder. My flies would not win a fly-tying contest. However, they look beautiful in the mouth of a big fish.

SURF CANDY—Bob Popovics

Hook: Straight eye, standard length, #2 to #2/0.

Wing: Blend several colors of Ultra Hair with some flash to form the tail and body. Pinch material together, and epoxy over the hook shank to form the first body. This first body should be small with just enough epoxy to hold the body shape.

Eyes:	Use either stick-on prismatic eyes with black pupils or stick-on yellow eyes with black pupils.
Gills:	Painted red with a marking pen; use the pen to add other details to the fly.
Body and head:	Apply a second coat of epoxy over the body; this will form the full-size body.
Length:	2–4 inches.

Bob's unique fly-tying techniques have revolutionized precise fly patterns.

GODDARD'S GLASS MINNOW—Dennis Goddard

Hook:	Straight eye, long shanked, #1 to #1/0.
Body:	Form the body by inserting the hook's eye through the middle of a 6-inch section of pearl Mylar tube. Use a dubbing needle to start the hole in the center of the Mylar section, slip the eye through the Mylar, and tie down at the eye. Then draw the Mylar toward the hook's bend and tie down both sections—one to the top, which will become the tail, and one on the bottom of the shank—but leave the middle section free. Color the top of the Mylar tubing with a green marker. Slide a dubbing needle between the shank and the Mylar. Do this to both the top and the bottom of the body.
Eyes:	Place stick-on eyes near the fly's head. Finish the body by applying epoxy mixed with fine glitter, and fill the space between the hook shank and the Mylar with epoxy while rotating the fly.
Tail:	After the epoxy hardens, pick apart the Mylar tubing that extends beyond the hook's bend to form the tail.
Length:	2–3 inches.

Dennis credits Matt Vinciguerra's Salty Beady Eye for inspiring the development of this fly.

POPPING BUG OR SKIPPING BUG—Bill Gallasch

Hook:	Straight eye, long shanked, kinked, #4 to #3/0.
Tail:	Bucktail or saddle hackle, and add flash to some poppers.
Body:	Cork or foam—both come preshaped, either tapered or straight. Glue or epoxy the body to the hook shank after tying on the tail. Paint or use as is, or paint and coat with epoxy for a stronger popper. Modern, single-cell foams are strong and do not require coating. The larger the face, the more splash the popper will make. Build several sizes for different conditions. For a slider, use a tapered body, reversing it so the small end faces the hook's eye.

Color: White, yellow, silver, blue and white, and red and white.

Length: 2½–6 inches.

POP-HAIR BUG—Lou Tabory

Hook: Mustad 9052S, #1/0 to #3/0.

Tail: Long bucktail, saddle hackle, or marabou, tied on at least ½ inch from the hook bend. Continue wrapping the hook shank with thread. Make tail 2–6 inches long, depending on hook size.

Body: Use either a preformed foam body or make a cork body. Cut a groove in the bottom, and hollow out the small end so the body will slip over the lump formed by the tail material. Cut the body in half using the front section. Spin deer body hair onto the hook shank, filling the gap between the tail and the hard popper body. Trim to the contour of the hard body.

Hollowing the large or face end, or cutting the face on an angle, makes it pop better. Cork is lighter and floats better, but is not as tough as foam. Glue the body to the hook shank. Paint if using cork.

Eyes: Paint on, or use stick-on eyes.

I tried this several years ago and it works well, adding better action to a hard-bodied popper.

GLOW SQUID—Lou Tabory

Hook: Mustad 34007 or 34011, #1 to #3/0.

Tail: Layer white, pink, and shrimp Kinkyfiber for a tail. Between the pink and shrimp Kinkyfiber, layer pink Come's Alive and hot pink Fluoro-fibre.

Body: Wrap hook shank with white or tan Dan Bailey's Sapp Body Fur from bend to the hook's eye, and tie in half a dozen strands of pink or pearl Come's Alive along the side of the body.

Eye: Glue on a big plastic eye near the hook's bend at the base of the tail.

MERKIN CRAB FLY—Del Brown

Hook: Straight eye, standard length, #1 to #2/0.

Tail: Pearl Flashabou and six ginger hackle tips, flared.

Legs: Rubber bands.

Body: Alternating tan and brown strands of yarn, or Polarfiber tied in with bright green thread.

Length: 1–1½ inches.

You can alter this fly to make a blue claw or green crab by using different color combinations.

MARK'S BABY BUNKER—Mark Lewchik

Hook:	Mustad 34007/3407, Daiichi 2546, Tiemco 811S.
Tail:	Craft fur or Polafibre, purple or pink; pearl Krystal Flash.
Body:	Pearl Flashabou or other flashy body wrap with a pearl flash.
Beard:	Craft fur or Polafibre, white or yellow.
Wing:	Craft fur or Polafibre. Blend the purple and white craft fur with pearl Krystal Flash. Mark the back with permanent marker in blue, gray, or black. Make the fly 2–4 inches long.
Eyes:	Solid plastic—black on yellow or black on red.

WORM HATCH FLY—Lou Tabory

Hook:	Mustad 34007, #4 to #1.
Tail-wing:	Marabou—red, orange, or black tied in at the hook's middle.
Head and eye:	Spun deer body hair to match tail color in front of wing. Add a black nose to red and orange flies. Trim head flat on the bottom and round on top, leaving some longer hairs for more action.

Make the fly 2–3 inches long and about ¼ inch thick when wet.

Retrieving and 18
Presenting the Fly

There are basic rules to follow when adding action to a fly. There are times when the right fly action is letting the fly settle to the bottom. When I talk about *retrieves,* I really mean presenting the fly to the fish and making the fly act or look right so a striper will take it. In most cases, you want to simulate the bait, but there are times when you break the rules.

Many anglers use a trial-and-error method, using different retrieves until one works. This is not a bad technique and is effective when your plan fails. Actually, it is a good idea to employ different retrieves, particularly at slow times, to keep your confidence up. However, there should be some logic used when selecting a retrieve for a fly or line type, or when fishing different types of water.

Throughout the book I have suggested different retrieves for different water types, but to fully understand retrieves, we should cover the important ones and see how they work.

There are several basic ways to retrieve. Most of the time, I use a two-handed retrieve with the rod tucked under my casting arm. Some anglers prefer a one-handed retrieve, holding the rod in the casting hand, stripping the line with the noncasting hand. Most trout anglers started with a one-handed retrieve and continue to use it in the sea.

Using a one-handed retrieve works well when fishing a short line, just casting and letting the fly drift with little or no retrieve. Making very long strips is easier with a

Both one- and two-handed retrieves work well.

one-handed retrieve. Some anglers believe they must use the rod to hook fish and never consider trying a two-handed retrieve.

I feel the two-handed retrieve is far superior for most fishing situations, even for sight casting. With two hands, I can give more action to the fly, using a greater variety of retrieves. Two hands are much better for clearing the line when a fish runs. When working the fly, line control is much easier. When clearing the line, if you have the rod under your arm, there is less chance of the line tangling with the reel and rod butt. Holding the rod under your arm also gives the casting hand a rest.

Basic Guidelines

There are some fundamental guidelines that determine what speed to move the fly. These are general rules and should be used only with an open mind. At night, a slower, less active retrieve is usually more effective. In the daytime, move the fly faster with much more action. In faster-flowing water, fish the fly with a slow retrieve or let it dead drift, using just pulls of the hand without taking in line. In slow current or slack water, try many speeds. Fishing the fly downcurrent in a fast flow might require a very fast retrieve just to maintain contact with the fly. Fast upcurrent retrieves look unnatural. Letting the fly just hold in a downcurrent lie, adding short quick pulls with the hand, can be very effective.

Using two hands to hook a fish is effective; I feel in most cases it is the best hooking technique.

The way fish feed will give a hint about fly action. Stripers that crash the surface, feeding aggressively, are chasing fast-moving baits. Fish that leave subtle rings, or are finning and tailing, are feeding on small, slow-moving foods. Match your fly's movement to the way the fish are feeding. If matching does not work, however, work the fly in a totally different manner.

Watch the Foods That Stripers Eat

Watch the bait to see how it moves in different conditions at every opportunity. The more you can simulate bait movement, the better an angler you will become. Watch how a crippled baitfish moves and swims. Along with effective fly construction, working the fly so it acts like a wounded baitfish, darting and rolling in the water, will bring more strikes. All gamefish are drawn to a crippled bait because it is easy prey. Fishing a floating fly with a sinking line below a thick school of bait can be deadly. Using 1-foot pulls with long pauses will make the fly dart down then float up like a wounded baitfish trying to rejoin the protection of the school. If you can get the fly to swim out of the school and hang just outside the healthy baitfish, it will attract attention.

Start the retrieve with hands together, gripping the line with the bottom hand and holding the line loosely with the top hand.

Different Retrieves

A steady retrieve using short, medium, or long strips gives the fly a constant flow. This retrieve is effective and will work at any speed. It is a good retrieve to use at night in a slow to moderate current. If fish are nipping the fly and then dropping it, a steady retrieve helps you to feel the fish.

Another retrieve for nipping fish is to make two short, fast pulls—pause—then make two long pulls and pause. Repeat the process. This break in rhythm seems to work very well. I started doing this last summer, using different speeds and lengths of retrieve when fish were sipping small baits and were tough to hook. I believe the change in rhythm either makes the fish strike more aggressively or catches them off guard. Use different speeds, pauses, and lengths of pulls to find one that works. This retrieve takes concentration and some time to learn because there is no set pattern.

Long, fast strips are effective with big flies and with sinking lines in fast currents. With a bow in the line, or when fishing deep, a faster retrieve allows you to feel more takes. A long, fast pull seems to trigger a striking response in stripers. Although a one-handed retrieve is better for this action, I have perfected a good two-handed system for this. It takes some practice, but once mastered, it works well. (See the illustrations for more details.) I grab the line with both hands, one hand above the other, gripping the line firmly with the lower hand. Then I pull my hands apart, directing my

Pull down with the hand gripping the line, and raise the hand holding the line loosely. Then repeat the process. Note the arrows showing how the hands pull apart.

right hand down into the basket while my left hand pulls up and away from the basket. The right hand holds the line firmly; the left lets the line slip. I keep a loose grip with the left hand so the line slips through the hand, but I can lock onto the line if a fish strikes. This generates about an 18-inch to 2-foot strip that I can work right out of a basket and still keep the rod under my arm. Use this retrieve only with smooth lines. Rough, thin lines will cut your hands.

Make the Fly Dance

Pulsating the fly works well when casting at different angles to a flow and is very effective in calm water. To get a fly to pulsate, give a sharp pull, and let the fly pause before making another sharp pull. Flies tied with active materials and buoyant flies pulsate better. In fast currents, a fly with good action will pulsate even without moving forward if you keep applying short, sharp pulls, then let it pause. Using a very slow, pulsating retrieve is one effective way to fish a fly upcurrent in a fast flow.

A pulsating retrieve makes small flies and epoxy flies dart. Even if the flies don't have active materials, they will still have an inviting action. Some anglers use Clousers this way, fishing them like a bucktail jig. A bouncing, hopping, or bolting action can trigger a striper to strike.

Popping Bugs and Surface Flies

Getting a bug to make a good splash on the surface takes the right action and good fly design. Test the popper at close range to be sure it pops. If the bug does not pop well with a short line, it will be tough to fish. A good popping bug should splash easily.

There are several ways to work a bug so it pops well. If you hold the rod with one hand, lift the rod slightly while pulling the line with the retrieving hand. Lifting the rod while giving a sharp, long strip should give the bug a loud splash. With a two-handed retrieve, use the long strip technique I described above. Another way to employ the two-handed retrieve is to grab the rod and the line up by the first stripping guide with the casting hand. This still leaves the rod under the arm, but now you can use the rod and the strip to pop the bug. Raise the rod tip sharply, about 2 feet, as you pull with the noncasting hand. The casting hand should let the line slip while raising the rod. This gives good action to the bug and still leaves two hands to hook the fish and handle the line. This is another way to work a fly with long, fast strips. I have my good friend and fine fly angler, John Posh, to thank for this technique.

When working a popping bug, try using various speeds while trying pauses of different lengths between pops. Sometimes a hard pop with a long pause will bring fish from a distance to investigate the action. In calm water, a soft pop or just a slight bubble might work well. A surface fly with a spun deer-hair head pushing a big wake can also be very effective in calm water. Small, fat poppers worked with a steady pop-pop-pop are also fish-getters in flat water.

In choppy water, work a popper more slowly, letting it surface before trying to pop it. In rolling water, you must give the popper time to work—to float back to the surface. Even a big-faced bug will not pop well unless the cupped front of the bug is above the surface.

Dead Drifting, Swinging, and Slipping the Fly

There are situations that require advanced fishing techniques when you need to finesse the fly. In *Inshore Fly Fishing,* I had only enough space to touch briefly on finesse fishing. Here I can delve into it more deeply.

Retrieving is a form of presentation. Drifting the fly, or letting the fly swing or slip back into the current, is also a form of presenting the fly. There are times when getting the fly to flow with the current into a certain lie at the proper depth is the only way to take fish. I believe there is no need for a classic, drag-free float because even small, juvenile baits can swim. But getting the fly to dead drift or to swing like a bait flowing with the tide is important. This is particularly true when fishing estuaries, because they continually produce or shelter many types of small bait. In shallow water, a portion of this fishing will be with short casts using a floating, intermediate, or clear sink-tip fly line. Perhaps the 10-foot clear-tip is the best line for finesse fishing.

The standard straight-across or quartering downcurrent cast followed by a drift will work in some circumstances, but mending the line might be necessary to fish some locations properly. After casting, roll cast some loose line upcurrent. What you are doing is removing the belly that the current creates in the fly line. This belly will drag the fly across the flow and not let it drift with the current. In some locations, it may be necessary to mend several times to keep the fly flowing down the run you want to fish, or to let the fly settle into the water column. Sometimes, I like to cast above a drop-off and keep mending line until the fly is just flowing into the hole before adding action to the fly. This makes the fly settle into the hole, then swing, rising up as if it's trying to escape. When fishing into a drop-off, most strikes occur right on the drop-off's edge or as the fly flows through the hole. With level bottoms, expect strikes at any time. When fishing constant flows with level bottoms, keep working small sections of water, trying different mends at different angles to the current. If you want to increase the speed of the swing, throwing a mend downcurrent will allow the flow to grab more of the line. Mending downcurrent makes the fly swing down the flow quickly, then turn uptide with a snap. This rapid change in direction can be very effective.

In stronger current, try a faster-sinking line, casting it across the flow, then make a roll cast to feed loose line downcurrent. Just as the fly swings into the deeper water, begin to retrieve. You will get an effect similar to mending in slower water and will fish the fly much deeper. This is also effective in bigger, deeper, water with midsize to large flies. To get the fly deeper, cast quartering upcurrent, roll the middle of the fly line downcurrent, and let some loose line feed as the line and fly sink. As the line begins to sweep below your lie, start a hard, fast retrieve. This allows the fly to sink deep, swing across current, then dart up toward the surface. A swinging, rising fly will bring a fish bolting up to strike. You will be making longer casts and handling more line here than in shallower, slower water.

At the time the fish hits, you might be retrieving the fly, but it is the drifting, swinging, mending, or slipping of line that sets up the strike. This is true when fishing rolling water along steep beaches, from rocky cliffs, and in many rips, where you must spend a good portion of the cast setting up the right presentation to fish only a small section of water. Even when fishing smaller, slower water, you might need to drift the fly 15 feet to cover just several feet of water.

Even a simple drop-back action can be deadly in faster current. Many times at the end of a swing, anglers just retrieve quickly upcurrent to cast again. Not fishing out each cast is a habit that we all get into when fishing a hard current. If fishing fast current, it is wise to allow the fly to settle back in the current on some casts. Let the fly

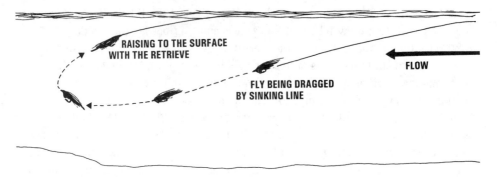

RAISING TO THE SURFACE
WITH THE RETRIEVE

FLY BEING DRAGGED
BY SINKING LINE

FLOW

Making a large mend downcurrent will allow the fly to sink, swing, and rise quickly to the surface when the retrieve begins.

drop back several feet, and keep adding short pulls to make the fly dance in the flow. Use this technique when first fishing a location, perhaps for ten or fifteen casts. Then do it every few casts after that. A striper might follow on the first several casts, then turn off as the fly heads upcurrent. If the fly flutters back, the fish might take.

This technique works well even for casting downcurrent to a drop-off. Land the fly in the shallow water just above the rip line. Let the fly settle into the drop-off while shaking the rod tip to add action to the fly. Beware: When a strike occurs, there will be a direct connection between you and the fish. A hard hook-set will part the line like a rifle shot.

Mending, drifting, and swinging the line and fly all take practice. You will spend some time experimenting before getting the feel of setting up the line, and even then, expect to miss fish. Remember, this is not like a steady retrieve when the fish usually hook themselves. When you are setting up the line, many times there is too much slack to feel the fly. If a fish hits with too much slack line, you may never know the fish was there. In daylight, if you see a swirl or a subsurface flash near the fly, or if you see the line move, try setting the hook. Do the same with any slight tug or tightening of the line. You must be ready to strike at any moment. A good nymph fisherman will feel at home with this angling. Once you begin to master these techniques, you will hook some fish by instinct, developing a sixth sense not only for hooking fish, but for knowing where fish hold and how to place the fly to take them. **Learning the water** is the key to advanced fishing. Once you know where the fish lie, fishing for them should become instinctive.

A good way to practice retrieving and to learn how the fly works in different situations is to cast a bright fly in clear moving water. Watch the fly's action, how it flows, at what depth and speed it moves, and what effect different retrieves have on the fly. See what mending does to the fly's action, where it sits in the water column, how it moves with the current. Try different flies and different-density lines to determine how they react.

We still have much to learn about fishing salt water. For years, I have used fresh-water techniques in the sea, but until recently I gave it little thought. Perhaps I am too instinctive when fishing; I only begin to think when I write. It is important that we keep trying new and different fishing methods, to learn better ways to fool fish. But equally important is to know the basics and to keep using them, because they work. This is what makes fly fishing fun. There is always something new and another challenge to address.

Fly Casting 19

*P*erhaps the biggest misconception in saltwater fly fishing concerns casting. Some anglers are intimidated because they cannot cast a long line. Yes, there are locations and circumstances that require longer casts. Sight casting to fish in shallow water is the most demanding. Here you need speed and accuracy, and at times distance, but not a 90-foot cast. Seventy feet is about the maximum distance at which I want to present a fly to a sighted fish; anything over that is a Hail Mary. If you factor in the wind, the moving boat, and the erratic path of a fish, long casts are not wise. Most sighted fish are taken with 40- to 60-foot casts.

There are times and places when a 40-foot cast might be too long. In low light or darkness, stripers feed close to shore, frequently in very shallow water, and will feed right next to a boat. Lack of casting skills should never prevent an angler from enjoying striper fishing with fly tackle. However, becoming a better caster will increase fishing possibilities and make the angler a better fly rodder. In the sea, we sometimes fish with big flies and heavy sinking lines and need to fight brisk winds. Becoming a better caster will make fishing easier and allow you to fish most environments.

Learning to cast is not difficult, but for some it can be a chore. Even very good athletes might have problems learning to cast. Bad habits are hard to break. For those who struggle—and there are plenty who do—get some help. There are good videos and books that help, and for some, a casting school or clinic is a necessity.

When starting, use balanced tackle; the fly-line weight should match the rod. If you have trouble feeling the line in the air or loading the rod, use a larger line size than the manufacturer recommends. Never try to learn at night; the first saltwater fly-casting experience should be during the day without a fly, unless you are a proficient caster.

You are actually line casting, not fly casting. The line carries the weightless fly. This is why weighted or bulky flies are hard to cast. The line must carry them out. Sometimes anglers have problems casting because they try to use a light line to cast a big, heavy fly. An 8-weight line will not cast a bulky fly very well. Some of the problems casters have come from using the wrong equipment for a given purpose. This is part of matching—or balancing—your equipment.

I will not attempt to teach basic casting in this book. My goal is to give advice to improve your casting and to offer some hints to make casting easier. If you are working too hard, you are not using the tackle correctly. Most anglers use too much force, applying too much power to the rod. A cast should be smooth, with enough power to drive the line and fly a given distance.

Grip the rod with the thumb on top of the handle. This grip gives the best control and allows for more power without taxing your hand. Stand so your noncasting shoulder is at about a 60-degree angle to the casting direction. This allows the use of the whole body rather than just the wrist and arm. Like golf, tennis, or baseball, you might use your hands and wrists to swing, but you employ the whole body to add power to the stroke. Fly casting in salt water requires some strength. If you use just the wrist and arm, you will tire quickly.

Lifting a Floating Line from the Water

You begin by raising the rod slowly upward, and lifting it to about a 45-degree angle in front of you. This moves the line, breaking the water's grip on the line. It also begins to bend the rod, loading it to prepare for the backcast. This first movement of the rod should be in one motion and should follow right back to a 45-degree angle on the backcast. The first sweep of the rod lifts the line from the water while making the backcast with one clean stroke.

Loading the Rod

On both the forward cast and backcast, you must first load the rod to prepare it for the cast. You push or force the rod in the direction of the cast, holding the line in the air with the rod. For a normal forward cast or backcast, the force should be directed to a location about 8–12 feet above the water's surface. The backcast might be higher when fishing from shore to prevent hitting the fly and line on obstacles. The rod bends, then carries the line through the air, building speed as the rod travels either forward or backward. The longer you can hold the line in the air on a straight plane in the direction of the cast, the more force and speed the cast will develop. Think of the line as a long, thin spear attached to the rod tip; you are throwing that spear from the rod tip. With the rod loaded, you direct the line on a straight plane toward a spot above the water. At this point you need only stop the rod cleanly to throw a good cast. This is called the power, or casting, stroke.

Timing

Watch the backcast. Just before the loop opens, begin the forward cast. This is also true with false casting. The loop should be just rolling over when you start the casting stroke. Watching the backcast will help to develop timing and put your body in the proper position to make a strong cast. Watching the backcast, even at night, will also eliminate the danger of being hit in the face with a wandering fly.

Loop Control

Throwing a tight loop, or controlling the loop's size on both the forward cast and backcast, is an important part of fly casting. When you cast a narrow, smooth loop, it means that the rod was loaded properly, then stopped in the correct position. The power, or casting force, is moving in the right direction, and the rod is throwing the line without excessive force. Excessive force will either open the loop or cause it to be lumpy. Most anglers who overpower their tackle drive the rod tip down on the forward cast or backcast. The rod tip must come to a smooth, clean stop. If the tip dips down, it opens the loop, and it can put waves in the line as well. Not stopping cleanly and overpowering are the worst faults of most casters.

For a normal cast, the right-handed caster should stop at about 1 o'clock on the backcast and at about 10 o'clock on the forward cast. A left-handed caster will stop at 11 o'clock on the backcast and at 2 o'clock on the forward cast. Stopping at about a 45-degree angle on both casts will produce a good loop.

Changing the Casting Plane

If you want to change the casting plane to cast to a higher or lower location on the water, you need to stop the rod in a different position and direct the force in a different direction. For a lower forward cast, when casting into the wind, pick a spot on the water—say, 50 feet out—and direct the power stroke toward that spot. You will stop the rod lower on the forward cast and keep a higher backcast. For casting downwind, make a lower backcast and a higher forward cast. Remember, the fly line is a spear, and you must cast it in a straight line. If you keep the rod tip traveling on a straight plane toward the casting location, the line will remain straight, but if the rod tip travels in an arc, the cast will lose most of its power. When changing the cast's elevation, it is important that you change the casting plane to keep the rod tip traveling in a straight line toward the target.

The Fly Line Should Be Straight When Landing

When the line lands on the water's surface, it must be straight, unless you purposely add slack line or mend line on the cast. (I will mention mending later in the chapter.) This gives a positive retrieve and maintains constant contact with the fly. If you make a good positive stop on the forward cast, the loop should turn over and land in a straight line. If the line piles up, either you are applying too much power, or the loop is opening up. A headwind will blow back the line's tip section and pile up the leader. When casting into the wind, shorten the cast so it turns over with more force. This is very important at night, when feel becomes your only link to the fly. At night, if the cast does not clear the fly line from the basket at least 50 percent of the time, reel in some of the line. I stop the line with my noncasting hand to be sure the cast turns over. At night, shorten the cast to be sure that the line is landing straight.

Roll Casting

I use a roll cast constantly when fly fishing in salt water. When I'm casting from jetties, on crowded beaches, or under normal conditions, the roll cast is usually the first cast in my routine. In crowded locations, the roll cast is the only safe cast to use, because it never travels behind you. Using a roll cast allows you to fish the fly right to your feet without retrieving too much line.

Begin the roll cast with 20 feet of line outside the rod tip. Raise the rod up just behind your head, to about the 1 o'clock position if you are right-handed. Keep working the fly, using the rod tip to add action; once the line stops, drive the rod tip toward a spot just above the water about 40 feet away. The two key parts of a roll cast are the rod's stopping position and stopping the line. If the line does not stop before casting, the cast will land in a pile. Not stopping the rod tip high enough above the water will pile up the line as well.

Once you make the roll cast, pick the line up, make a backcast, and begin casting normally. If a fish takes the fly during the raising of the rod, make a hard roll cast; you will hook most of the fish that strike close. (See Chapter 20, Hooking, Fighting, and Landing Techniques.) Using a roll cast and keeping 20–30 feet of fly line outside the tip will eliminate many false casts. The fly will be in the water fishing for much longer with less casting effort.

When roll casting, the hand must be above and behind the head, with the rod in the 1 o'clock position.

When casting sinking lines or big flies, the roll cast is a must. If the line is underwater, you cannot pick it up. A sinking line might require several fast roll casts in succession to bring the line to the surface. The trick is to pick up the line as soon as it hits the water. *Do not let the line sink.* When the line lands on the water, begin the backcast. With a big fly, make the backcast before the fly hits the water. With big flies and poppers that are hard to pick up from the water, make a high roll cast, pushing the line into the air. Direct the roll cast's power as you would a normal forward cast, to about a 45-degree angle. This will force the roll cast into the air. As the line jumps off the water, make a backcast, then begin casting.

When you roll cast, each roll, each cast, puts a half twist into the fly line. After an hour of fishing, the line will begin to tangle from the twisting caused by roll casting. It is a good practice to alter casting sides, using an off-shoulder roll cast on every other cast to remove the twist. You make an off-shoulder roll cast by just reaching the arm across your body and casting from the other side. This puts an opposite twist in the line.

Dealing with the Wind

I briefly mentioned casting into and with the wind. The key is to shorten the cast if the wind is causing problems. For some anglers, a wind at their backs can be difficult.

If you do not make a strong, low backcast, a tailwind will stack up the line. I believe that for many casters, a headwind is easier to deal with, because most anglers make stronger forward casts than backcasts. When choosing a fishing location, try to pick one where you can cast at an angle to the wind and not fight it directly. With a strong wind at your back, try making a high roll cast, getting the line up into the air, and letting the wind do all the work. If there is a strong wind blowing over a jetty, I just get down low on the lee side and make roll casts.

When casting directly into the wind, keep the loop tight, shorten the cast, and shoot it low. Usually the wind will put the fish onto the beach, so casting a long line is unnecessary. When fishing from a boat, position yourself to use the wind, casting downwind at an angle.

Trying to fish when the wind blows into the ear on your casting side is difficult and dangerous. When you're making standard casts, the wind will keep blowing the fly against your body. The best solution is to turn around when casting, making the forward cast your backcast and vice versa. In other words, you are backcasting to the fish. This technique also works well when fishing from a boat if both anglers want to work the same water without casting over the boat. Backcasting to the fish allows safe fishing when the wind is blowing the fly into your body. It also helps to develop a stronger backcast.

Use the backcast as a forward cast when the wind is blowing into your ear.

Double Haul

This is the toughest technique in fly casting. It is hard to teach even one-on-one. You are pulling the line with the noncasting hand to add speed and power to the cast. It is very effective when casting into the wind and for sight casting when you want more speed. It also takes some of the work from the casting arm. Most casters pick it up just by feel. The secret is not to make a hard, sharp haul. The haul should be applied at the same time as the power stroke. If the loop tangles, or if the end of the fly line flips over or under the loop, the haul was too hard or was made at the wrong time. The trick is to make a smooth, short, soft haul, like pulling a cork from a hundred-dollar bottle of wine. If you are having problems double hauling, work on a single haul first, then put them together.

Casting Heavy Sinking Lines and Big Flies

Some anglers have problems casting heavy sinking lines. Trying to cast a very tight loop or using too much force causes the lines to pile up and collapse. Use a longer, slower power stroke to open the loop. And do not try to hold too much line in the air. Thirty to 35 feet is all that most anglers can hold, particularly with a 500- or 600-grain head. With a very heavy line, I apply just enough power to keep it moving, throwing a 3- to 4-foot-high loop. It is really a lob. These lines are so heavy, they cast with little effort. You can pop them with a tight loop, but the cast must be crisp with no extra power; otherwise, they tangle.

A slow lob also works well with big flies. Sometimes when casting big flies, a fast, tight loop will open too quickly, before the line has traveled very far. A slow-moving loop will carry a big, wind-resistant fly farther because it drags out more line before the loop opens up.

Casting Shooting Heads

You cast a shooting head in the same manner as a big sinking line. The best length for a head is about 28 feet. This is the size that most anglers can handle. If you want a head for casting longer distances, lengthen the head. But for most fishing situations, the shorter heads work better and are easier to control.

Hold the head just outside the rod tip, leaving about 2–3 feet of running line beyond the tip. If the head is a floating or intermediate line, you can cast it like a weight-forward, using a clean stop to shoot a small loop. If the head is a heavy sinking line or a lead-core, use a slower push with the rod, and open up the loop slightly. Try different power strokes until you find one that shoots the line cleanly without too much speed or tangling. Most shooting heads cast better with a slower-moving loop.

Only the better casters can shoot a clean, tight loop with a fast-sinking shooting head. If you have problems with a shooting head, try casting with several feet of the head inside the rod tip. This will affect the distance somewhat, but it helps the novice throw a smoother line.

Try to make the head turn over at the end of the cast. If the cast is falling to the water before it has turned over, grab the running line to stop it, and lift the rod. This should cause the head to turn over and straighten the leader. As in a standard cast, if the line slaps the rod at the cast's end, the front section of the line usually rolls over and lands straight. If the line is landing in a heap, try lifting the rod at the cast's end. If the cast still piles up, use less force.

Develop a Routine

Casting and presenting the fly to a sighted fish—or to water that you believe holds fish—should be second nature. It should be executed without thinking. At first, casting and presenting the fly will require most of your attention. However, once you develop a system—a routine—it will make fishing easier.

Start by stretching the line, checking the leader to be sure it's sound, and checking that the hook is sharp. After working out some line, I always roll cast first, then begin false casting and shoot the line. With a sinking line, I usually make a roll cast, a backcast, and one false cast, then present the fly. With a heavy sinking shooting head, I might roll cast twice to bring the line up, then just lob a slow forward cast. (For sight-casting information, see Chapter 6, Flats and Shallow Water, Mud, and Sand.)

Mending, or Manipulating the Line after Casting

Some fishing situations might require mending the belly—or running-line section—of the fly line to make the fly fish in a certain location in the current or to settle it deeper in the water column. After making a cast, use the rod tip to throw loose fly line either up and across or downcurrent, or into a flow of white water to make the fly track in a certain manner. Usually you roll cast the loose fly line after the cast has landed. When using sinking line, you must mend quickly, before the line begins to sink. You can make some mends in the air before the line hits the water. Just after you make the forward cast, when the loop is still flowing out, flick the rod tip to either side to throw a mend in that direction.

Mending line is for advanced fishing. I use it in locations that require precise fly control—usually when I'm making short casts and fishing the fly to swing it above a holding location, or to keep the fly flowing in a section of water. A good example of mending is when cliff fishing, where you might need to throw the belly of the line into moving white water to keep the fly flowing in a desired location. Mending can overcome some flows in smaller surf, but it will not work in big, booming waves. However, mending line is a technique that works only sometimes in finesse situations. I use it in perhaps 5 percent of my fishing, if that. It does not apply to many fishing situations and will drastically affect success when used in the wrong environment. Use mending in the right situations, but use it only when basic techniques fail. There are anglers who believe mending can replace a sinking line. They're wrong.

Speed Casting into Breaking Fish

Sometimes getting the fly into feeding fish quickly is the only way to catch them. There are days when feeding fish stay on the surface for only a brief time. One problem with fly fishing is getting the fly to the fish quickly. Using a stripping basket, with the line coiled inside the basket ready to cast, will help make a faster delivery. This works both from the beach and in a boat. You see the surface action and move toward it, ready to cast. As when casting to sighted fish, have some fly line outside the tip, and use the same technique of holding the line and casting to present the fly.

From a boat there is another method that will present the fly as quickly as a spin cast. As you run toward the fish, have the angler trail some fly line, about 35 feet, outside the rod tip. When you reach the fish, cut the motor and have the angler make a cast with the line trailing in the water. The caster must use both the boat's forward motion and the water's resistance to make the cast. The casting arm and rod should be pointing back toward the trailing line. As the boat slows, the caster should force the rod forward, using the same power stroke as for a long forward cast. Once the rod is loaded, the tip must travel in a straight plane toward a target just above the water, and the stop must be clean. Because the rod stroke is so long, keeping a straight plane and stopping the rod high are essential to making a good cast. If you drive the rod tip down, it opens the loop, destroying the cast. The amount of line you trail beyond the tip will vary depending on the caster, the type of line, and the fishing conditions. Some casters can handle 50 feet of line, but in windy, choppy situations with a sinking line, a shorter line might work better. With the line trailing back behind the boat, approach the fish so the caster does not have to throw the line over the boat. With a right-handed caster, I run straight toward the fish, cut the motor, and turn quartering

When approaching fast-moving fish from a boat, try letting the line trail behind the boat, using the boat's flow and the water's resistance to make the cast.

to the right before running into them. This allows the caster to throw a quartering cast over the bow, keeping the line away from the boat. It also glides the boat past the fish, not into them. A straight-in approach makes casting difficult and retrieving almost impossible, because the boat's forward motion runs over the line.

The secret to fly fishing in the sea is selecting locations that fit your casting skills and using only lines and flies that you can cast easily. Then, keep striving to become a better caster so you can fish those difficult locations and handle those hard-to-cast lines and flies. Good fly-casting skills come with practice and more practice. Take the time to become a good caster. It will make fishing more fun.

Hooking, Fighting, and Landing Techniques

20

S tripers have fairly firm but hookable mouths. Setting the hook into even a big fish is not difficult. Most of the flesh from inside the mouth to the beginning of the stomach will hold a hook well. If a striper inhales a fly and closes its mouth, and if you can make a clean strike, the fish is hooked. The trick to hooking a fish is to let the fish take the fly. I believe most anglers strike too soon, before the fish has the fly in its mouth.

There are days and situations when fish are picky and do not hit the fly aggressively. These are the times when striking quickly at just the right moment is the only way to hook fish. I have watched fish follow, inhale, and drop a fly in less than a heartbeat. In shallow, clear water with bright sun, stripers can be very finicky and not feed normally. If you see a fish following your fly and the fly disappears, strike quickly. Under these conditions, it will not hold the fly very long. But this is not the way stripers usually feed. Most of the time, they are positive strikers.

Wait for a Solid Take

Stripers usually come up behind the fly, taking with a quick turn of the body. A larger fish will inhale the fly with the suction of its big mouth and gills. I have let stripers grab the fly and swim with it without hooking the fish; surprisingly, some fish held it a long time. When they are feeding actively on midsize to large baits, they are easier to hook; let them eat the fly. When you feel the first pressure of a fish, keep retrieving until the line tightens. Striking too soon might take the fly away from the fish. This is true with larger fish when they are inhaling the fly. The first resistance you feel could be the fish sucking the fly into its mouth. Striking when you feel that first sensation before the line tightens will result in many short strikes. In most situations, I wait until the line tightens in my hands before attempting to set the hook. Only when sight fishing, or when I'm mending line to dead drift the fly, would I try to set the hook by sight or by feeling just a slight touch. *I want a positive connection before striking.*

If you set the hook using the rod, be doubly sure that the fish has the fly. Striking with the rod moves the fly many feet if you miss, usually beyond the fish's range. Setting the hook with a two-handed retrieve will not move the fly very far. You might get several chances to hook up, because the fly stays close to the fish.

Hooking with Two Hands

Fishing with the rod under the arm has many advantages; perhaps the biggest is hooking fish. There is no more positive way to hook a fish than by using two hands to keep tightening the line, then making the final set with a straight pull. You can never make a better, more positive set with a rod—never. If you choose to strike with the rod, use the butt section, the first 4 feet of the rod, to set the hook. Trying to set the hook with the tip seldom works. The best way to set with the rod is making a straight pull with the rod and the stripping hand. Do not raise the rod.

I seldom use the rod to set the hook. If I'm holding the rod, roll casting and working a short line around structure without retrieving, I use the rod to hook the fish. Also, if a fish takes the fly and keeps gliding toward me and I cannot tighten the line fast enough, I'll use the rod. This happens when sight fishing. Sometimes you see a fish take the fly and keep coming toward you. With the rod under the arm, grab the line and rod at the first guide and sweep the rod to one side, striking hard. Remember, to gain quick control of the fly line, reach for the first guide—the line is always there waiting for you.

Hooking Finicky Fish

There are days when fish nip at the fly, grabbing with just their lips. I noticed a period last summer when fish were feeding on small, 1-inch-long baitfish on the Rhode Island reefs. It was a clear, calm, sunny afternoon, and at times you could watch the fish take. When the current's flow slackened, the fish would just sip the food. Most fish drifted toward the fly and nipped it without a positive take. When you could not watch the take, hooking some fish was difficult because you needed a quick hook-set. Once the flow increased, the fish took more positively. During slack water, most fish were hooked right on the inner lip area, which is unusual for stripers. Most of the time stripers grab the fly and are hooked well inside the mouth—regrettably, too deeply in some cases. This subtle feeding lasted for several weeks until the baitfish grew and became more mobile. It shows that fish will feed differently when the bait is not mobile.

When you're fishing for finning and tailing fish, or fish that are just dimpling on the surface taking small immobile foods, hooking them can be tough. This subtle feeding occurs when baits like shrimp or crabs hatch, or when juvenile baitfish appear. The way a fish feeds is a clue to hooking technique. When fish are sipping, feeding casually, you must concentrate and be aware of every pull, tug, or touch on the fly line. Watching for line movement and activity near the fly's location is also important for hooking picky fish. If fish are finicky and I see any activity around the fly or feel even a slightly different sensation in the line, I make several quick pulls with both hands. At these times, the anglers who have developed a sensitive feel will outfish the freshmen five to one. Luckily, this is not normal feeding procedure for stripers.

Crashing the Fly

When fish are aggressively attacking the fly, many anglers strike too soon. Fish busting a surface popper are difficult for some anglers to hook. The trick is to wait for the line to tighten; do not pull when you see the splash. Stripers frequently miss poppers on the first try or hit them with their tails. Let the fish grab the popper or the fly when they are chasing it. If you are having trouble hooking fish when they chase poppers, look away once the fish rushes the bug. This will force you to feel for the take.

This is also true with a rod-tip explosion at night, or when a fish rushes a surface fly in calm water and you see the wake. The tendency is to pull too soon, before the fish has the fly. A rushing fish wants the fly. If the fish doesn't miss, it will hit like a freight train. Let the fish eat the fly before setting the hook.

Fish feeding aggressively usually hook themselves. Setting the hook too hard on explosive strikes will pop the tippet. The excitement of a topwater take might cause you to lock up and pull. Remember that with a floating line and surface fly, you have a positive link to the fish with no slack line. If the fish takes the fly close, then turns away, just a gentle pull sets the hook. When fish are close and take a fast-moving fly, you need to hook with soft hands.

Sinking Line and Too Much Slack

Hooking fish at the end of a long cast or when fishing a sinking line requires a fast take-up. You must retrieve quickly to tighten the line when you feel the strike. Sometimes you might retrieve as much as 15 feet of fly line before the line is tight enough to set the hook. I have felt fish take the fly and needed to retrieve hand-over-hand for what seemed like half the cast to hook the fish. The combination of current, sag in the sinking line, and the fish swimming toward the angler can create a tremendous bow in the line. The bow must be removed before hooking the fish. You might get away hooking some fish with a curve in the line, but for consistency, keep taking in line until it there is a solid connection to the fish.

When mending line on a short cast, some anglers like to use the sweep of the rod to hook fish. If the fish are close and there is little slack, do not strike hard. A gentle sideways stroke of the rod will set the hook. I prefer hooking with my hands, because I can gauge the tightness and stop quickly before shocking the tippet. Mending on a long cast with sinking line creates both slack and a bow in the line, and demands a fast take-up to tighten the line. Even experienced anglers miss some fish, and probably do not feel half the strikes. There is just too much time without contact with the fly.

The Best Rod Position

Point the rod toward the line and fly and keep it low. If you hold the rod under the arm, the rod's weight should naturally keep the tip down. From a boat or a high perch, the rod tip should rest below your feet. In current, swing the rod, pointing it at the fly.

Keeping the rod low, pointed straight at the fish, will increase your hooking percentage.

If the rod is properly positioned, there should be no slack line between the rod tip and the water. The only exception is when fishing from a very high location, where there is too much distance between rod tip and the water. There is no way to avoid this. If you can, keep the rod tip in the water on a fast retrieve; it prevents the line from jumping with the long hard pulls.

Hooking with a Roll Cast

If you use a roll cast, there will be times when a fish takes the fly during the setup of the cast. If a fish takes with the rod in the air, make a hard roll cast. With a sharp hook, you will hook most, if not all, of the close takers. With this technique, you can work a fly very close without making numerous false casts. When roll casting, raise the rod and lift it shoulder high with the tip pointing back at a 45-degree angle, as if to make a backcast. As the rod rises in front of the angler, it creates slack line, which creates a problem setting the hook. With the rod in the air, you do not have enough arm reach to set the hook. If the rod is in or near the roll-casting position when the fish takes, make a hard, quick roll cast. The mechanics of a roll cast drive the line backward even though the rod is traveling forward. If a fish takes the fly when the rod is in the air, roll casting is your only option to set the hook; it is a fairly effective way to hook a fish when the angler is in an awkward position.

If a fish takes when the rod is raised in front, before moving to the roll-casting position, you have two options. Either must be exercised quickly. If the rod is too high to attempt setting the hook with the rod tip, sweep the rod backward and try roll casting quickly. If the rod is low enough, use the tip to try setting the hook. Both attempts are desperation measures only and not the best techniques for hooking fish.

Use Sharp Hooks

The key to positive hook-set is a sharp hook. All hooks should be sharpened before placing them in the fly box. While fishing, check the points constantly to be sure they remain sharp. Locations like steep beaches and rocky structure—where the fly might drag through the sand and gravel—or hang-ups on hard bottom will quickly dull the point. Anytime you hear or feel the cast hit something, check the hook point. If the hook is dull or damaged, either change the fly or sharpen the point. I carry two noncorrosive hook sharpeners: a ceramic stone and a diamond-surfaced tool. The diamond-surfaced tool is faster for big hooks and major work; the fine ceramic stone is better for touch-ups and small hooks.

Some hooks come presharpened from the manufacturer, but all require maintenance to keep a good point. There are several ways to sharpen a hook. The fastest and best way is to triangulate the hook point. Filing both sides of the point on the barb side of the hook on a 45-degree angle forms a short cutting edge on the top of the hook point. Then file the hook's underside to create two short cutting edges on the bottom of the hook. This forms a triangular shape with three cutting edges. To create four cutting edges on the point, file both sides of the bottom on a 45-degree angle similar to the top. Four cutting edges are perhaps better for tarpon, but for stripers a good, sharp triangulated hook works well.

I prefer a shorter, sharpened point because it is more durable. Long, thin points bend and break too easily. Usually I sharpen just the end of the point, about ⅛ inch. I want the point to stop on flesh and drive in. I feel that long cutting edges are unnecessary for hooking stripers, and they are not as durable.

Barbless Hooks and Hook Penetration

Crushing down the barb on a hook makes penetration much easier. On some hooks, it cuts the diameter of the point in half. Most straightened or bent hooks occur when the hook is not driven in to the bend. Hooks with large barbs are harder to drive home in the tougher sections of a striper's mouth. Not only do barbless hooks penetrate better, they are safer to use and much easier to remove.

I do not use hooks larger than #4/0, and I use that size only when I'm fishing heavily dressed flies if the material will eliminate the hook gap. I have landed bluefin tuna in the 40-pound class and tarpon as large as 80 pounds on #1/0 hooks. If a #1/0 hook drives into solid flesh, it will not straighten and will not pull out. Yes, a #2/0 or #3/0 hook will give more bite and is a better choice for bigger flies for large fish. But to use #6/0 or larger hooks is ludicrous. They are too heavy, too hard to drive home, and do too much damage to the fish; I shiver to think what a #6/0 would feel like in my neck.

The First Run

Clearing the fly line is the major concern after hooking a fish. Anglers lose fish when they try to clear the loose fly line that builds up between the stripping guide and the reel. If the fish bolts off quickly, let the fly line flow freely, applying just enough hand pressure to control the line. Here is the advantage of having two hands to manage the line. Using a stripping basket, I hold one hand near the stripping guide and the other just above the basket. I use both hands to pinch the line lightly, to keep it flowing but not allow it to fly wildly about. Using an open hand or, as some anglers suggest, making an O with the thumb and first finger, allows the line to run out with no control. I want to control the line at all times, for several reasons. If the line flies out of control, it can tangle easily. And if the fish hits close or makes a quick, short run, then stops, the line will keep flowing, either emptying the basket or dumping it from the boat deck into the water. Either way, you are in trouble. Be sure to control the line on the

When a fish runs, you must clear the loose fly line so you can fight the fish from the reel.

first run, and get the fish onto the reel. The only time I will fight a fish using my hands to grip the fly line is when a fish runs for structure immediately after the strike. Be careful: This can alter your fingerprints.

I handstrip small fish in, pinching the line to the rod with the first finger of my casting hand while stripping with the noncasting hand. It is the same technique used to land trout. This method works well—even for fish in the 24- to 28-inch range—in locations without current. Handstripping the fly line into a basket saves time. Otherwise, you are constantly pulling line off the reel and putting it back into the basket before casting again.

Hand Pressure to the Drag

Once the fish begins to take line from the reel, use your hand to apply pressure to slow the run. If the reel drag is preset at a firm setting, 6 pounds, use only light hand pressure. I set my drags to about 3 or 4 pounds with a straight pull off the reel. My main concern is that they do not overspin when the fish stops running. Setting the

Use the palm of your hand to feather the spinning spool of the reel.

drag too tightly might cause a problem with a long-running fish. As the line on the reel spool's arbor diminishes, the drag increases.

Most reels have exposed spool rims, so the outside rim of the spool is not covered by the frame. Use your palm or thumb and first finger to apply pressure to the spinning spool rim. There is no better drag than a seasoned hand. Your hand can apply a variety of drag settings—from clamping down to free spool—faster and better than any machine. When reaching for the spinning spool or reel handle, leave your hand open, grabbing with the face of the hand. The fast-spinning handle can crack bones in your fingers. The palm and face of the hand are more durable and are better protected.

Use the palm at first to slow the spool, then apply the thumb and first finger to control the drag. Some anglers use the palm to cup the spool and the handle to add drag. This works when the fish is tired and the runs are slow; with a fresh fish, this technique takes practice. Learning to apply drag with the hand will make fighting and landing fish easier.

To apply hand drag to reels without an exposed spool, reach in and add pressure with your finger to the inside of the spool. Use the first two fingers of the reel hand. Using finger pressure against the line will burn the skin quickly.

While fighting the fish, *never touch the drag*. It might seem too loose, but keep using your hands to apply more drag. The only adjustment I will make is to loosen the drag if it seems too hard—never tighten the drag. With the heavy front section of a floating fly line inside the guides, the resistance of the drag could double with a full bend in the rod. If you adjust the drag to the feel of the thin backing running through the guides, it might overtax a worn leader.

Clearing the Line Yourself

Don't judge a fish by its first actions. Oftentimes, a big fish will not run, catching the angler off guard. I once hooked what I thought was a big codfish while fishing a section of rocky cliffs in Maine. There was this heavy weight with little activity, and I thought the fish was big, but it never ran. When the fish finally surfaced and I saw the big tail of a striper, I knew this was a tough fish. After surfacing, the fish swam to my left and began heading slowly for the bottom. I was like a small child with a leash trying to stop a golden retriever heading for a large bowl of food. The line parted when the fish ripped it on the structure.

Because it did not run, the fish gave me time to clear the line onto the reel. After hooking the fish, I had a chance to back up on the level structure, clearing the line. Sometimes a big fish will wallow in one location on the surface, its tail throwing water like a broken fire hydrant. If a fish does not make an immediate run and you believe the fish is large, use that opportunity to clear the line yourself. This works well along an open beach when you can slowly back up, slipping line from the basket. If you have the time, clear the line at your own pace before the fish runs. In difficult wading areas and from a boat, you must let the fish run to clear the line.

Which Hand Should You Use to Reel?

There is perhaps more controversy about which hand to turn the reel handle with than about what is the best fly. I cast with my right hand and reel with my left. Why change hands to fight the fish? Actually, I reel with both hands but prefer the left. My advice to students is to use the hand that works better. Many right-handed spin anglers reel with their left hands; why change? I want the right hand, my strong side, to pull on the fish. Reeling is not as demanding as lifting. This decision is totally a matter of personal preference; reel with whichever hand you wish to use.

Applying Pressure

Proper rod angle is important when fighting a fish. A high rod angle is useful only when a fish is in or around structure. A high rod applies little pressure to the fish. When a fish has the line around structure, a high rod might clear the line and will reduce leader and fly-line damage because there is little pressure on the tippet. I use a high rod angle only in desperation or for a dramatic photo.

To apply firm pressure, use the butt section of the rod—the first 4–5 feet—to pull on the fish. When applying pressure properly with a 9-foot rod, the first 4 or 5 feet of the rod should be straight. The top half of a fly rod has little lifting power, particularly

When a fish runs, or when a fish is close, hold the rod to one side to apply pressure from different angles.

7- and 8-weights. Heavier rods have better lifting power. With an 11-weight, you can use more of the rod's butt section for lifting, but it is still the lower half of the rod that does the fighting.

When a fish runs, hold the rod off to one side at a 45-degree angle. This puts the line at a slight angle, to one side of the fish, making it harder to gain line. If there is current, tip the rod to the downcurrent side. This increases the line's angle to the fish and begins to force the fish into the current's eddy. Whenever possible, try to lead a fish into the back eddy of a current. When current is not a factor, hold the rod to the side that is more comfortable. An angler who fights a fish with the rod in the right hand should tilt the rod to the right.

Moving the Fish

When it stops running, begin to move the fish immediately. A tired fish will search for a place to hide or to rub its head to dislodge the force that is gripping its face.

Although we like to make them seem human, a fish does not rationalize that it is hooked to a line and plan to cut the line to free itself. The fish has something stuck in its mouth and rubs against the bottom or structure to remove it. Permitting a fish to mill around lets it recover its strength and allows it time to reach cover.

A big striper is not easy to move, particularly if the fish is in a current. The key is to turn the fish so you are pulling it headfirst. There are two ways to pull on a fish effectively. With either technique, use the body to set up the lifting stroke. As in casting, the body is what generates the power in the arms. When pulling on a fish, start with legs first, using a steady rhythm and lifting the fish with your whole body, not just the arms. If you use only arms and wrists, you will tire quickly.

The hardest but most effective way is to use the butt section of the rod, pulling toward your body with your arms, with one hand on the grip and the other cupping the reel. Tilt the rod slightly upward while stroking the rod into your body as your body moves backward. Think of the rod as a short lever, and imagine that you are pulling that lever into your body while lifting the tip slightly. You make the initial pull with your legs, your upper body, then your arms, and finally lift with your wrist. This is the best way to gain the most line per stroke, but most anglers will find this tiring.

Another way is to place the rod butt against your body and lift by raising the rod. You basically stroke the same way, pulling with the legs first, then the upper body, then both the arms and the wrists, but the rod butt is the fulcrum and remains in one location. This gives a shorter stroke but is much less tiring.

With either technique, the rod should never rise above a 75-degree angle. If the fish is straight down below the angler, which occurs frequently when boat fishing, the rod should stay below 45-degrees. A high rod decreases the pressure on the fish and increases the chance of rod breakage.

Pumping the Fish

Once you have stopped and moved the fish, keep it coming by stroking, then quickly dropping the rod, reeling in the gained line, and stroking again. This is called pumping. You are lifting the fish, gaining line with the rod while using the reel only to take up the loose line. Trying to gain line with the reel does not work. Pumping is a steady series of moves, pulling then reeling quickly to gain line. Once the fish is coming, with its head pointed toward you, take as much line as possible. A big fish recovers rapidly after the first run. If you do not recoup enough line, the next run could put the fish beyond a controllable distance, possibly cleaning the spool. After that first long run, pumping is necessary to gain every precious yard. Usually from a boat you can follow the fish, but from shore or in locations that prevent moving the boat, stopping the fish and gaining back line are essential for landing a big fish.

When fighting a fish from a small boat, you must put the rod tip into the water to get a longer pull when lifting.

Pump in a fish by lifting the rod, then lowering the rod while reeling in the gained line, then repeating the process.

Follow the Fish

When a fish gets beyond 150 yards, control becomes difficult; there is too much stretch in the line. At this distance, too many things can happen. Weed can build up on the line, the fish can tangle the line or leader in structure, or a boat or another angler can cross your line. Whenever possible, stay close to the fish by following, either walking or moving the boat.

I watched an angler fighting a big fish from a boat early one calm morning. The fish took the fly on a shallow bar right on top of a reef and bolted into the deeper water on the opposite side of the structure. As it ran through the shallows, the fish threw water like a frightened seal. This fish was big. The angler held the rod high as his partner just stood watching, his tongue hanging out. He could have been licking stamps in a post office. The boat was anchored. By the time the angler's partner came to life, pulled the anchor, and followed, the fish had covered several hundred yards, wrapping the line into three different pieces of structure. As I watched, the boat motored from one location to the next, hopeful that the fish would still be hooked up. At the last location, a stream of four-letter words signaled the loss of a lifetime fish.

This happens to shore anglers as well. With the excitement of a big fish, rigor mortis sets in, and by the time the angler reacts, the fight is over. In some locations, time is critical. In fast currents, a fish can quickly build a head of steam, and backing melts from the spool. Staying ahead of the fish is the key to landing trophies.

From shore, begin to move as soon as the fish runs, and keep pace with the fish. The shorter the distance between you and the fish, the better control you have. In most locations along a beach, particularly on steep beaches, walk to dry ground when fighting a fish. Walking is easier, there is no chance of being hit by a wave, and the high ground gives more control over the fish. On most beaches, you're only a few steps from easy walking; moving quickly in water is difficult.

This is very important on a crowded beach to prevent other anglers from crossing your line. Particularly at night, other anglers would not know there is a hooked fish in front of them. Remember, there might be spin anglers casting several hundred feet from the shore, so let them know there is a hooked fish coming down the beach. Most anglers are polite and are happy to give another angler room to fight a fish. But you must tell them what the fish is doing.

For prompt pursuit of a fish from an anchored boat, use a release anchor system on the anchor line. Attach a loop to the end of the anchor line. To this, hook a lobster buoy. I make up a lobster float with a loop at one end and a snap at the other and snap it to the anchor line. When hooking a big fish, I just throw the line and float overboard and follow the fish. The other benefit is coming back to same location without resetting the anchor.

When the Fish Is Close

There is a special feeling, after fighting a big fish for a long time, to getting fly line back onto the reel. It's a small victory; the fish is close, there is better control, and you can begin to plan landing the fish. It is also a time for caution. As the line shortens, there is less stretch, so there is less room for error. It is a time for soft hands, a time to use modest pressure. Even if the fish appears beaten, it will probably have one good punch left. If the fight has lasted a long time, the leader is at less than full strength—it could be quite worn.

On a calm beach, unless the hook pulls out, the fish is yours if you don't panic. Keep the fish off balance by changing the rod angle from side to side. This will turn the fish over, affecting its balance. Beware: When the fish begins to feel the confinement of shallow water, it will probably bolt. That first touch of bottom along a shoreline can give even a "dead" fish new life. The fish might take only 30 feet of line, but if you lock up on the drag, the fish will break the leader. When the fish makes that last surge, let it run, using only light pressure. This should be the last real burst of power, and when the fish stops, it will probably turn on its side. Apply pressure, still with soft hands, turning the fish to face the beach. If you can see that the fish is facing toward the beach, back up quickly, walking sideways, holding the rod level with the sand and parallel to the beach. When a tired fish is facing the beach, you can sometimes slide the fish right into shore with one quick move. If the fish turns, gain some more line, turn the fish into the beach, and try again. Always leave at least 10 feet of fly line outside the tip. There are times when I will land a fish with 25–30 feet of fly line outside the tip. Once the fish is beached, hold a bend in the rod and walk toward the fish, keeping a tight line and reeling as you walk. With the fish facing you, every movement of the water or the fish will push it farther up onto the beach.

Fighting Fish from Rocky Cliffs

Landing a fish from surf-battered, high, rocky cliffs is more finesse than power. You will not outmuscle a fish, so you must outmaneuver it. With a big striper, you will need some help from the fish and some luck as well. Planning is critical when landing a fish that is always near structure. Find a good, safe landing location that is big enough for you to lead a fish into and is away from the surging waves. I look for a crack or channel in the rocks that leads well back from the breaking waves. Look for several pools where you can move a fish from one location to the next, using the waves to lift the fish from spot to spot. The backsides of points that break the heavy force of the waves are also good landing spots. **Never,** ever attempt to climb down the front face of a cliff to retrieve a fish. It is better to lose the fish than to lose your life.

After hooking a fish, try to move toward the landing location. If the fish goes the opposite way, try to turn the fish, using rod angles to make it swim in the right direction. Keep the fish up off the bottom, but do not bring it too close to the rocks until you reach the landing location. This is a game of cat and mouse, keeping a fish away from structure while leading it to a small landing spot. With big fish, you are the mouse.

When a fish gets behind a ledge, hold the rod high, giving the rod a full bend. A full bend puts little pressure on the leader. If the leader or line rubs on the structure, there will be less damage. Fluorocarbon is very durable, so it is the only tippet material I use for structure fishing. As long as the fish holds behind the structure, keep holding the rod high, letting the surging water move the fish. Be patient; wait the fish out. I have stayed with fish for 5 minutes before they finally cleared the structure. If you keep feeling the fish move, there is hope. Usually, once you can work the fish from one lie and keep its head up, there is a good chance of landing it. Even with better-size stripers, once you spin them around and get them confused, you can control them.

By the time a fish reaches the landing spot, it is usually docile, and you can just lead it using the flow of waves. Some of the channels I use for landing are too narrow for the fish to turn in, so they can only move forward.

When a fish gets around structure, keep the rod high with a full bend to decrease the pressure on the tippet.

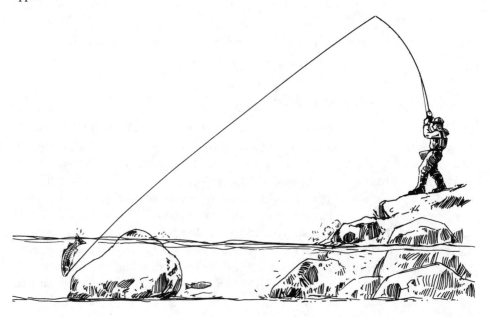

I use 20-pound tippet and 10- and 11-weight rods. With schoolie-size fish, I just pick up the fish hand-over-hand with the leader. To release the fish, choose a deep location, and wait for a wave to surge up close enough to set the fish gently into the water. The water here is so rich with oxygen that the fish bolt quickly away. I have never seen a fish go belly-up in this water. I'm using heavy tackle and I land the fish quickly, so they are strong when I return them.

Fighting Fish from Boats

Fighting fish from a boat is basically the same as when shore fishing but the lifting angle is different, because many times you are lifting the fish straight up. Any fish is tough when you're trying to lift it. Most anglers try to fight and lift a fish using the same pulling stroke that they use from shore. From a boat, the last portion of the fight usually involves bringing the fish up from below the boat. When lifting a fish up, the tip of the rod should be in the water at the start of the stroke, unless the boat is large. (See photo on page 245.) From most small boats, some portion of the rod will touch the water; with my 20-foot Action Craft, 3 feet of rod disappears below the surface. This way the butt of the rod is doing the lifting, not the tip section. As

Captain Pat Keliher is holding the rod high to grab the leader after the fish is tired. This is a poor rod angle for fighting and lifting fish.

when fighting a fish from shore, the front section of your rod should be straight. When lifting, lift the rod tip from the water, then reel up the gained line. The water surface gives you a starting and stopping distance for the best stroke. Heavier rods have more lifting power. With an 11-weight, the stroke will be longer and higher.

Lifting too high can break fly rods. A high stroke puts pressure on the front section of the rod. In rolling seas, concentrate so the rod does not rise too far above the water's surface. If the boat rolls backward when you're lifting the rod, be sure to drop your hand to keep the rod low, or you will have graphite splinters.

In flowing water, a drifting boat neutralizes some of the current advantage for a fish. The shore angler does not usually have this luxury, but the boat angler can move with the current. If it is safe to drift with the tide, always follow a running fish to stay within a good fighting distance, particularly in places with structure, where control is critical to landing a good fish.

When motoring after a fish, move slowly, allowing the angler to maintain pressure and control. Do not overrun the fish and create slack line. After the first run, let the boat drift, running the motor only if the fish makes another long run or heads for structure. Once the fish is near the boat, lift the motor and be sure that any loose gear is stowed away. As when bringing a fish into shallow water when shore fishing, the fish will react when it sees the boat. Expect a last bolt of energy from a big fish. Most fish will circle the boat, and some will swim under it. When a fish swims under the boat, be prepared to act quickly, moving to either end to clear the line to the other side. Use the rod to sweep the line around the bow or stern to fight the fish from the other side. If the fish goes under the boat's middle, you may need to stick the rod in the water to clear any obstacles underneath the boat. This is usually not a problem in smaller boats. Keep the rod from touching any part of the boat. A rod under pressure, with a full bend, can break if it touches a hard object.

If hooked from an anchored boat in current, fish are usually tired from the long fight up the flow. And if they do run, it will be downcurrent, away from the anchor line. With a big fish, I always throw the release anchor to eliminate any chance of fouling with the anchor. A fish that wraps the fly line around the anchor line usually breaks off.

In all these locations, use the same techniques when fighting small to midsize fish. In most cases, you can land smaller fish easily without taking the precautions that you would with big fish. Small stripers are not that strong, but the water they live and feed in makes them a worthy foe.

Handling the Fish

Once a striper, even a big fish, is tired, handling it is not that difficult. Grabbing a small fish firmly by the lower lip usually calms the fish so it is easy to unhook and release. You can do this with big fish, but you must have good hand strength. When wading or fishing from a boat, this is standard procedure. There are two considerations when reaching into a fish's mouth: Is the hook barbless, and is the fish a striper? At night, be sure it is not a bluefish you are reaching for when grabbing the lower jaw. A thumb, like a mind, is a terrible thing to waste.

Never touch the lungs, the red gill area under the gill plate. If the fish is hooked deep, carefully try to work the hook out without touching or damaging this location. If you must reach into this area, do so cautiously, with a small pair of forceps. Any damage to this area, even slight, will kill a fish. If a fish bleeds from other locations, it will generally survive; if the gills bleed, it's usually fatal.

From shore, unless you are wading on a large flat, drag the fish onto dry ground. If the fish is small, handle it by the lower lip. With a big fish, remove the hook without lifting the fish. Then grab the lip and support the fish's body with your other hand to carry it. Stripers have several sharp weapons that demand attention. A deep puncture from a spine can send an angler to the hospital. The dorsal fin has nine to ten sharp spines that will penetrate a rubber boot. Each pectoral fin has one spine, and the outer edge of the gill plate is razor sharp. The mouth, however, is like gritty sandpaper, ideal for handling.

The best way to handle a striper is by the lower lip.

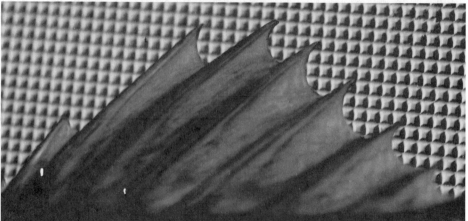

The pectoral, dorsal, and anal fins of a striper are armed with sharp spines that can inflict a savage wound.

When landing a striper from the beach, never push it with your foot or let a wave slam the fish into your leg. A striper becomes defensive if rolled on the beach and stiffens its body, exposing all its spines. Trying to grab or stop a tumbling fish in white water is like reaching into a bag of wet cats. Once a fish settles down, it is not a problem. Take an extra second and be sure to hold the fish firmly. Most anglers get stuck when dropping the fish or reaching for one that's moving.

Many times, unless the fish is very large, grab the leader first, slipping your hand down the leader to grab the lip or the fly. Even with fish in the 20-pound class, grabbing the leader works well. A tired fish does not have the strength to break a 16-

pound tippet. I do not advise lifting a big fish with the leader, but in the water, holding the leader and unhooking and releasing the fish is standard procedure. The less you handle the fish, the better it is for everyone.

Landing Tools

There are different tools that work for landing a swimming fish. The only landing tool I would now use from shore is a BogaGrip. It has a strap that slips over the wrist and a good handle. Once it grips the fish, there is no slipping, and the tool's head will spin so the fish can't wrench it from your hand. There is a flared collar that you pull back to open the rounded jaws. You snap the jaws around the fish's jaw, release the collar, and the fish is held fast. It is the best releasing tool on the market, and it will also weigh the fish. It is a very popular landing tool for boat guides as well. With a BogaGrip, you can leave the fish in the water when unhooking and releasing.

Landing nets are probably the best tools for landing a big fish from a boat. A net will scoop up a fish when it is still lively. They are cumbersome and take up space, but nets have landed many trophies that might have slipped away.

The BogaGrip is a good, safe, humane way to land a striper. Captain Dan Marini of Chatham, Massachusetts, lands a nice fish for Peter Alves, fishing manager of Fishing the Cape.

A net is a big scoop. To land a fish, put the net in the water and have the angler bring the fish toward the net. With the rod, lead the fish's head into the net and scoop, with one motion, from head to tail. Do not chase the fish with the net or try to scoop from the tail. When buying a net, plan for a big fish. Small fish fit into big nets; the opposite is not true. Each year, be sure that the netting has not rotted and has no holes.

The major advantage of a net is not having to bring the fish into the boat. Scoop the fish and just hold it alongside the boat, remove the hook, and release the fish. Any device that reduces handling increases the fish's chance of survival. Gaffs are illegal in some states and too dangerous for most anglers to use.

Releasing

The secret to a trouble-free release is fighting the fish properly. If you pressure the fish aggressively, it will bolt from your hands when you put it back into the water. Stripers are hardy fish, more durable than most gamefish. The difficulty lies in fighting a big fish on light tackle or not applying enough pressure once the fish is beat. When a fish turns on its side, push hard to get the fish in quickly. With a very tired fish, every minute counts. Most stripers, even those that seem dead, will come back with proper care. Hold the fish by the tail and work it back and forth in the water to

Release a fish by holding the tail and moving the fish back and forth through the water to let it revive.

help it breathe. Keep the fish upright and be sure that the gill plates are moving as you force the fish through the water. If there is current, push the fish into the flow. The white water around cliffs is excellent for releasing fish because it is so full of air. I have put fish into sheltered gullies along cliffs, and they spring to life, swimming off quickly.

Hold the fish until it swims from your hand. There is nothing worse than watching a fish sink out of reach and turn belly up. As a fish comes to life it will tighten, and the fins will flare out. You will feel the fish wanting to swim—its tail begins to beat. I want the fish to pull from my grip.

A fish is not worth your life. There might be locations where you cannot revive a fish properly because it too dangerous to approach the water. Do the best you can, but in these locations, fight the fish so that when you dump them into the water they are lively. Along the cliffs, I have walked several hundred feet to find a good release location. It is your responsibility to take the time and effort to release a fish properly. If you feel that a fish will die, and it is of legal size, bring it home. Stripers are fine table fare, and there is nothing wrong with keeping some fish for dinner. Legal fish that are damaged, particularly those hooked and bleeding from the red gill area, should be kept.

Stripers have firm, white flesh when cooked. The taste is exceptional. Although stripers do hold up well in the cool months, it is wise to keep fish on ice and clean them promptly. On a hot sunny day, storing the fish on ice in a cooler is a necessity. Part of fishing the sea is enjoying the catch. I do not keep many fish in a season, but they are always a treat, and if a keeper is in poor condition, the fish should be used rather than wasted.

There are times when we all have wasted a fish. A small, nonlegal striper that is severely injured will probably die. All anglers have let fish go that they knew would not possibly survive. It is not a good feeling, any more than hitting a wild animal with a car. However, this is part of fishing, and if you have taken every precaution to save the fish, then just accept it as bad luck. As responsible anglers, we must all strive to release fish so they are healthy. Fighting and landing a fish properly and quickly, using heavy-enough tackle, and using barbless hooks will increase the fish's chances of survival. Every fish is special and should be treated that way.

Tides and Weather (21)

*E*ach day along our coast—actually in the sea throughout the world—the tide rises and falls twice. Each location is different; both the depth and the amount of the tide change will vary, sometimes significantly. The distance from Martha's Vineyard to Cape Cod Bay is less than 30 miles, but the tide in Cape Cod Bay is 9 feet, and the tides around the Vineyard average only about 2½ feet. In areas with big tides, the difference from high to low tide is drastic; a fishing location will change completely. The rising and dropping of water levels moves the bait, and the stripers follow the food. Feeding is easier for fish in flowing water, and a falling tide will force bait to leave a safe location and move into the waiting trap of gamefish. This constant flow of water makes our fishing interesting; without tides, the sea would be a massive lake with little character.

What Creates Tide?

The sun and moon are the major forces creating tides. The moon's effect is 2.17 times greater than the sun's. Full moons and new moons create higher tides—or "spring tides"—and stronger currents. Half-moon tides—or "neap tides"—are the smallest tides. When either a full or a new moon occurs at perigee, there will be a higher tide and a stronger current. Tides and current are not as strong when full and new moons occur at apogee. During a new moon, the midday tide is higher than the night tide; with a full moon, the opposite is true—the night tide is the larger.

Tides, both incoming and outgoing, do not rise or fall in one steady flow, but move in several stages. The tide begins to rise, then slacks for a short period, ebbs slightly, and then starts to rise again, repeating this process several times before reaching the high. Then it reverses this process on the falling tide. A drop in flow does not always mean the end of a tide. Boatmen and waders should always consult tide charts and watches.

What Alters Tide?

Both weather and wind affect tide. With higher-than-normal pressure, tides are lower. When the barometer is low, tides during both high and low water are higher than normal. When a major storm brings very low pressure, high water and flooding can occur, and currents will be extremely strong.

In the Atlantic, tides increase in size and flow later when the wind blows strongly to southward or eastward. When winds are northward or westward, tides are lower than normal and occur earlier. Wind will alter water depth and currents in back bays and sounds. Give strong winds serious consideration if water depth and sea conditions can hamper your angling.

Tides and Fishing

Tide is important to anglers because it creates water movement and alters the contour of the land and water. Some locations have good fishing on all tides, but one phase of the tide might produce better fishing. There are some general rules about tides that will help to determine how, when, and where to fish a location. These rules are for initial research and are never set in stone; only time on the water will determine how to fish a spot. Along with finding fish, tide knowledge is important when wading or running a boat, because water depth can make the difference between a safe and a dangerous outing. Throughout the book, I have mentioned tides and how they influence fishing. The following is just a refresher and some good basic guidelines.

Openings that flow into open water are most productive just after the flow begins to run either in or out of the opening. That first hour of flow can bring hot fishing. The flow running through an opening will always have a lag time from the actual tide. A small opening filling a large backwater will still be flowing in several hours after high tide; the water level inside the opening never reaches the same height as the open water. The lag time will be about the same at low tide. A spring tide increases the lag time because there is more water to move.

Large shallow areas that run dry or have little holding water will have better fishing on a coming tide. Most flats become active as the sea fills the shallows, exposing feeding areas lost to the fish on the falling tide. As the tide covers a flat, baitfish begin to move into the shallows for protection, while bottom-dwelling baits become active. On a rising tide, stripers are bold, with no fear of being trapped; as the water level on the flats drops, the fish leave to search the edges and the deeper areas along the flats. On a low incoming tide, the edges of some flats will have heavy activity until the fish can move onto the flat. Tide is critical when wading the shallows in big-tide locations. Be sure to know the area well and know when the flood begins.

Places with heavy tides can offer excellent fly fishing during slower water. Without bait to bring the fish up, stripers in fast, deep rips might not be reachable with fly tackle. But once the tide slows, fish will begin to move up in the water column searching for food. Big rips produce exceptional fishing at slack or just as the flow begins. During spring tides, this period of slow water will not last long, so move quickly. In a location with a series of rips several miles long, keep moving down the flow to find a slower section of water.

Ocean beaches are good on the last 2 hours of incoming and the first 2 hours of outgoing tides. However, there are many factors, such as wind, wave size, bait type, and time of year, that will affect the activity on a beach. Beaches can run hot and cold with no influence from the tide.

The time fish move into a small estuary might be short, offering only an hour or so of good action. A log is important to predict the precise time to look for fish. Small waters usually have short windows of opportunity during a tide.

The time of year might make some locations better on certain tides. In spring and fall, big estuaries provide warmer water than the surrounding areas. Both inside the system and around the mouth, the water will be a few degrees warmer. These warm spots will hold bait and attract fish. In the spring, big stripers seek the outflows both for more comfortable temperatures and for the big baits that move into these areas. In the fall, the outflows offer a warm holding area on outgoing tide and have good concentrations of bait flowing out with the tide. Around big systems, the outside area will have a large section of warmer water when the outflow spills into open water.

How to Predict Tide

Each day, the tide advances approximately 50 minutes; therefore, a location with the right tide and hot fishing at 11 PM will have those same conditions at midnight the following day. This 50-minute change might vary because of time of year, moon phase, or wind, which could accelerate or delay a flow, particularly in smaller waters.

A tide chart is the safest way to predict tides accurately. Reading a tide chart seems simple, and for many locations, it is. Most open areas of water in a given location have approximately the same tide, predictable to within several minutes. For example, from Portland, Maine, to Provincetown on Cape Cod, there is little difference in the tides, and the tides in between can be predicted from a Boston tide chart. Yet Wasque Point and Menemsha have a 2-hour difference, and they are less than 20 miles apart, on opposite ends of Martha's Vineyard.

River systems, inlets, flats, and large sections of rips will require time to learn the tide's effects on the flow and depth. Water around Nantucket can be confusing, having both high and low tides and east and west current flows. In the locations I have fished near Eel Point, the flow changes direction about 1 hour before low tide. I thought the tide had started in when the current turned, but the water level kept dropping. Tides and current flow do not always coincide.

The *Eldridge Tide and Pilot Book* is a very useful tool. It not only gives tide information from Nova Scotia to Key West, Florida, but offers knowledge of current flows and speeds, moon phases, sun rising and setting times, and wonderful information on tidal effects. No traveling angler should be without it.

Keep a logbook for exact records on each regular fishing spot, marking tide, wind, moon phase, and weather. This information will be invaluable in locations with long tide lag times and small fishing windows.

Weather and How It Affects Fishing

Approaching weather systems can make a significant impact on fishing. Before and after a large weather system—even a hurricane—fishing can be excellent. Fish feed heavily before the weather and then again after the system departs. They seem to know that during the storm, feeding might be difficult, and they react to changes in pressure. Cold fronts with sudden temperature drops usually put fish down in the spring and summer but can turn fish on in the fall. Dark and rainy days, particularly in the summer along warmer-water areas, might cause fish to feed all day long.

Watch for thunderstorms that might produce high winds, hail, and lightning. Whether boating or wading, find a safe place to hide. If wading in an area with no shelter, set your rod down, walk 50 yards from it, and get low to the ground. Graphite rods are excellent conductors of electricity.

Wind is important to long rodders, making fishing tough if the direction is wrong or the force is too great. Approaching weather fronts generally produce onshore winds; with exiting fronts, the wind blows from the west to the north, usually hard, for a day or more. Learn to watch the weather and predict the winds, then fish locations with favorable winds. Learn also to know when strong wind will blow out some fishing areas. The wind can be your friend if you learn to use it.

Cold weather creates uncomfortable fishing conditions, but the fishing can be hot. In late fall, severe cold fronts can produce excellent fishing, and some anglers are so enthusiastic they fish all winter long for stripers.

Keep a close eye on the horizon for approaching weather.

The following section offers some hints on cold-weather and winter fishing. Most of the advice is on safety and keeping warm; the fishing is fairly basic.

Cold-Weather Striper Fishing

Stripers feed actively even throughout the winter in the warmwater outflows of some electric power plants. For the hardy angler, this is an all-winter event, but use this advice for late-fall fishing as well. If you wade, the first consideration must be safety; know the area well, and never wade in deep locations with fast currents. It's smart to fish with a partner and wear an inflatable life vest. From a boat, watch the weather. Be sure that the radio is working, and bring spare batteries; a cell phone is better. Remember, low batteries die quickly in the cold; put fresh ones in before each trip.

Dress Properly

Dress well, using many layers. Even on a warm day, bring extra clothing. Thick, 4 mm neoprene waders and long underwear keep the cold out even in frigid water, and the neoprenes are safer because they act like a wetsuit. When boat fishing, wear a full rain suit over layers of fleece to cut the wind. Good insulated boots are a must, and bring several pairs of gloves if it's very cold: one waterproof pair for pulling the anchor, one heavy pair to keep warm, and two fishing pairs in case one gets wet.

On balmy winter days without wind, you might be able to fish without gloves, but bring them anyway. Keep the gloves warm, particularly neoprene. Cold gloves make your hands colder. Bring several pairs because the water off the line constantly soaks your hands. I prefer fingerless fleece for most fishing, and full-fingered light neoprene gloves for very cold conditions.

Fish Low and Slow

The angling is simple, mostly bottom dredging with a fast-sinking line. The Depth Charge and Teeny-style lines in 250–400 grains are the best choice for this fishing. An intermediate line will work in shallow water, but with any current, the faster-sinking lines are better. Patterns like Deceivers and Snake Flies 3–5 inches long with good breathing action work well, as well as Clousers that give an up-and-down bucktail jig action. Black, white, and chartreuse are effective colors. You might see surface action, mostly deeper swirls from fish feeding below the surface, but continue fishing low and slow. Be sure to keep working the warmer water. In some locations, the hot water moves, depending on wind and tide. Knowing the water flow and tide is important— you must research each location.

Fish the Strike Zone

Fly tackle is effective because a fly holds longer in the strike zone. Pausing at different levels, use a countdown system, letting the fly line sink before retrieving, until you find the right feeding location. Once you find the best depth, keep working it. This is also true any time you fish deeper holding water.

For fly tackle, 9- and 10-weight outfits work well, with reels that hold 100 yards of backing. In the cold water, most fish are slow and will not make long runs. And be sure that the fish are lively before releasing them.

Best Times

Actually, the colder periods are better because they concentrate the fish in the warmwater locations. The most frigid part of the winter can provide hot fishing.

Cold-weather striper fishing is a good, inexpensive way to beat the winter doldrums. If you dress right and practice safety, winter striper fishing can be fun.

Protocol and Etiquette 22

ctually, this should be called common sense and good manners, or the golden rule. There are times when fishing gets crazy, with that run-and-gun boat race to reach breaking schools of fish or crowding for that small key spot at the mouth of an estuary. Boat anglers and shore anglers alike must practice good manners when fishing. There is no excuse for cutting off another boat or crowding other anglers to reach their spots. Fishing is supposed to be fun, but competition and greed can spoil a good day.

Some guides feel they must be aggressive to get their clients into fish. That is no excuse. Actually, they are the ones who should set the example. The guides must teach the freshman anglers. Both their clients and new anglers look to the professionals for guidance. If guides run around like jerks, so will the anglers who learn from them.

Here is a list of simple rules to follow and some suggestions that might make everyone's fishing better. I'm sure to some this might seem insulting. If it does, be thankful; that means you are well mannered.

When fishing from a boat, give the shore fishermen room. The wading angler is confined, sometimes to a very limited area, while the boat angler has numerous opportunities. You should stay well beyond the casting range of the shore anglers, and never run the motor near their area.

Crowded areas demand cool heads and careful angling to prevent injuries and still allow fishing. If everyone is courteous and level-headed, congested areas can still have good fishing.

I have watched anglers cast over other boats to reach the fish. There are times when boats pack up and might get close. Wind affects different boats differently, and in the heat of battle you can find yourself next to several craft. Be patient if you cannot reach the fish when others can. Move only when you will not spook the fish and will not cut another angler's line. Every boat operator must watch other anglers to see if they are fighting fish. The boat that cuts off a shore angler's line is totally inconsiderate.

When wading, fishing a rip, give another angler enough room so your lines do not cross, and never infringe on another's casting space. There are locations that warrant close fishing, but never crowd the other angler. Wading anglers generally can fish much closer than boat anglers. During the annual one-night fly-fishing contest, Lobsterville Beach on Martha's Vineyard can be a picket fence of anglers, but everyone knows each other. Along a beach, three rod lengths is good spacing. If you're fishing across from another angler, your lines should never cross.

When fishing along a busy beach, be aware of your backcast. Non–fly casters do not realize that a backcast might extend 50 feet behind the angler. When walking behind another fly caster, I like to pass just behind the other angler, telling him or her that I'm crossing the casting path.

There are locations where a fly rodder must use good judgment when fishing. At the end of a popular jetty or point, one fly rodder might occupy the space of several anglers. The fly angler using a conventional backcast requires too much space, the room of perhaps five spin anglers. The only way to fish a location like this is to use a roll cast, so other anglers can fish close by. It just gives fly fishing a bad name if one angler hogs the space that many anglers could use.

Several boats working a rip at the same time need to keep a safe distance both below and to the side of other boats—at least several casts away. At times there might be one hot spot that holds fish. If everyone works together, you can hopscotch—taking turns to fish, then drifting down to let another boat work the sweet spot. In heavily fished rip areas, anchoring is discouraged. If you like to anchor, fish off to one side away from the popular location. If there is a crowd, I generally prefer to stay out of the competition, and many times I can find good fishing by myself.

In shallow water, outboard motors frighten fish. With flats fishing becoming so popular, some shallow-water locations are overfished. As more anglers pound the flats, we all must tread lightly. Plan your fishing to minimize the use of the outboard. Run around rather than across a flat, even when you are leaving. Each time a boat runs over a flat, it spooks the fish. Too much traffic will drive the fish away for good. On the flats, you must give extra room for both wading and boat anglers. If a boat is poling a flat that you planned to work, go in behind the boat, fishing another path on the flat. Never cut in front of a boat or a wading angler.

At night or in low light, never intentionally shine a light on another angler's boat or at a wading angler. The light might affect their fishing, and it will affect their night vision.

If you are doing well, try to help others by giving fly-pattern information, as well as telling them how you retrieve the fly. I will help the decent anglers, but I will not help belligerent jerks.

When running up to a school of feeding fish, avoid motoring over them. Sometimes several boats can hook up on a school of fish. Don't be the dummy who drives them down. Gliding into the school with the motor cut, or drifting into them, is the best way to approach a school of fish.

Choosing a Guide 23

A guide can make or break a fishing trip. A good one can turn a fishless day into a great day of fishing. Remember that even though you are paying the bill, a guide is a person, not a servant. The good ones will work hard to make your day a pleasurable one. But guides with big egos can also ruin what would have been a productive fishing day. Never let a guide beat you up mentally or physically.

Guided trips are a big help when learning a new fishery. For most anglers, this is the optimum way to fish a location if you have only few days. Guides are not gods—they cannot walk on water, although I've met a few who believed they could. There is no guarantee in fishing. And just because you are fishing with a guide doesn't mean you will have a great day of catching. The important thing is to have a good day, a good trip, and a good time. For the most part, a bad day's fishing with a guide is the fault of the angler—from choosing a guide, to preparation, to the level of angling skills. If planned properly, guided trips can be fun and productive. Here are some thoughts to make a guided trip better.

Outfitters will offer the services of several guides. When booking with an outfitter for the first time, ask to talk with your guide directly. That old cliché, "You're getting my best guide," is often used, and if you are booking for the first time, you probably are not. If the person doing the booking is uncooperative with your request to talk with the guide directly, I would not book. Independent guides are usually better established, although I know some very good guides who work with outfitters.

Beware of the big come-on: advertisements or stories that tell of many large, near-record fish that got away. And statements of how many years of fishing experience the guide has, or claims of being the best, are just so much rhetoric. These are the same guides who will tell you that they killed them the day before—when you are having a slow day.

The good guides don't need to boast—their clients do it for them. *Word of mouth is the best way to find a guide.* Guides who have mostly repeat customers are good—that's why the anglers come back. Steve Huff, the famous Keys guide, has a 5-year waiting list: He's the best. Stay clear of guides who keep changing their client base—there is a reason for it. Guides who exaggerate, have poor manners, or race around beating up their anglers go through clients quickly. A slow day of fishing is generally not the reason for an angler switching guides. Good guides will tell you that fishing is slow or even call off a trip. The greedy guide will go out and make excuses. Several anglers I know went out with a flimflam local guide, and after a 2-hour drive, were greeted with the guide saying: "The fish are small, but we can use 4-weights to make it sporty." One angler's answer was, "If I wanted to use a 4-weight, I could go trout fishing."

What Should You Ask or Tell Your Guide?

Be honest about your fishing skills. Remember, you will not be as good as your best day, especially if sight casting, when you have to put the fly in front of a cruising fish. The excitement alone will affect the best caster. Most guides will check your skills before you actually fish, but a fair evaluation beforehand helps them plan the day. Tell your guide about any concerns you might have. I do not like casting over the boat, particularly over the guide. I would rather pass on a fish than hook someone.

What tackle and gear should you bring? Rain gear, sunglasses, a hat, sunscreen, and extra clothes are the basics to take along. If you plan to wade, bring wading gear; some guides do provide waders, but they will not fit like your own. Some shoes mark up a boat deck, making cleanup difficult. Sneakers work well for most warm-weather fishing; in cold locations, winter boots with light-colored soles will keep your feet warm and dry and the boat clean as well.

If you like to use a stripping basket, bring your own along. Most boat guides don't use them. Some guides don't like them. I bring a basket everywhere. If you prefer to fish with a basket, use it.

Who should provide lunch and drinks? Orvis-endorsed guides supply everything for you. Discuss this beforehand so no one goes hungry; a starved guide is an unhappy one. Remember, bring extra water on hot days.

If you have any special medical needs or diet, are handicapped, or are older and not very agile, be sure to inform the guide. They need to plan their fishing days.

Mention your goals and the type of fishing you expect to experience. Some anglers are trophy hunters; others just want to catch fish. Some anglers want to use a day's guided fishing as a learning experience, to familiarize themselves with a type of fishing or to learn how to fish a location. Some guides are good teachers—others just want to catch. Be sure to make it clear if you are planning an educational session.

Those who prefer to bring and fish with their own tackle must be sure it is the right tackle and is in working order. You will frustrate the guide by fishing with junk, and there will be bitter words if you lose a good fish. And the guide will be justifiably mad if he or she works hard, only to lose a big one because of your poor tackle. In some locations, bragging rights are important to the guide.

How to Help the Guide

When first meeting a guide, try to put him or her at ease. Say you are there for a fun time—yes, it would be nice to hammer the fish, but a good time is the reason you are there. This takes the pressure off, particularly if the guide is young or inexperienced. Even some old salts might soften to this approach.

When working a shoreline with breaking surf, everyone must watch for a rough wave that could catch the boat. Most guides are careful, but it does not hurt to voice a concern if you think the boat's in danger. If I'm not happy, I let someone know quickly.

Before casting, be sure your backcasting area is clear. Even if the guide tells you it is fine to cast over his or her head, I would not. Although some guides don't like them, I use barbless hooks. I have had tremendous success with them, and barbless hooks are much safer.

Be ready to move when the guide says go. There is nothing more irritating than waiting for someone who is never ready. This begins at home by having your tackle and gear in order. And be ready to move quickly if the boat is nearing a risky situation. When fishing hazardous waters, the guide will instruct you beforehand about emergency actions, such as when fishing rocky locations, where motoring close to structure might require a speedy departure if a big wave builds up outside. This is one time when a guide who screams at a client is doing so for everyone's welfare.

Move slowly and carefully around the boat, especially if the guide is up on a poling platform. And the bigger you are, the slower you must move. In a very small boat, one wrong move could spell disaster.

Listen to what the guide says, and do it. It's fun to try your own techniques, but if your methods or flies are not working, respect the guide's advice.

If a problem arises, say a personality conflict, try to defuse it with humor. But if that dilemma persists, it may be best to cancel future days. Most guides are easy-going, but there are still some tyrants who think they can abuse anglers and still have them coming back the next day or the next year. Those days are over—there is too much competition and too many good guides. There has been more than one –angler who canceled a week's trip.

Things to Do Before Fishing Each Day

Cast for several minutes to warm up if you are sight fishing. This will help you to improve your timing, loosen up, get some confidence, and show the guide how you cast.

Have the terminal tackle all set, with sharp hooks, clean new leaders, and all knots in good shape. Stretch and clean the fly line to take out the coils, and check the drag. All these preparations are a must. Be sure all your tackle is set and ready to go.

Fishing with a guide should be a pleasurable time, not a dreaded chore. It should not be thought of as an expensive day on the water. A guided trip should be a fun day's fishing, when the angler learns and both guide and client have a good time. Guided trips should be special events, days that you cherish, not times of irritation. Picking the right guide and being prepared will help make your next guided trip a memorable one. Remember, you are the one choosing the guide—if you have a bad day, look in the mirror.

Guides

Below is a list of guides with whom I have fished, or seen in action on the water. They are all guides I would send a friend to for a day's fishing. My criteria for a good guide include someone who is polite on the water, does not beat up the clients, and does not boast or stretch the truth. I know there are other good guides, but I will only recommend guides with whom I have had personal contact. It is impossible to say on a given day who is the best guide. If I had to pick just one of these guides for stripers, it would be Bill Herold, because of his experience and time on the water; Glen Exstrom, Fairfield.

New Jersey: Dick Dennis, Bay Head; Chris Goldmark, Cape May and Culebra, Puerto Rico; Bill Hoblitzell, Sandy Hook.

New York: Joe Blados, Southold; Barry Kanavy, Seaford.

Connecticut: Steve Bellefleur, Stonington; Scott Bennett, Darien; Steve Burnett, Mystic; Ian Devlin, Rowayton; Bill Herold, Greenwich; Joe Keegan, Niantic; Pete Kriewald, Westport; Emmett Pizzoferrato, Mystic; Dan Wood, Waterford; Glen Exstrom, Fairfield.

Rhode Island: Johnny Glenn, Watch Hill/Block Island; Ed Hughes, Snug Harbor; Mike Kenfield, Newport; Ray Smith, Newport (shore guide); Gregg Weatherby, Newport.

Massachusetts: Chris Aubut, Westport; Bob Benson, East Harwich; Rich Benson, East Harwich; Jaime Boyle, Martha's Vineyard; Barry Clemson, Plum Island; Fred Christian, Marblehead; Mo Flaherty, Martha's Vineyard; Cooper Gilkes, Martha's

Vineyard (shore guide); Karen Kukolich, Martha's Vineyard; Dan Marini, Chatham; Mike Monte, Nantucket (shore guide); John Pirie, Beverly; Dave Rimmer, Newburyport (shore guide); Leslie Smith, Martha's Vineyard; Dave Steeves, East Harwich; Ken and Lori Vanderlaske, Martha's Vineyard (shore guides).

New Hampshire: Dave Beattie, Portsmouth; Dave Beshara, Salem.

Maine: Pat Keliher, Brunswick; Dave Pecci, Topsham; Julian Rubenstein, Thomaston.

Join the CCA

The Coastal Conservation Association is an organization that is doing something to preserve and protect our fishery. The CCA is the best friend the recreational angler has. Become a part of the CCA and help to protect not only the striped bass, but other fish, the baitfish, and the environment as well. Without the support of all anglers, we will lose the striper again. Those of you who have recently started enjoying the excellent fishing for stripers might not know that only a few years ago, the striper's future looked bleak. Because of overharvesting, their numbers were so low that fishing for stripers was not the wonderful experience it is today. If we are not careful and do not protect our fishery, it will again decline. Do your part. Join the CCA and help protect a great sport and a great fish.

> As this book goes to press, concern is growing about the lack of striped bass in the 30–50-pound class. Few anglers take these trophy fish on fly tackle, but now even conventional anglers are seeing fewer of these fish beacuse thay are frequently targeted by both commercial and sport fishermen. I feel that too many big breeders are being taken, and that this will seriously affect striper stocks in the future. We will have a serious management problem to address in the coming years if we want to improve our stocks of large stripers. We all must keep fighting to keep the striper fishery strong.

Bibliography

Bay, Kenneth E., and Hermann Kessler. *Salt Water Flies.* New York: J. B. Lippincott, 1972.

Brooks, Joe. *Fly Fishing.* New York: Outdoor Life Books, 1958.

International Game Fish Association. *World Record Game Fishes.* Fort Lauderdale: The International Game Fish Association, 1995.

Karas, Nick. *The Striped Bass.* New York: The Lyons Press, 1993.

Kreh, Bernard "Lefty." *Fly Fishing in Salt Water.* New York: The Lyons Press, 1997.

McClane, A. J., ed. *McClane's New Standard Fishing Encyclopedia.* New York: Holt, Rinehart and Winston, 1998.

Meyer, Deke. *Saltwater Flies.* Portland: Frank Amato Publications, 1995.

Mitchell, Ed. *Fly Rodding the Coast.* Mechanicsburg: Stackpole Books, 1995.

Tabory, Lou. *Inshore Fly Fishing.* New York: The Lyons Press, 1992.

Tabory, Lou. *Lou Tabory's Guide to Saltwater Baits and Their Imitations.* New York: The Lyons Press, 1995.

White, Marion Jewett. *Eldridge Tide and Pilot Book.* Boston: Marion Jewett White— Robert Eldridge White—Linda Foster White, Publishers, 1999.

Index

Page numbers in **boldface** type refer to photographs. Those in *italic* type refer to illustrations.